DATE DUE

OC 7 '97	DE 18 06		
NO 6 '97			
NO 25 '97			
MR 19 '98			
JY 14 '98			
JY 30 '98			
DE 18 '98			
MY 25 '99			
NO 15 '99			
DE 6 '99			
MY 23 '00			
DE 5 '00			
DE 5 '02			
MY 20 '04			

Dickinson and Audience

Dickinson and Audience

Edited by
Martin Orzeck and
Robert Weisbuch

Ann Arbor
THE UNIVERSITY OF MICHIGAN PRESS

Copyright © by the University of Michigan 1996
All rights reserved
Published in the United States of America by
The University of Michigan Press
Manufactured in the United States of America
♾ Printed on acid-free paper

1999   1998   1997   1996   4   3   2   1

A CIP catalog record for this book is available from the British Library.

Library of Congress Cataloging-in-Publication Data

Dickinson and audience / edited by Martin Orzeck and Robert Weisbuch.
        p.   cm.
     Includes bibliographical references.
     ISBN 0-472-10325-3 (acid-free paper)
     1. Dickinson, Emily, 1830–1886—Criticism and interpretation.
   2. Women and literature—United States—History—19th century.
   3. Authors and readers—United States—History—19th century.
   4. Reader-response criticism. I. Orzeck, Martin, 1951–   .
   II. Weisbuch, Robert, 1946–   .
   PS1541.Z5D475   1996   96-18592
   811'.4—dc20   CIP

*The editors and contributors wish
to dedicate this volume to
Richard Benson Sewall,
for his lifetime contribution to
American letters,
especially to Dickinson studies.*

Contents

Introduction: Dickinson the Scrivener

Robert Weisbuch and Martin Orzeck

In Herman Melville's story "Bartleby the Scrivener" the mysterious title character takes a position as a copyist in a law office and soon thereafter refuses his employer's request to perform his appointed task with a simple repetitive "I would prefer not to." A supine, undeliberate rebel by introducing the principle of preference into a Wall Street America where one must do as told and must obliterate the personal self implied by preference—what could be more self-abandoning than the task of mindlessly copying the words of others, words themselves based on a system more and more its own abstract entity?—Bartleby stands accused by his boss, the rich man's lawyer, who narrates the tale, less of lassitude or of crime than of causing him enormous frustration.

Dickinson as poet is akin to Bartleby as scrivener. She appears to have elected herself to a job she will not perform. "Publication—is the Auction / Of the Mind of Man—," she wrote in grand refusal. "Thought" belongs to the "Heavenly Grace" that gave it, and grace precludes "the Merchant." We must by Dickinson's unambiguous command "reduce no Human Spirit / To Disgrace of Price—."[1] And, more simply, in response to Thomas Wentworth Higginson, the editor of the *Atlantic Monthly* whose advice on poetry Dickinson sought and then dismissed, when he offered advice as well on marketing the poems, Dickinson replied that the notion of publication was more foreign to her than "Firmament to Fin—."[2]

Like Bartleby, whose subjunctive phrase masks an iron determination, Dickinson "would prefer not to," and her preference, too, can create a maddening annoyance. "This is my letter to the World / That never wrote to Me—" (441), she claims, as if abused, but is the real situation not the reverse for those who would respond to the poetry, our letter to the poet who never wrote to us? Dickinson seems at times not to write for us—seems, that is, not only by her stated and practiced choice for artistic and personal privacy but also by the internal qualities of the poems finally pried postmortem from her, to enforce with a special literalness the dictum that the lyric poet never addresses an audience but only can be overheard. Just as Melville's lawyer learns only by barest rumor the circumstances of Bartleby's past, so we are denied in the poems the circumstances of their utterance. We overhear a searing account of the internal upshot of events, but the events themselves are conspicuously absent, an "omitted center," by Jay Leyda's phrase.[3] And yet, by a final comparison, just as the other law copyists find themselves employing Bartleby's "would prefer" much as they oppose him and much as the lawyer himself becomes maddeningly obsessed by his refusing scrivener, so too a huge multitude of readers have found themselves not repelled but attached by Dickinson's refusals.

Even so, if the eventual publication of Dickinson's poems constituted something of a crime against the poet, do we not extend the offense by this collection of essays? What in the name of sanctity are we doing here in a volume on "Dickinson and Audience"? The title might seem a cruel joke on its contributors and more cruel still to the poet who inspired it. In fact, we can list several reasons against the existence of this topic. (1) Dickinson explicitly disdained a public audience for her work. (2) She conceived of that work as directed solely "White—Unto the White Creator—," with whiteness here, not entirely Melvillian, implying the transparent and transcendent, that not marked by the soil of earthly merchandising and what we might call the capitalist ego. (3) Once she was published her words were traduced by conventionally bound editors, the lawyers of this tale, and, despite the attempts of subsequent editors to restore the poems to their original state, Dickinson never will be published accurately because of the sincerely unprepared state in which she left her work. (4) The content of many of the poems praises silence over all utterance. And (5), in stern practice of her adage that "Subjects hinder talk" (L 397), the strategy of all of the poems precludes the kinds of circumstantial fillings-in that an audience reasonably might expect.

Yet each of these objections can be met. In fact, each of these apparent prohibitions against considering Dickinson in relation to audience provides an opportunity for doing just that. For instance, a large number of the poems began their lives included in letters to friends. The letters themselves, wonderfully empathetic and yearning, in turn, for intense response, speak to a special desire in Dickinson for "fit audience if few," in which *few* means the one-to-one that alone allows for intimacy. And, while the inclusion of poems in some of those letters in no way compromises their anti-occasional status (the relation of poem to letter or to addressee is often obscure, and even where it is plain the poem spreads quickly beyond the ostensible occasion to an all-of-life pattern), this is proof that the poems were offered to an audience and bear the mark of communication. The poems are anything but the usual communication and, in fact, meaningfully refuse what we expect in writing to provide an alternative. This is a major insight in the essay in this volume written by David Porter. Like Bartleby, who apparently was made disconsolate by an earlier employment in the Dead Letter Office, where the usual forms of communication (scriptural as well as personal, with a pun on *Dead Letter*) had failed, Dickinson too means to say something by an alternate speech to a deafened world, as and by becoming a puzzle.

Further still, some of the writers in this volume question whether Dickinson did not half-desire wider publication, a not-impossible surmise concerning a poet whose best poems often openly conflict with one another in meaning. It is perfectly possible to argue, without recourse to a charge of hypocrisy, that Dickinson did and did not wish to keep the poems a private affair among herself, God, and a few friends. Truly, the poems were left in handwritten form, with hasty punctuation and even a list of variant words with a final choice unmade. But the poems also were left in packets, as if by design. The nature of the revisions—in most, usually, the overall structure of the poem remains unchanged, while individual words are nominated and dismissed—provides insight into the working of her patterning mind, whereby design precedes detail; otherwise, the raw state of the manuscripts does not so much preclude a more or less scrupulous printed representation, as Thomas Johnson's editing in 1955 and the subsequent surge in interest in Dickinson proved, as it does offer editorial theorists a particularly rich set of problems and choices. Finally, Dickinson's praise of silence as indicative of deepest emotion is met by her many praisings of poetry itself as wrung silence, the winning of words to the same effect. And the nature of her own language, in refusing the circumstantial and biographical, does not prohibit but, rather, creates a uniquely intimate response, as if the withholding of gossipy details provides an archetypal autobiography in which all of us find our lives. As another of our contributors, Rob Smith, documents, readers have personalized their readings of the poems almost hilariously, and, while this anthropomorphism is often revelatory of every romantic myth and gender blunder in the culture, it is also testimony to the communicated intimacy of Dickinson's work. But that is not surprising, for the Dickinson of the poems, "not myself," she told Higginson with a professional's confidence, but "the Representative of the Verse" (L 268), does not initiate outer action but responds, like a reader herself, to an unnamed something-out-there. And it is the responding, the reading, that finally means more than the initiating event.

Put plainly, in no profound way does the poet's history or her art preclude the topic of Dickinson and audience. Instead, it offers magnificent challenges to the usual lexicons of reader-response theory and to the study of public reception. Reading becomes as or more essential than what is read. Audience is not only a who but a what, not so much you as you are in your daily mind but, instead, a new you not so far from that divinity who provided the grace of thought. Or perhaps to say this is to enlist in the Dickinson vision without enough of a struggle to stay outside the circle of its eye and "I." But that is yet another of the problems that Dickinson creates. Indeed, there is the unsettling sense as one considers Dickinson and audience that she has visited this subject first, anticipated its conventions, and constructed traps that drop us into an ignorance higher that the sure knowledge we might reach by a likelier poetry, into a darkness more enlightening than the noons of others.

Editorially, we have arranged our collection of essays into three groupings to uncover the poet's theoretical, her epistolary, and her more broadly public and historical sense of an audience. The reader should not be misled by these discrete groupings, however, into thinking the contributors are working at cross-purposes, or putting their own polemical carts before their horses, so to speak. Dickinson, probably more than any other American writer of her century, invites the diversity of critical approaches we seek to apply to her poems and letters. Indeed, one of the most telling differences between Melville's "pallidly neat, pitiably respectable, incurably forlorn" scrivener and the Amherst poet is the length (and volume) of the paper trail she left behind, and, when dealing with a body of work as richly complex and challenging as hers, we do well always to remember there is more than one Emily Dickinson. As our most distinguished contributor, Richard Sewall, remarks in his National Book Award–winning biography of the poet, "There may in fact be as many as there are biographers"—or as many as there are critics, we might add.[4] But for our own expository purposes we have chosen to present three who are primarily concerned with the problem of audience.

"The bridge of faith has no pier," as one of us has written elsewhere, echoing the opening line of Poem 915, "Faith—is the Pierless Bridge."[5] As a supreme artist of compensation, however, Dickinson translated her lack of certainty into a chief motive for writing as much as she did. Her poems often seem to be expressed toward a conceptual audience that, while it cannot always be delineated as precisely as contemporary readers would like, constitutes "A first Necessity," as we tell our composition students all the time. She must have been writing for someone, yet each of the first five essays in this volume undertakes in its own way to explore an aspect of Dickinson's marvelously skeptical and resourceful approaches to composing poems for "Nobody" in particular and the rhetorical and grammatical consequences of her endeavors. As David Porter argues, there is the "mystery of why Dickinson did not revise and further the mystery of her conception of audience." Among the problems raised by these related questions is the tendency of critics to provide historical contextualizations or biographical storifications of their own for the poems rather than to examine what makes them so intriguing to us in their unrevised (and unrevisable) state. Porter charts the territory between "madeness" and "saidness" in Dickinson's poems—texts that often startle us with the power of their utterance while baffling us with a "glorious ricketiness, more authentic to her than finish."

For Charlotte Nekola the poles of Dickinson's ambivalence toward a conceptual audience are the "demand of [her] individual genius" to express itself in great poetry and the conflicting "cultural gender expectations" that limit female writers of her generation to forms "such as sentimental verse and domestic or pious novels" or even to silence, a virtue often praised by the poet herself. In a similar vein Robert Weisbuch sees the poems as "Nobody's" business, seeking not so much to confirm the "good old universalized reader" of the humanist tradition but, rather, to expose (or possibly to obliterate) the myth of ego identity, that "bland assurance of the first-person pronoun and the certainties of personal boundary." Virginia Jackson also sees challenges to the reader's selfhood implicit in the poems from their earliest public presentation in the 1890s. For Jackson "Dickinson's privileged self-address entitles her to the definition of lyric poet in its purest form," whose "structure of address . . . is one in which saying 'I' can stand for saying 'you.'" Finally, Rob Smith provides his own nice reversal to our discussion of Dickinson's concept of audience by making a century of male criticism following her initial publication the target of the poet's rhetoric of irony.

"Reading Seductions: Dickinson, Rhetoric, and the Male Reader" uses Poem 1206, "The Show is not the Show," as "a neat summation of a Dickinson aesthetic of reception that assumes what is of interest is not the response but, rather, the attitude assumed by the responders and that the reading is less valuable than the subsequent exposure of the readers in the course of their analyses."

Still, in spite of all these testimonies to Dickinson's ambivalent posturings toward audience, there remains the indisputable evidence of over a thousand published letters, not to mention the fact that "many [other] letters are known to be irrecoverable," as Thomas Johnson noted in his 1958 edition of *The Letters of Emily Dickinson.*[6] More than two hundred and sixty different poems appear in the context of her written correspondence, enough certainly to give weight to the argument that their recipients constituted the major portion of the poet's contemporary audience. And, though the relationship between given poems and the letters in which they appear still occasions critical debate, there is no denying that her correspondence at least offered the poet a kind of "writer's workshop, in which the developing artist would likely experiment with her persona, formulate a durable reader-writer relationship, and sample various images and image clusters that might then reemerge meaningfully in the poems"—so Martin Orzeck argues in "Dickinson's Letters to Abiah Root: Formulating the Reader as 'Absentee.' "

Moreover, there is no denying certain crucial relationships were formative for Dickinson, and none more so than those she had with other women. For Betsy Erkkila the poet's sister-in-law, Susan Gilbert Dickinson, "more than any other . . . was the presiding presence in the birth chambers of her poetic art." In "Homoeroticism and Audience: Emily Dickinson's Female 'Master' " Erkkila concludes that throughout the years of their relationship "Sue continued as sister-spirit, witch-goddess, erotic center, and muse at the very sources of Dickinson's poetic creation." Yet another shaping influence was exerted by Mrs. Elizabeth Holland, who, according to Stephanie Tingley, "became for Emily Dickinson the ideal friend Ralph Waldo Emerson defined and described in his essay 'Friendship,' " one before whom the poet could "think aloud." Richard Sewall finds in the poet's late friendship with Helen Hunt Jackson "Emily Dickinson's perfect audience": "Here at last was someone, and someone of literary stature, who believed in her, recognized her greatness, and was willing to work not only *for* but *on* her poems." The fact is that Dickinson led a richly creative life of the mind through her epistolary relationships—not one of deprivation and frustrated desire but, rather, one that enabled her to upbraid Higginson for asking if she never felt want of employment: "I never thought of conceiving that I could ever have the slightest approach to such a want in all future time. . . . I feel that I have not expressed myself strongly enough."[7]

It is significant that Dickinson turned to the same Higginson, however, "to ensure her enduring reputation, indeed, her immortality," as Robert Regan points out in "Dickinson's Elected Audience." She would have been well informed by Emerson's essays that it is often the poet's lot to endure "flights of censure," to be "hissed and hooted" by the multitude, but, like her comparably obscure contemporaries, Jones Very and Frederick Tuckerman, Dickinson sought to secure her fame posthumously. Still, the historical Dickinson is a mid-nineteenth-century poet, as Willis Buckingham reminds us in "Emily Dickinson and the Reading Life." Consequently, in studying the period poetry reviews of the 1840s and 1850s, he discerns the antebellum cultural imagination from which Dickinson the reader, and soon-to-be writer, of poems was to emerge. The degree to which that culture was publicly aware of Dickinson's aspirations is a subject revisited by our final contributor, Karen Dandurand. In "Dickinson and the Public" she raises the question of just how widely known Dickinson was during her lifetime, asserting that "a larger audience than we have thought was aware of her as a poet during at least the last two decades of her life, though members of this audience usually maintained some reticence about commenting publicly on her, in keeping with the private channels through which they had come to know her work."

If there are as many Dickinsons as there are Dickinson biographers and critics, we have her own prolific and enigmatic creativity to thank for that. In studying one of America's two truly great nineteenth-century poets, who wrote to a world that was "*not* Conclusion," we find the problem of audience as beckoning and as baffling as it must have seemed one hundred years ago, when her poems elicited their first widespread public reception. From a late-twentieth-century perspective that tends to theorize more while mythologizing less, we can still be intrigued by questions as basic as "Who did she write for?" "Why didn't she publish more?" And, of course, "Who was her 'Master' "?—that wonderfully engendered nineteenth-century term used so craftily and so subversively by her much admired Charlotte Brontë in *Jane Eyre*. Whether our answers to these questions discover more about the critic than they do about the poet, they finally reveal that the proper answer to her initial letter to Higginson asking if her poetry is "alive" remains a resounding yes.

NOTES

1. Poem 709, in the one-volume edition of *The Poems of Emily Dickinson,* ed. Thomas H. Johnson (Boston: Little Brown, 1960). Unless otherwise noted, the poems are reprinted in accordance with Johnson's choice of variants in this edition. References to this edition appear in the text, with the poem's number placed in parentheses.
2. Letter 265, in *The Letters of Emily Dickinson,* ed. Thomas H. Johnson and Theodora Ward, 3 vols. (Cambridge: Belknap Press of Harvard University Press, 1958), vol. 2. References to this edition appear in the text in parentheses, with the abbreviation "L" followed by the number of the cited letter.
3. Jay Leyda, "Introduction," in *The Years and Hours of Emily Dickinson,* 2 vols. (New Haven: Yale University Press, 1960), 1:xx.
4. Richard B. Sewall, *The Life of Emily Dickinson* (New York: Farrar, Straus and Giroux, 1980), 532.
5. Robert Weisbuch, *Emily Dickinson's Poetry* (Chicago: University of Chicago Press, 1975), 177.
6. Thomas H. Johnson, "Notes on the Present Text," in *The Letters of Emily Dickinson,* 1:xxiii.
7. *Letters,* 2:474.

Part 1:
"The Pierless Bridge": Dickinson's Concept of Audience

Faith—is the Pierless Bridge
Supporting what We see
Unto the Scene that We do not—
Too slender for the eye

—Poem 915

Dickinson's Unrevised Poems

David Porter

After his first encounter face to face with the poet the noted man of letters Thomas Wentworth Higginson declared, "I am glad not to live near her."

In a letter to his wife describing the hour-long interview in which Dickinson, fully mature at age thirty-nine, had talked incessantly, Higginson included a succinct account of his experience: "I never was with any one who drained my nerve power so much. Without touching her, she drew from me."[1] The poet's performance for her audience of one, at a time when she was seeing no one outside the family, is especially significant in light of the mannerisms that mark her written performance in the poems.

The single most brilliant commentary on the nature of those mannerisms is R. P. Blackmur's brief essay "Emily Dickinson's Notation," which appeared in 1956, prompted by the publication of Thomas H. Johnson's variorum edition of the complete poems.[2] Blackmur's stunning analogy would be notorious in these days of heightened gender sensitivities if it were widely known. He wrote that "it sometimes seems as if in her work a cat came at us speaking English," adding "it comes at us all voice so far as it is in control, fragmented elsewhere, willful and arbitrary, because it has not the acknowledged means to be otherwise." His judgment is that "her disorder is her own," and his incisive survey of the irregularities, her "resourceful barbarism of the soul," initiated or anticipated much of what is enlightening in later analyses, including criticism that deals with the reader's role. His basic assertion linking the notation of poetry and music, that is, everything that actually appears on the page, including spacing and punctuation, applies specifically as well to Dickinson's texts: "The point is that the notation is always inadequate, by itself, in predicting performance or reading. As the poet was saying much more, so the reader is left with more or less to do for himself as the notation wills him or fails him."

Between this profound, sensitive view of the generative processes within written poetry and the more common view, exemplified by John Updike, that what is mainly needed in Dickinson's case are regularized texts of her work in type, lies the hard question of Dickinson's concept of her audience and, in turn, her intentions regarding publication. Updike, commenting on the "disfiguring" typographical "eccentricity" of the printed, revised text (1986) of James Joyce's *Ulysses,* writes: "What we have here, as in the almost unreadable Thomas H. Johnson transcriptions of Emily Dickinson's manuscript poems, is a mistaken scholarly fidelity to holograph mannerisms that were never meant by the author to be translated into type."[3] But Thomas Johnson had, in fact, said much the same thing in his introduction to the variorum edition concerning the poet's idiosyncratic dashes and possessives and her spelling and capitals: "Quite properly such 'punctuation' can be omitted in later editions, and the spelling and capitalization regularized."[4] In conversation with me later, however, Johnson allowed that "regularizing" Dickinson's mannerisms was not advised because it eliminated from the poet's habitual expression very real but hard-to-identify qualities. Thus, the question of Dickinson's conception of her audience is inseparably involved in the process of transcribing the holographs into type. In that form the poems, to use Mikhail Bakhtin's terms, are the crucial factor in a three-role drama, the artistic work being the one in which the relation of the creator and the contemplator is fixed.[5]

Had Dickinson sent off a batch of her poems for possible publication, their spelling and punctuation irregularities unrevised as well as the elided syntax, peculiar noun classes, and invented verb forms, the editor's reply would have been, "My Dear Miss Dickinson, There are striking passages here, and we will gladly print the poems once you have finished them and the lines have a syntactic clarity." The editor's problems to this day are the constant affair of translators, who must labor at the hazardous boundary between attempting somehow to convey the mannerisms and yet produce intelligibility. Because languages have distinct grammars, they have equally distinct occasions for irregularity. The Japanese translator Masako Takeda writes that she is asked why she does "not present Dickinson as she is, that is, translate her into 'chaotic' Japanese." Her answer indicates the root level of the English language at which Dickinson, like Gerard Manley Hopkins, composed: "As English and Japanese have so large a gap, 'chaotic' Japanese would have completely different aspects from what comes out of 'chaotic' English."[6]

The extent of Dickinson's idiosyncratic language practice is reflected in the fact that she wrote one of the two oddest lines in American literature. Ralph Waldo Emerson wrote the other in his greatest, most demanding essay "Experience." Their two lines illustrate once again how misleading the practice of putting authors and their works into stories, "storifying" them—whether historicist, psychological, or feminist—can be. Emerson's sentence is: "And yet is the God the native of these bleak rocks."[7] All readers who I know construe the sentence in a quick naturalizing process as referring, incorrectly, supposedly in Emerson's darkest philosophical moment, to blasted life, declaring starkly, "And yet God is the creator of these bleak rocks." In its intricate textural function, however, quite to the contrary, the sentence actually reads as the truth that Emerson had set his heart on. It is paraphrasable this way: "And though people don't like to hear it, subjectivity, that is, Temperament, one of the lords of life, is the natural condition of our state of separate existences." Emerson's earnest implication is that Americans must hold hard to this condition of self-trust and possess this "axis more firmly."

Dickinson's weird line begins one of her better-known poems, which, significantly, was not published until 1929 and, then, with only two of the original twenty dashes, as here, and with periods demarcating the sentences:

This was a Poet—It is That
Distills amazing sense
From ordinary Meanings—
And Attar so immense

From the familiar species
That perished by the Door—
We wonder it was not Ourselves
Arrested it—before—

Of Pictures, the Discloser—
The Poet—it is He—
Entitles Us—by Contrast—
To ceaseless Poverty—

Of Portion—so unconscious—
The Robbing—could not harm—
Himself—to Him—a Fortune—
Exterior—to Time—

(Poem 448)

Quite aside from the excision of the expected pronoun—it appears conventionally in line 10—the poem's opening line, containing the indispensable subject phrases, is a phonological din on top of a deictic hopscotch. From the line's outer boundaries it reads inward as clashing markers: *This/That, was/is, a Poet/It.* The line abruptly yokes two habitual Dickinson genres, the epitaph and the definition. We know what she means, of course: the poet is the one who extracts amazing sense where others find only the familiar. Avoidance at the outset of the generic pronoun that is masculine in specific contexts, but not here, is hardly significant as the poem forms its values. The fugitive syntax of this beginning, quite unlike the recoverable lack of two pronouns (*he* and *him*), a verb (*is*), and a period stop (*him.*) in the final stanza, resists, to be sure, any paraphrase more simple than this: for us to be able to say of someone in eulogy that "This was a Poet," the person must have been one who is able to distill amazing sense from our ordinary experiences.

The problem is not that the poem is too advanced for its time but, rather, that it is unprintable as it is. No editor until 1929 approved it. Why do we? Are not such poems, given their syllabic constraint, in which more belligerently than in most poems in English, syllables are at war with syntax and lines at war with sentences, unrevisable? Such circumstances indicate what is almost universally overlooked: the mystery of why Dickinson did not revise and the further mystery of her conception of her audience. What did she think poetry was? Not least of all, the circumstances raise the question of her understanding with her sister Lavinia, who, after Emily's death, burned the poet's private papers but not the poems from the locked box in the bedroom. Did Emily say to Lavinia, "Don't burn the poems because by 1929 the audience will tolerate these quirks of mine." Whatever Dickinson *storia* one writes, it must account for the opening line of "This was a Poet" to see how the line in turn dismantles the historicizing and ideologizing that would naturalize it by conscripting it. We must deal, that is, with what Blackmur called "a cruel freedom which will not itself be tampered with"?

While historical contextualizing or biographical storification does not equip readers to retrieve the controlling syntactical logic in the problematic poems, that logic exists for the most part and is almost always grammatical in form. It is most strikingly apparent in Dickinson's aphorisms. Karl Keller, in a favor to all readers, collected seven full pages of these gnomic shafts that he calls "axioms."[8] They are a riveting demonstration of Dickinson's clarity of syntax when she chose:

> Impossibility, like wine, exhilarates the man who tastes it.
> Possibility is flavorless.

> Satisfaction is the agent of satiety, want a quiet commissary for infinity.

> The most intangible thing is the most adhesive.

She was masterful in the skill. It explains, I believe, why her verses, which I have called miscellaneous and unmanageable, with the fascicle arrangements the chief example, evincing intensity without a controlling project, are, in the end, triumphantly unmanageable.[9] Like cult performances in other arts that join cliché to cliché in unpredictable ways—in Dickinson's case the simple hymnal forms, the vernacular voice, ready-to-hand subjects of love and separation, delight and despair—her poems, often at the same time elliptical, lacking technical or grammatical finish, identifiable speakers, definite referents or titles, exemplify, to borrow the apt term of Umberto Eco's, what may be called "glorious ricketiness."[10]

To frame our recognition of this rare merging of ramshackle form and piercing originality we shall do well to consider at a deeper level, in this present era of discomfort with the concept of "art" itself, the actual nature of poetry. For poetry worthy of its heritage rests not upon historical definition or mere expression of emotion but, rather, upon the central paradox of language itself, that unique intersection of what nature gives us and culture instills. Language, at the same instant, is both law abiding and infinitely creative. Because it is rule governed, each of us, on the basis of astonishingly piecemeal and disorderly sound stimuli coming from others—mainly "motherese" while one is pushed in a shopping cart, shall we say, through the supermarket—solves the mystery of its grammar and internalizes this program by the age of four. Because the grammatical structure is generative, we say and understand sentences every day that we have never heard before. Theoretically, then, while the heavens hold billions upon billions of stars, there are more sentences even than stars. As a consequence of this creativity, there exists a vast linguistic expanse that is still unuttered. It is the poet who, phrase by phrase, opens up that territory that lies waiting. In that yet-to-be spoken land occurs always the overthrow by art of existing representational conventions. In this colonization are the surprise and the satisfaction that enlarge our capacities and that we call art. Dickinson is unsurpassed at this, extracting to our repeated surprise an exact language from the layers of words that already cover all things. As Joseph Brodsky remarked somewhere of the poet's task, "What provides you with subject matter is your own language, and that's all."

The territory Dickinson colonizes for her audience displays yet a further paradox that derives from the basic nature of poetry: poetry is simultaneously something *said* and something *made*. In Dickinson's case, at the core of her work is the almost continual opposition of her (so it seems) urgent meaning to the madeness of her verses. As for the objective, we remember the dramatic statement she made to Higginson in that first interview in the Amherst parlor: "If I read a book [and] it makes my whole body so cold no fire ever can warm me I know *that* is poetry. If I feel physically as if the top of my head were taken off, I know *that* is poetry. These are the only way I know it. Is there any other way."[11]

When madeness dominates in the conflict with saidness—as in limericks or pop rock lyrics—we have the banalities of doggerel. It is our interpretation, of the sort I am attempting here, that lifts Dickinson's work out of the amateur's realm of folk practice into the art world. As Arthur Danto asserts convincingly of visual art, "Only in relationship to an interpretation is a material object an artwork."[12]

Madeness in Dickinson's poems is essentially a spatial function. It begins with her minimalist form, which is often in exhilarating conflict with replete reality, that is, with the mute universe of things and relations that are nonlinguistic and that lie outside of poems. Her touchstone verse in this regard is five lines long, twenty-seven words:

> To make a prairie it takes a clover and one bee,
> One clover, and a bee,
> And revery.
> The revery alone will do,
> If bees are few.

(Poem 1755)

Within her telegraphic poems the play of language is essentially spatial: high-density single words and figures intensify the already constraining hymnal form, with its syllabic count, short lines, and brief stanzas. In appearance, strikingly so in the holographs, single words are more substantial than line layouts, and the very presence of the text on the fascicle page is emphatic as it fills the space to the margins. Appropriately, the first edition in 1890 creates a new kind of presence for the tiny poems by beginning them with outsize letters and placing each in a sky of white margins.

Despite the minimalist scale, with its drastic elimination, we as readers find ourselves not transported to the end of poems in strict linear fashion as simplistic reader-response theory would have it but, rather, retracing our steps repeatedly, identifying pronoun referents, finding subjects for the verbs, restoring syntax. This spatial movement of the reader's eye and mind together prolongs the process of readerly engagement. Though the poems are compact, they require complicated movement by the spectator. We legitimately wonder if those syntactical and referential difficulties are a reflection of Dickinson's own spatial awkwardnesses. She told Higginson that she couldn't tell time until she was fifteen and was afraid to ask because she didn't want her father to find out.[13]

The spatial functions that occupy the reader involve, then, both brevity and conflict. The brevity is in the hymn form, the further reliance on sharply focused, unelaborated figures, and, most impressively, in her characteristic first lines, notable in our literature for their engagement and suspense. Yet the difficulty of reference, both inside and outside the poem, involves the opposite process of slow retrieval and matching. Further conflict occurs as lines win out over sentences, syllable count blocks syntax and inflection, and unconventional punctuation impedes meaning.

One of Dickinson's pivotal poems on poetics will serve as an example of both the retracing necessary through the poem's spatial layout and of the syllabic-metric distortion of syntax. The subject of the opening sentence, Poetry, is placed suspensefully at the end of the first stanza and then, by enjambment, doubled as subject to include Love and then, by analogy in the final line, tripled to include God. The possessive displays Dickinson's own punctuation.

> To pile like Thunder to it's close
> Then crumble grand away
> While Everything created hid
> This—would be Poetry—

Or Love—the two coeval come—
We both and neither prove—
Experience either and consume—
For None see God and live—

(Poem 1247)

The spatial retracing is strictly linguistic in the second stanza as the reader
sorts out the referents for *two, both, neither,* and *either* and seeks the logic
by which *None* enfolds the prior *We.* All this spatial travel by the reader—
and I have by no means completed the chart of it—occurs within just
twenty-two words at the close. As for syllabic count distorting syntax in
this regular eight-six hymnal form, the clause in the line before the last—
"Experience either and consume"—must be expanded by the reader to
restore the elided syntax so that it reads intelligibly "[If We] Experience
either [Poetry or Love,] [We are] consume[d] [by it]." I leave unat-
tempted the question of whether experiencing poetry or love, as asserted
by the analogy to seeing God in the final line, can cost life itself.

Dickinson's best-known poem, "Because I could not stop for
Death," has comparable spatial difficulties, the initial entry occurring in
the opening word, *Because,* which inaugurates the cross-cutting motifs of
time and emotion that readers strive to understand. The opening eight
lines are a space-time-tonal complex:

Because I could not stop for Death—
He kindly stopped for me—
The Carriage held but just Ourselves—
And Immortality.

We slowly drove—He knew no haste
And I had put away
My labor and my leisure too,
For His Civility—

(Poem 712)

Only earnest effort on the reader's part will get at the source of the
mystery of the undescribed joining of Death and the I-speaker that domi-
nates the poem. In the connector *Because* resides the shocking relationship
of *I* and *Death,* their linked actions, but the actual dying, the coition, is in
that *And* at the beginning of line 6. The poem's drama, quite apart from

the striking figure of the country gentleman and, later on, the gazing grain and the horses' heads, takes place in those two connectors, *Because* and *And,* and it is only through the reader's spatial travels back and forth that the event comes to be known.

The hard question that I am addressing, posed a different way, is this: What did Dickinson seek to preserve at the cost of intelligibility for her audience? The challenge is manifest in poem after poem. Here are the eight lines of a poem in fascicle 21, written in 1862 or before, not published until 1935, the final four lines of which are a syntactical puzzle to be unscrambled only when the function of the opening word, *Sweeter,* is understood, when the space is retraced, not to a parallel *better* employed in lines 1 and 3 but, rather, in a typical Dickinson liberty, to be shorthand for "more sweetly." That adverbial function produces a sentence, the final one of three to be discovered amid the thirteen dashes, that, fully expanded, would read: The surmising robins never gladdened a tree more sweetly than when confronting a solid—that is, a permanent and heavenly dawn leading to no ordinary day.

> Dreams—are well—but Waking's better,
> If One wake at Morn—
> If One wake at Midnight—better—
> Dreaming—of the Dawn—
>
> Sweeter—the Surmising Robins—
> Never gladdened Tree—
> Than a Solid Dawn—confronting—
> Leading to no Day—

(Poem 450)

Comparable puzzles mark the closing stanzas of the important poem that begins "I think I was enchanted" (593) on the transforming magic of Barrett Browning's lines, for example, and also mark the figurative closing of the following love poem, in which the female speaker is evidently asked by her lover if he will suffice for her. Here are the closing lines:

> Withdrew the Sun—to Other Wests—
> Withdrew the furthest Star
> Before Decision—stooped to speech—
> And then—be audibler

> The Answer of the Sea unto
> The Motion of the Moon—
> Herself adjust Her Tides—unto—
> Could I—do else—with Mine?
>
> (Poem 643)

What will our provisional paraphrase be? Perhaps this: The sound of the sea adjusting her tides to the motion of the moon was more audible than my answer to my lover as I adjusted my tides to him.

As a final example of the type, the compaction of Poem 982 is so absolute that, unless the spatial retracing is assiduously undertaken, the poem's bitterly ironic judgment on the Calvinist measurement of human-kind is unattainable. The version that follows is the fair copy sent to Sue, distilled by the poet herself quite deliberately from earlier and longer packet versions. The "No Other" that begins the poem omits the actual subject, Thought, which must be inserted by the reader as the implied but absent parallel to *remembering* and *Contemplation:*

> No Other can reduce
> Our mortal Consequence
> Like the remembering it be nought
> A Period from hence
> But Contemplation for
> Cotemporaneous Nought
> Our Single Competition
> Jehovah's Estimate.
>
> (Poem 982)

Mapping the syntax requires the reader to attend to the "No Other . . . But" construction at the center. The fully recovered sentence, then, has this meaning: Nothing so diminishes our thought of life's importance as remembering that it will be over in a short time, unless it is God's estimate that even now our mortal lives are nought.[14]

The answer to the basic question I have posed concerning the poet's priorities appears to be that Dickinson chose to preserve the intensity of the performance at the cost of effortless intelligibility for her audience. That practice can be seen as a radical mode of deconstruction—what all poems do to some extent—and not simply in the vague metaphoric sense in which the term is almost invariably used by critics and theorists but, instead, in its demonstration of the enriching contest between figure and logic in the structure of language itself. Dickinson composed mostly by rigid adherence to the formal requirements of syllabic count and line length and lexical dominance rather than syntax and intelligibility. Another way to say this is that for this poet evocation took precedence over description, the poem, as she declared starkly to Higginson about having her head taken off by poetry, being a *source*, not a *record*, of experience. In short, this is the sensationalist principle of poetry. Dickinson's refusal to title her poems is the overarching sign of this.

Feminist biographical and ideological historicizings of Dickinson, the effort through storification to connect her poems to social issues on the outside, fail to discern the characteristic linguistic practices that identify Dickinson's verse. Furthermore, stereotyping her as a subversive player in a simple Manichaean sexual allegory, rationalizing her troublesome poems by biography, fails, perhaps most notably, to preserve the poet's compelling strangeness. The most basic fallacy is to insist on the referential function of the poems as if they were ordinary communication. Gender studies have yet to study, instead, perhaps the most promising aspect of Dickinson's art; the connection between the miscellaneousness, the ricketiness, and the ways in which a woman's writing is sometimes distinguishable from a man's—nonlinear, shorter, organized in fragments, the product of work patterns and objectives that do not lead to a single totemized object.

Whatever approach readers take to her work, the significance of those textual realities must be taken into account: the special experience of reading the Dickinson canon that produces in the reader no overall order of the poet's perception, the way printing misrepresents her work as orderly and decisive, and the generic elements her poetry lacks, including titles, selection and categorization, magnitude, finishedness, a dialogue with history, a hierarchy of claims, an ars poetica, and technical development.

Yet Dickinson seems to have shared the exalted view of poetry with her younger contemporary Stéphane Mallarmé, who wrote: "One desire of my epoch which cannot be dismissed is to separate so as to attribute them differently the double state of the immediate or unrefined word on the one hand, the essential one on the other." He emphasized both the desire for and the indirectness of the supreme word: "Languages are imperfect in that although there are many, the supreme one is lacking: thinking is to write without accessories . . . the immortal word is still tacit."[15] Blackmur correctly enlisted Dickinson "as a member in good

standing" in the movement of modern poetry, noting the spiritual aspira-
tions beyond common language that Dickinson possessed ("the Word
made flesh"), and wrote, quoting Marcel Raymond, that "poetry in this
time . . . 'tended to become an ethic or some sort of irregular instrument
of metaphysical knowledge.' "[16]

Perhaps Robert Frost, in a single stroke, got to the heart of the
willfulness and doggedness on Dickinson's part that makes the poems
unrevisable:

> Since she wrote without thought of publication and was not under
> the necessity of revamping and polishing, it was easy for her to go
> right to the point and say precisely what she thought and felt. Her
> technical irregularities give her poems strength as if she were saying,
> "Look out, Rhyme and Meter, Here I come."

Elsewhere Frost distilled Dickinson's mode to a single marvelous sen-
tence: "When she started a poem, it was 'Here I come!' and she came
plunging through."[17] Poetry and love, Dickinson wrote,

> We both and neither prove—
> Experience either and consume—
> For None see God and live—.

Roman Jakobson was exactly right when he asserted that poems may
be grammatical or antigrammatical but never agrammatical. Agram-
maticality is mishmash, chaos. But deliberately ungrammatical poems
like Dickinson's release, as the nonsymmetry and disorder of a modern
city does, as collage does, surprise encounters, novel juxtapositions, fan-
tasy, transport, surrealism. An editor, then, in asking Dickinson to adopt
the conventions of the language for her readers' ease would have required
the poet and the poems to change character.

Do Dickinson's poems, then, succeed by their flaws? John Ashbery's
poetry is instructive. Poised between the splendid excesses of Romanti-
cism and the carefully offhand banalities of postmodernist iconoclasms,
his poems exploit with impressive freshness the agglomeration of literary
language, workaday conversation, and advertising hard sell that articu-
late our days, intricately deployed so that the nobilities Romanticism
celebrated—love and beauty, aspirings to the ideal—while never named,
are never out of mind. Evasion itself is a strategy of valuing the ideal.

Here are the familiar lines beginning an early poem, "The Tennis Court Oath," that do this:

> What had you been thinking about
> the face studiously bloodied
> heaven blotted region
> I go on loving you like water but
> there is a terrible breath in the way all of this
> You were not elected president, yet won the race

Ashbery's work, as Keith Cohen usefully writes, but with a needless neo-Marxist overlay, is "a frontal attack on the fundamental props of bourgeois discourse—continuity, utility, closure."[18] Dickinson's disjunctions are less systematic than Ashbery's but not the less significant.

Take this occurrence that italicizes the affinity of mannerisms and ricketiness and the question of the artist's intentions. While walking recently on the remote Wauwinet shore of Nantucket Island, I came upon some peculiar scratches left in the sand by a wave from the Atlantic. Stepping back, I saw they formed the following words:

> Much madness is divinest sense
> Much sense the starkest madness
> In this, as all, prevail.
> Demur, you're straightway dangerous.

Here was a Dickinson poem if ever I saw one, but without an iota of intention evident on any human being's part, leastwise hers. As I gazed, a second wave washed up and receded, leaving in its wake four more lines that I recognized as Dickinson's second stanza, characteristically flawed but effective in its frugal intensity:

> To a discerning eye
> 'Tis the majority
> Assent, and you are sane;
> And handled with a chain.

My itch to make sense of the lines was fully activated, as always, and there was not a moment's need in these oceanic circumstances to trouble myself with the question of authorial intention.[19] But, of course, the poem

on the beach never happened, and, furthermore, the poem as such is not
Dickinson's. It is, rather, Blackmur's version of the poem "Much Mad-
ness" seen "askance," as he says, with alternate lines printed in a new order
as stanzas and punctuation regularized. The actual poem, we know, is the
one that follows. If its distortion by the beach poem seems so limited, it is
because the sentence boundaries in the original are, typically, a puzzle.

> Much Madness is divinest Sense—
> To a discerning Eye—
> Much Sense—the starkest Madness—
> 'Tis the Majority
> In this, as All, prevail—
> Assent—and you are sane—
> Demur—you're straightway dangerous—
> And handled with a Chain—

(Poem 435)

Now, with the beach poem accurately revised, the question of inten-
tion is at the center of our attention. We shall profit by heeding, surely,
the reminder by the art historian Richard Wollheim that the artist stands
in front of his canvas, not behind it, seeing each brushstroke as he applies
it in relation to his other brushstrokes and to the edge of the canvas.[20] In
short, within every painter there is a spectator with choice—that is,
intention, ever so complicated but ineradicable. We must assume simi-
larly that Emily Dickinson stood not behind her sheets and scraps, reach-
ing over them to write what she could not see, but, in fact, saw each
word on the paper as she penciled it. Within Dickinson, we conclude,
there was not only a writer but also, most assuredly, a reader of what the
writer wrote. The consequences of this discernment oblige us to distin-
guish the nature of writing for an audience as distinct from exchanging
speech in conversation. There is, as it happens, a unique and singularly
revealing set of instances when we read what Dickinson wrote to a
special reader and then we hear her speak to him.

Dickinson's direct conversation with Thomas Wentworth Higginson in
1870 was an intense, compulsive affair, as we have noted. In that obliga-
tory communicative circuit she was unable to act with circumspection.
Her words came out in a torrent, all but uncontrolled. She began her
stopless monologue, Higginson tells us, by putting two daylilies in his

hand, saying, "These are my introduction," and then adding under her breath, "Forgive me if I am frightened; I never see strangers and hardly know what I say."[21]

The year before, however, when Higginson had asked her in a letter each of the pointed questions we would pose to her if we could, she was in exquisite control, mannered, mysterious, warm, candid, and, best of all, refusing to be banal, stunning in her conviction. When, for example, Higginson earnestly invites her to come to meet him in Boston, proposing the intellectual treats of hearing Emerson and himself lecture, adding disarmingly, "Don't you need sea air in summer," her reply is breath stopping in its finality: "I do not cross my Father's ground to any House or town." What follows below are excerpts rearranged, with emendations for coherence, of his exacting questions and her evident reply, however indirect, to each of them. It is her writing put, for contrastive purpose, into a conversational context.[22]

Higginson: I have the greatest desire to see you, but till then I can only rejoice in the rare sparkles of light from your poems and letters.

Dickinson: I am sure that you speak the truth, because the noble do, but your words always surprise me. Gratitude is the timid wealth of those who have nothing.

I never relax my interest in what you send to me, in the fine edge of thought which you bear. I take out your letters and verses, and I feel their strange power.

When a little Girl I remember hearing that remarkable passage and preferring the "Power," not knowing at the time that "Kingdom" and "Glory" were included.

I would gladly go to Boston to meet you. You must come down to Boston sometimes? All ladies do. I wonder if it would be possible to lure you to the meetings on the 3d Monday of every month at Mrs. Sargent's, 13 Chestnut Street at 10 A.M.—when somebody reads a paper and others talk or listen. Next Monday Mr. Emerson reads and then at 3:30 P.M. there is a meeting of Woman's Club where I read a paper on the Greek goddesses. That would be a good time for you to come, although I should still rather have you come on some day when I shall not be so much taken up—for my object is to see you, more than to entertain you. You see, I am in earnest. Or don't you need sea air in summer?

I do not cross my Father's ground to any House or town.

It is hard for me to understand how you can live so alone, with thoughts of such quality coming up in you and even the companionship of your dog withdrawn.

You noticed my dwelling alone—.

You enshroud yourself in this fiery mist and I cannot reach you.

"Seen of Angels" is scarcely my responsibility.

But if I could once see you and know that you are real. It brought you nearer even to know you had an actual uncle, though I can hardly fancy any two beings less alike than you and him. But I have not seen him for several years, though I have seen a lady who once knew you, but could not tell me much.

It is difficult not to be fictitious in so fair a place as Amherst, but test's severe repairs are permitted all.

It would be so easy, I fear, to miss you. I feel always timid lest what I write should be badly aimed.

My life has been too simple and stern to embarrass any.

It isolates one anywhere to think beyond a certain point or have such luminous flashes as come to you—so perhaps the place does not make much difference.

To an Emigrant, Country is idle except it be his own.

Her side of the transaction is finely manipulated, appealing in its strategies of give-and-take. What is revealed is the nature of writing that Dickinson understood superbly and exploited—that is, that writing releases language from its communicative function and allows other functions to operate, including, here in the flashes of gnomic authority and selective self-dramatization, the way it reveals as well as conceals and does so by writing's very design.

The ellipses and concealments in Dickinson's language and in her life pose a particular dilemma for audiences employing ordinary readerly strategies. "Our major device of order" in reading, Jonathan Culler

writes, is "the notion of the person or speaking subject, and the process
of reading is especially troubled when we cannot construct a subject who
would serve as a source of the poetic utterance." The reader, he adds
succinctly, reads the poem "as a gesture whose significance lies in the
context of a life."[23] Storifying, as we know well from Dickinson studies,
is a basic interpretive device, but, because the Dickinson context is a
mystery, it tends to be derived, in massive tautology, from the poems in
the first place. Yet the gap between life and writing is perhaps nowhere
wider than in the case of Dickinson. What, then, would regularizing of
the poems eliminate? In her poetics of evocation, we can say, she demon-
strated in a proleptic, surrealist way that sensation is not a syntactical
affair. It was her great insight, as it was for surrealism.

   Julia Kristeva's concept of the *chora* in art helps us to go a step farther
than this. She speaks of the "drive charge" that alters representation and
language. In Dickinson's irregularities what is established, then, is the
moment Kristeva conceives as the drive process breaking into text, dis-
turbing the sign and narrative "with all their lock-step, univocal serious-
ness." The breakthrough includes chance, which sometimes fortuitously
objectifies the dangerous motility of the instinctual experience. It also
includes for Dickinson's audience the laughter and the pleasure obtained
from the lifting of inhibitions.[24] Succinctly, what is preserved in the poet's
irregularities that so engage us is the performance of the thetic break into
language.

   Dickinson's glorious ricketiness, more authentic to her than finish,
was part of a manifest, if unstated, poetics in which the word, coming
into being, was made not semantic flesh but sensation. This drama of
incompletion, being essential, was to be preserved. Her poems partici-
pate in an incomplete universe, exploiting the virtues of nonclosure, and
no one knew this more urgently, as her axioms testify, than Dickinson.
The escape from convention, call it surrealist, appealed to her 1890 audi-
ences, who praised her poems for being "strange" and "powerful."[25] She
sought, as she implied in that unique letter to Higginson in 1869, to have
her poems represent the "mind alone," not to be auctioned off for publica-
tion or the revision that this would have required. The anathema of
closure and of desire fulfilled, the aura of spontaneous revelation, not
least the "spectral power" of writing, as she called it in the same letter,
were not to be compromised by an editor's syntactic clarity, for in those
willful contortions of language constrained by the primitive rigidities of
the hymn form, as in rickety collage, lay the possibility, not always

possible in the conventional, clear, and determinate, of taking the top of
her reader's head off.

NOTES

1. *The Letters of Emily Dickinson,* ed. Thomas H. Johnson, vol. 2 (Cambridge:
   Belknap Press of Harvard University Press, 1958), 476. Hereafter letters are
   cited by the numbers used in Johnson's volume.
2. Reprinted in *Emily Dickinson: A Collection of Critical Essays,* ed. Richard B.
   Sewall (Englewood Cliffs: Prentice-Hall, 1963), 78–87. This collection is an
   early portion of the broad and indispensable foundation Richard Sewall has
   provided for Dickinson studies over more than three decades. I am indebted
   to him beyond measure.
3. Letter in the *New York Review of Books,* 18 August 1988.
4. *The Poems of Emily Dickinson,* ed. Thomas H. Johnson, vol. 1 (Cambridge:
   Belknap Press of Harvard University Press, 1958), lxiii. Poems are cited in
   the text by the Johnson numbering.
5. Tzvetan Todorov, *Mikhail Bakhtin: The Dialogical Principle* (Minneapolis: Uni-
   versity of Minnesota Press, 1984), 21.
6. Masako Takeda, "On Translating Emily Dickinson into Japanese," in *After a
   Hundred Years: Essays on Emily Dickinson,* ed. Tamaaki Yamakawa et al.
   (Kyoto: Apollon-sha, 1988), 165.
7. *The Collected Works of Ralph Waldo Emerson,* ed. Alfred R. Ferguson et al.,
   vol. 3 (Cambridge: Belknap Press of Harvard University Press, 1983), 46.
8. Karl Keller, *The Only Kangaroo among the Beauty: Emily Dickinson and America*
   (Baltimore: Johns Hopkins Press, 1979), 171–78.
9. R. W. Franklin's facsimile edition of the fascicles, *The Manuscript Books of
   Emily Dickinson,* 2 vols. (Cambridge: Belknap Press of Harvard University
   Press, 1981), is exemplary textual scholarship and indispensable to Dickinson
   studies.
10. Umberto Eco, *Travels in Hyperreality* (New York: Harcourt Brace Jo-
    vanovich, 1986), 198.
11. Letter 342a.
12. Arthur Danto, *The Philosophical Disenfranchisement of Art* (New York: Colum-
    bia University Press, 1986), 39.
13. Letter 342b.
14. For a fuller discussion of poem 982, see my book *Dickinson: The Modern
    Idiom* (Cambridge: Harvard University Press, 1981), 27–28, 42.
15. *Stéphane Mallarmé: Selected Poetry and Prose,* ed. Mary Ann Caws (New York:
    New Directions, 1982), 75.
16. Sewall, *Emily Dickinson,* 87.
17. Quoted in Keller, *Only Kangaroo,* 312–13.
18. Keith Cohen, "Ashbery's Dismantling of Bourgeois Discourse," *Beyond*

Amazement: New Essays on John Ashbery, ed. David Lehman (Ithaca: Cornell University Press, 1980), 148.

19. I am indebted to Steven Knapp and Walter Benn Michaels for opening up literary theory to consideration of the poems some of us have found on ocean beaches. See Steven Knapp and Walter Benn Michaels, "Against Theory," in *Against Theory: Literary Studies and the New Pragmatism,* ed. W. J. T. Mitchell (Chicago: University of Chicago Press, 1985), 11–30.

20. *Painting as an Art* (Princeton: Princeton University Press, 1987), 39, 43.

21. Letter 342a.

22. Letters 330 and 330a.

23. Jonathan Culler, *Structuralist Poetics: Structuralism, Linguistics, and the Study of Literature* (Ithaca: Cornell University Press, 1975), 170, 178.

24. Julia Kristeva, *Revolution in Poetic Language* (New York: Columbia University Press, 1984), 25–26, 28, 48, 103, 225, 227.

25. Willis J. Buckingham, ed., "Introduction," *Emily Dickinson's Reception in the 1890s: A Documentary History* (Pittsburgh: University of Pittsburgh Press, 1989), xi–xxiii.

"Red in my Mind":
Dickinson, Gender, and Audience

Charlotte Nekola

The poems of Emily Dickinson stand as the strongest testimony to her desire to be known by language. Though she wrote many poems that rank silence, instead of speaking, as supreme virtue, it does not seem that she believed "True Poems flee" *all* of the time.[1] Her ambivalence over calling herself a poet, asserting the authority of a poet, and perceiving an audience for her poetry can be discussed as an issue of gender. Other factors certainly contributed to Dickinson's famous reticence, well discussed by other scholars, such as her position within her own family, the tradition of New England reticence, the influence of contemporary literary movements and writers, her own personal aesthetic, and her own stance toward finding an audience, among others. In addition to these surrounding influences Dickinson wrote at a time when the ideology of womanhood promoted ideals of passivity, silence, and domestic sainthood for white middle-class women, as feminist scholars have now amply detailed. Despite the many years that Dickinson seemed to reside in our cultural imagination as a disembodied poetic mythology, we are now coming to a perspective that can include her among other women who lived in her time. Like her female poet contemporaries, she faced the dilemma of self-expression in an unpromising era for women who wrote beyond the expected forms for "good" women, such as sentimental verse and domestic or pious novels. Her bold progress as a maverick poet may have been undercut or even aided by her quizzical stance toward finding an audience for her work—an ambivalence that can be seen as deeply rooted in the conflict between cultural gender expectations and the demands of individual genius.

Dickinson's ambivalence surfaces not only in those poems that praise silence, or in her spare and "slant" way of speaking, but also in her

31

disavowal of authority in her own poems. She will often make a broad claim at a poem's outset and then unravel that claim by the poem's end. Her poetic principles of circuity demark her from male contemporaries who wrote poetic manifestos that embraced openness and plain speaking, such as Emerson, Whitman, and Wordsworth. Certainly, these writers were not without their own ambivalences over their authority as male bards, as evidenced by self-subverting irony or identification with female figures. They were able, however, to compose poetic proclamations to place before their readers, in a way that Dickinson and her female poet contemporaries never did. Within the manifestos of Emerson, Wordsworth, and Whitman we can easily find language that highlights fitness between being a male speaker and being a man—a confidence not shared by Dickinson and her contemporaries such as Elizabeth Barrett Browning, Emily Brontë, Helen Hunt Jackson, and Mary Coleridge. These women worried about voice and audience in their poetry and often portrayed the female body as a site of that ambivalence.

The poems of Dickinson and her female contemporaries may praise silence, or the perfection of blankness, or snow language. They hope the poet will not be lost, or ruined, by a degraded world. Or they communicate an anxiety about "telling" as if the word, told and received, sullied the white landscape of silent perfection. To worry so much about speaking and telling suggests that female writers in her era were burdened by issues of entitlement: Were they entitled to use the words, or must they speak in snow language? Would being understood by an audience—those listeners and readers who belonged to the degraded world—mark the end of their definition as women, bring on confusion or lack of gender? Would female writers, then, be tempted to repudiate the need for audience? Suppose being understood, unconsciously, stood not for confirmation of one's gender, as it did in Emerson's joyous, "spermatic" language, but, rather, for the repudiation of it, the end of it?

Ambivalence often surfaces in Dickinson's poems whose subject is speaking. These poems may move toward a proclamation or seizure of language and bardic authority. They may insist that the speaker cannot be silenced, or they announce the speaker's ability to know the world through language and give it meaning. But these poems most often undo their own assertions by the poem's end. They attribute their claims to someone else; they unravel their definitions; they ask us to believe in the supremacy of deprivation and absence; they reduce their speakers to children or "small" figures on the road. It would seem that these ambivalent speakers find it hard to maintain a stance of authority; making a statement provokes so much anxiety that a disclaimer, however subtle, must be added or the claim must be undone. It is as if the speaker assures her reader that she is not claiming *too much*. Such poems point to the dilemma of female writers, trained in self-abnegation but required by their craft to make strong statements of self.

In "The Voice that stands for Floods to me" the speaker at first claims even more than immortal voice. She celebrates the phenomenology of language—which, for a woman, is perhaps one of the most daring assertions of all. It requires not only the right to speak but also the right to impose oneself and one's symbol-making systems:

> The Voice that stands for Floods to me
> Is sterile borne to some—
> The Face that makes the Morning mean
> Glows impotent on them—
>
> What a difference in Substance lies
> That what is Sum to me
> By other Financiers be deemed
> Exclusive Poverty!
>
> (Poem 1189)

Yet the speaker deflates the ecstasy of her own assertion. At first she rejoices in her own subjectivity and her facility with metaphor. Her native tongue is the voice that "stands for" floods; she reads the face of meaning. She distinguishes between herself and "them" of conventional ear. Ultimately, however, this powerful voice attributes her talent to some Higher Authority—the "Voice," the "Face." She still distinguishes herself as the Higher Authority's superior disciple, different from "them" and "other Financiers." But even this claim to her authority is strained by the second stanza. What others call "Exclusive Poverty" is really her grand "Sum." The speaker ends on two dubious propositions. First, as in so many other poems, she ranks, by proclamation, her experience as superior. The impulse to set up such deliberate hierarchies might imply a rejection of existing hierarchical relationships in language or culture. As such, her position is constantly adversarial; she becomes the permanently ornery speaker of wild proclamation, not easily believed. Second, she must carve her throne from poverty; she must proclaim that absence is presence, that someone else's idea of need is her idea of wealth. The queenship she derives from these assertions would seem to involve the intentional willing of denial in place of desire—a position difficult to maintain.

Dickinson also unravels some of her most adamant poems of definition by letting the final terms of the poem rest on a self-canceling paradox. When Dickinson boldly proclaims the absolute freedom of interior life and then defies consciousness, she leaves us only with a quizzical equation:

> No Rack can torture me—
> My Soul—at Liberty—
> Behind this mortal Bone
> There knits a bolder One—
>
> You cannot prick with saw—
> Nor pierce with Scimitar—
> Two Bodies—therefore be—
> Bind One—The Other fly—
>
> The Eagle of his Nest
> No easier divest—
> And gain the Sky
> Than mayest Thou—
>
> Except Thyself may be
> Thine Enemy—
> Captivity is Consciousness—
> So's Liberty.
>
> (Poem 384)

The soul behind the bone grants the speaker invulnerability. The self that has two selves can send itself flying in the face of exterior prisons. Yet this poem uneasily echoes the solution of the reeling brain of "They shut me up in Prose—" (Poem 613). It asks us to believe that captivity can be escaped by the self splitting from itself. The self becomes its own caretaker, impervious except to its own attacks: "Except Thyself may be / Thine Enemy—." This stance also makes the self totally responsible for its own freedom. It imposes the premium of individual transcendence as

solution to exterior constrictions, whether social or economic: it is some-
thing like declaring poverty best; it ranks what is left as supreme. The
difficulty of maintaining such a claim can be detected in the poem's last
comparisons: "Captivity is Consciousness— / So's Liberty." If captivity
is consciousness, liberty is consciousness—but liberty and captivity are
opposing terms that cancel each other's sense. Consciousness, then,
might simply be another void of nullity. We can interpret the equation to
mean that consciousness is both liberty and captivity, but this version also
leaves us with the definition of a paradox. How is the self to soar if
consciousness is only a riddle? It might be said that these poems talk
themselves into silence.

When Dickinson's speakers venture a claim of authority or voice,
they often diminish the size of their claim by trimming the speaker's size
down to something "small." The girl of "It was given to me by the
Gods" celebrates her wealth:

> It was given to me by the Gods—
> When I was a little Girl—
> They give us Presents most—you know—
> When we are new—and small.
> I kept it in my Hand—
> I never put it down—
> I did not dare to eat—or sleep—
> For fear it would be gone—
> I heard such words as "Rich"—
> When hurrying to school—
> From lips at Corners of the Streets—
> And wrestled with a smile.
> Rich! 'Twas Myself—was rich—
> To take the name of Gold—
> And Gold to own—in solid Bars—
> The Difference—made me bold—

(Poem 454)

The splendor of self-possession, of owning a gold name, of perceiving
one's difference, belongs to the child. She both appropriates language—
takes the name of gold—and owns gold. This is not the mute, adult
Queen of Poverty; this is the speaking child of possession. But, still, the
wealthy self is only a child of the past.

Similarly, the ecstatic speaker of "I taste a liquor never brewed" (Poem 214) claims herself privy to the wine of pearl, air, and dew. This rapt "Inebriate," however, becomes only "the little Tippler" by the poem's end. Dickinson's speakers are often most emphatic when they insist on some reduction of desire, or denial:

> A modest lot—a fame petite—
> A brief Campaign of sting and sweet
> Is plenty! Is enough!
>
> (Poem 159)

Could her assertions have been so strident if she had not insisted on the small life? How long can we believe repeated claims that the small life is really the large life?

"A Tongue—to tell him I am true!" seizes speech vehemently. But it undercuts its own claims in several of the ways we have so far discussed. First, it proclaims the urgent need to deliver a message to an unspecified "Him." It seeks permission to speak by using a convention of love poetry: telling the "other." Second, it builds a strenuous claim for the importance of its own message—in this case, a heretical message of power. Third, it diminishes the magnitude of its claim by assuring its readers of the speaker's small size:

> A Tongue—to tell Him I am true!
> Its fee—to be of Gold—
> Had Nature—in Her monstrous House
> A single Ragged Child—
>
> To earn a Mine—would run
> That Interdicted Way,
> And tell Him—Charge thee speak it plain—
> That so far—Truth is True?
>
> And answer What I do—
> Beginning with the Day
> That Night—begun—
> Nay—Midnight—'twas—
> Since Midnight—happened—say—

If once more—Pardon—Boy—
The Magnitude thou may
Enlarge my Message—If too vast
Another Lad—help thee—

Thy Pay—in Diamonds—be—
And His—in solid Gold—
Say Rubies—if He hesitate—
My Message—must be told—

Say—last I said—was this—
That when the Hills—come down—
And hold no higher than the Plain—
My Bond—have just begun—

And when the Heavens—disband—
And Deity conclude—
Then—look for me. Be sure you say—
Least Figure—on the Road—

(Poem 400)

It is this poem's *insistence* on voice that makes it important: "Tell Him!"
"Say . . . This," and "My Message—must be told." It plays on the con-
vention of a love poem; the speaker must tell him that she is "true." But it
never claims, like the usual love lyric, that she is true *to him*. The use of an
indefinite *He* to receive this message foils the audacity of the speaker's
claim. It appears that she wants to deliver a message of fidelity to a lover,
but she actually proclaims the authority of her own voice: "I am true."
The speaker values her own voice and weighs it in terms of gold, dia-
monds, and rubies. But she cannot speak for herself. To get the tongue
she needs the gold fee; to put the message across she needs to pay the
messenger boy and lad.

It seems that the voice cannot be claimed, then, without cost *to the
speaker,* or perhaps without a male metaphor or medium as conveyer. The
poem unfolds the speaker's final claim through a very convoluted path
involving fees and messages. It struggles through obstacles to confes-
sion. When the earth is leveled, the Heavens disbanded, and Deity
concluded, this speaker will remain. But she adds her disclaimer:
"Then—look for me. Be sure you say— / Least Figure—on the Road—."

The speaker who dares to outlive earth, heaven, and God, more eternal than the eternal, assures us that, if she is heretical, she is still very small. Perhaps this humility only amplifies her claim: to be smallest is largest. But it also backs out of the audacity of its assertions. Perhaps it attempts to adjust an assertion of self for an audience nervous of women's authority or women's subjectivity. This audience may well have included herself.

Initially, all of these poems proclaim that the speaker can speak or must speak. Yet they deny the full weight of their claim by the poem's end. They do not rank silence over speaking, but they do censor their own speakers. The progress of Dickinson's discourse in many other kinds of poems could also be said to court silence or negate language. Some, like "Come Slowly—Eden!" find landscapes of fulfillment only to encounter irrationality and silence; the humming bee is "lost in Balms" (Poem 211). Many offer such strenuous claims of denial that the poem's language seems harnessed to improbable renunciations: "The Tint I cannot take—is best—" (Poem 627), "A *Wounded* Deer—leaps highest—" (Poem 165), and "Undue Significance a starving man attaches / To Food—" (Poem 479) are all examples. Poems that dare to define often do so only by negation: " 'Heaven'—is what I cannot reach!" (Poem 239) or "This World is not Conclusion" (Poem 501). Poems such as "I'm ceded— I've stopped being Theirs—" (Poem 508) define self by negation. Many more poems rank states of nullity as supreme, such as poverty over wealth, silence over speaking, absence over presence. That the activity of a poem would involve the creation of these deliberate hierarchies of denial suggests a speaker who deeply suspects her own authority.

Perhaps Dickinson's poems of undoing point us toward an answer to one of the most important questions for female poets of the nineteenth century: How does one claim self, voice, or ego when trained in a cult of self-denial? In these poems the self does get as far as speaking. But at the point of speaking ambivalence begins. The poems' speakers begin to talk but will not claim *too much;* they will name only the crumb, only the mute or the wound, as their own. Or, if they announce their authority, they eventually unravel their own claims. Definition begins with negation. Desire is approached only to be denied. The hesitations and silences of such a poet would not appear to offer what is traditionally known as bardic authority: the ability to proclaim, state, name, or impose one's vision upon the world at large. A female poet such as Emily Dickinson may have gotten little help from the poetic manifestos of her male predecessors and contemporaries, who broadly claimed the poet's right to speak in the world.

Emerson, Wordsworth, and Whitman: How to Speak

Ralph Waldo Emerson prizes "beauty not explicable" in "The Poet"; William Wordsworth settles "Intimations of Immortality" on thoughts "too deep for tears"; Walt Whitman's 1855 "Preface to *Leaves of Grass*" asserts that "to be is just as great as to perceive or tell." These tributes to the unexpressed surface in their works, but they do not become part of a major debate on the value of speaking and silence. Nor are they tangled in a great deal of ambivalence about whether to speak at all. Emerson's and Whitman's comments were addressed to those not lucky enough to be poets, in the spirit of democratizing the vistas of the inarticulate. Wordsworth's darker thoughts might have been too deep for tears but not for words.

Emerson, Wordsworth, and Whitman all wrote manifestos justifying the ways of their writing to an audience, they assumed, that was there. No such sustained prologue to her own poetry or consideration of poetry in general exists in Dickinson's work. After visiting Dickinson, T. W. Higginson wrote home to his wife that Dickinson thought poetry true when it took off the top of her head; this is as much as we know.[2] The existence of Emerson's, Wordsworth's, and Whitman's guides to their poetics has provided readers and critics with a certain amount of confidence. These writers had the audacity to tell their readers how to read their writing—an act of ego, crucial in ensuring that their audience would follow the innovations of their work. Given their view of the representative role of the poet, they could even present their proclamations as public-spirited acts.

As David Porter points out, Dickinson left us no ars poetica.[3] We have no such manifestos written by female poets of Dickinson's era. It is difficult to think of any essays by female poets to explain their poetics until very recently. Yet this absence is predictable in a culture that advocated silence for women. To break that silence with heretical poetry was courageous; to be able to justify the form and content of that poetry as well as write it may have been very improbable for Dickinson and others. It is tantalizing to imagine what a different course the critical reception of Dickinson's poetry might have taken had she first explained the method of what others often termed madness.

Emerson's, Wordsworth's, and Whitman's manifestos celebrate self and celebrate speaking. Their assertions soar; they deem the poet supreme, language potent, and speaking essential. They do not row between the extremes of the syllable-less sea and volcanic utterance, as Dickinson's ambivalent speakers do. Teller, utterer, singer, arguer, are the roles of Emerson's articulate poet. Whitman's poem finds a fit language and escapes the silence of the unsaid. Emerson's poet becomes a conduit to the natural and eternal through his ability to speak in symbol, and Wordsworth's poet is a "translator" of "real life."[4] In short, Emerson's, Wordsworth's, and Whitman's poets embark on a promising voyage of language; they do not cast about for a syllable-less sea.

These writers not only proclaim the power of poets, poetry, and language, but they also recommend the best ways of speaking. Dickinson's most sustained counsel on this matter was to tell the truth but tell it "slant." Emerson's, Wordsworth's, and Whitman's advice opposed this tactic radically: tell *directly,* not slant. The poet, says Emerson, is "the man without impediment, who sees and handles what others dream of."[5] Whitman claimed an ideal language capable of translating experience exactly; nothing would be lost between medium and message: "The greatest poet," he said, is "the free channel of himself. He swears to his art, I will not be meddlesome, I will not have in my writing any elegance or effect or originality to hang in the way between me and the rest like curtains. I will have nothing hang in the way, not even the richest curtains. What I tell I tell precisely for what it is."[6] Wordsworth praised the poet with no impediment, defining poetry as "the spontaneous overflow of powerful feelings" (25), written in "the very language of men" (8). Emerson, Whitman, and Wordsworth easily claim that art could approach life, language equaled reality, the poet could speak without a medium, and that the self spoke to others.

Dickinson's poetry most often does not reflect these propositions; at times it implies almost an opposite impulse. Art belongs not to life but, instead, to hothouse life on the shelf. Language might be inferior or superior to reality but not simply equal. She disparaged the "real" language of the world's babblers and looked for the perfect language of silence. Her poems are more at home with interior dramas of the psyche and imaginary landscapes than in the "world." She more often spoke indirectly than directly; there are many kinds of impediments, curtains, and obstacles in her poetry. Her poems sometimes block understanding with their difficult analogies, multiple personae, conceptual landscapes, dashed lines, and other palimpsestic techniques. The speakers of her poems often divide their authority among multiple speakers, escape to incoherence, or disclaim their authority by a poem's end.

Emerson's, Wordsworth's, and Whitman's essays assumed and directly addressed an audience. What had their assertions of the supremacy of self, their conceptions of themselves as representative poets, to do with the ideal of self*lessness* for women? The idea of an audience for one's work, a public, or publication implying an audience could have seemed foreign, perhaps dangerous to women. Contemporary ideas of womanhood warned that the world was false and home was true; a woman making her way in the world would find a wasteland. Women may have unconsciously feared becoming gender*less* by being received by that world or by being received and understood by an audience. There were complex cultural reasons for women to seek and fear an audience at the same time. One can only wonder if an aspiring female writer, reading these texts, believed that they spoke to her own experience, unless it was an out-of-gender experience.

To find language or poem, according to Wordsworth or Emerson or Whitman, the poet needed the world. Dickinson may have written that publication was the auction of the mind of man, but how else was one to find a public audience? Two important distinctions can be made between Dickinson's ambivalence toward the idea of audience and the attitudes toward audience expressed in the essays of her male contemporaries. First, these writers did not quarrel with the ideas of publication and audience: the possibility of a listening public did not become an issue to debate. Second, these writers assumed that their audience existed and that this audience would tolerate much instruction on the form and content of poetry. Emerson confidently wrote that "the world seems always waiting for its poet" (761).

In *Preface to the Lyrical Ballads* Wordsworth ennobles himself, the vocation of poetry, and his own poetic style while inviting in the rest of the world: the poet sings "a song in which all human beings join . . ." (18). Similarly, Whitman prepares his readers to applaud his poetry by defining an American bard amazingly like himself and his own verse. His poet, like his poetry, spans the continent and catalogs diversity. The poet, he says, not only describes reality but also points to the connection between reality and the soul; the poet shows the relevance of his work to the reader's own life; the poet does not moralize. All of these goals inform his own verse. At times Whitman even addresses readers in the imperative, telling them how to read and live. Praising the value of apparently artless composition, he tells his reader that "you shall stand by my side and look in the mirror with me" (418). He flatters his readers by telling them that everyone can be a poet. His democratic view claims every man a poet, or at least as good as a poet, since perceiving is as good as telling. But this vista also works as a massive seduction for his audience: he praises them, he praises the poetic goals he writes by, and he praises their language, the American language, as fit. But this divine coherence between speaker and listener would be impossible for those with no audience in the first place and for those who shrank from the public arena.

Coherent, too, was the male poets' relationship between their own gender and their perception of language. They were men and spoke the language of men. In a journal entry in 1841 Emerson calls for "a spermatic book."[7] This is what a woman would have read in the "Preface to Lyrical Ballads": the poet "is a man speaking to men" (13). The best language is that "really used by men" (4). The best poems were written by "a man who, being possessed of more than usual organic sensibility, had also thought long and deeply" (6). The poet must avoid "unmanly despair" (15) when he feels inferior to "that which is uttered by men in real life" (14). Whitman frames the generative quality of language in specifically masculine terms, like Emerson's spermatic words: the poet "spreads out his dishes . . . he offers the sweet firmfibred meat that grows men and women" (414). The poet is heir to "lawgivers," who in the world of 1855 would most likely have been exclusively male: "The sailor and traveler . . . the atomist chemist astronomer geologist phrenologist spiritualist mathematician historian and lexicographer" (419). These lawgivers build language; their "construction underlies the structure of every perfect poem" (414).

It is difficult to imagine how women read themselves into Whitman's conclusion: "always of their fatherstuff," he said, "must be begotten the sinewy races of bards" (419). One test of literature is whether it will produce spermatic men: "Will it help breed one goodshaped and well hung man, and a woman to be his perfect and independent mate." This manly poet inherits macho language as well; the English and American languages together provide expression from "tough stock, brawny enough and limber enough and full enough" (426). There are no essays among contemporary female poets exuding this kind of confidence, or fitness, between one's gender and language.

Speaking and the White Election

Trouble over speaking and audience marks the work of Dickinson's female contemporaries. In their poems that discuss poets, or how a woman or poet should speak, Elizabeth Barrett Browning, Helen Hunt Jackson, Emily Brontë, and Mary Elizabeth Coleridge all debate the value of being heard. While Emerson, Wordsworth, and Whitman sent their ideal poet out to meet his waiting world, these female poets sometimes denied the worth of an audience. Yet their poetry does not point to a complete absence of desire for what they denied. These women continually lament the unexpressed. They write about what they *would* have said. Or they create strange dramas of voice and voicelessness, often expressed in mysterious states of whiteness. Remaining silent—or speaking—might be portrayed as a sanctuary or a horror. The buoyant claims of voice, ego, and authority in the poetic manifestos of male contemporaries are not apparent in these works. To make such claims the poet may resort, as Dickinson did, to the mysterious "white election," a high, white, and blank status that transcends an audience so completely that it may remain unheard, unknown, misunderstood, or unread.

Elizabeth Barrett Browning was very well-known in her time, extremely prolific, and much admired by Dickinson. The contemporary ideal of selflessness for women and the idea of world as void were at odds with a female poet's success. When Browning writes about poets this dilemma shows: she praises anonymity and humility as virtues of the poet. Poets in her poetry are reminded to trim their own egos and to remember that the world will misuse them.

Browning's 1850 "Mountaineer and Poet" compares an anonymous goatherd to poets who pursue "eminence."[8] She warns fame-seeking poets that

> Ye are not great because creation drew
> Large revelations round your earliest sense,
> Not bright because God's glory shines for you.
>
> (197)

Browning's poem "A Vision of Poets" was written, she explained, to show the "necessary relations of genius to suffering and self-sacrifice" (127). Curiously, her objective also defines the poet as a "good" woman. The poet does not merely exist or sing or claim multitudes; she must suffer and deny herself. The poem reports that poets die for Beauty "as martyrs" did for Truth (11.290–91). Thirty-nine ghost poets, from Homer to Coleridge, including Sappho as the only woman, present themselves in the narrator's vision. The ghosts show a wound, or dripping blood, in the place where their hearts should be (11.427–29). The narrator's spiritual guide, in the form of "the lady," tells us what ideology told women: "*World's use* is cold, *world's love* is vain, / *World's cruelty* is bitter bane" (11.436–37). It is as if Browning adapts the fate of poets to the life prescribed for women: they should expect devastation in the world, once their words are told.

Dickinson's American contemporary Helen Hunt Jackson wrote mostly sentimental and conventional verse. Though widely published, she preferred to sign her poems "Anonymous." Not surprisingly, her poems portrayed anonymity as virtue, fame as vice, and the world as peril. The best audience was no audience. "The Way to Sing," for example, recommends the bird's song as ideal; it has no listeners: "No mention of the place or hour / To any man."[9] Like Browning, Jackson casts the unknown shepherd as best poet. It may be that women's anonymity found an apt projection in this figure; Dickinson's hunter-assistant in "My Life had stood—a Loaded Gun" comes to mind. In Jackson's poem "The True Ballad of the King's Singer" a king on a hunt chances upon a lonesome shepherd. The shepherd sings an unearthly, beautiful song. The king brings the shepherd to court and commands him to perform. With his opportunity for fame the shepherd becomes mute, and the king's court begins to jeer. Fortunately, the devil plays for the shepherd in court, and the true poet/shepherd escapes back to his mountain. Hunt's message serves the anonymous female poet well: the best poems die under public scrutiny and thrive in isolation.

And what of the female writer who does manage to become famous? One of Browning's tributes to the notorious George Sand attempts to make the poet's reputation "stainless"; another poem hopes that the future will "unsex" her. She also wrote a tribute poem to Felicia Hemans, a popular poet of sentimental verse. Hemans herself warned against fame for women. Browning still found it necessary to dim the shine of Hemans's own fame. In "Felicia Hemans" she ranks heavenly silence over earthly singing. The poem's speaker advises the departed Hemans to "Take music from the silent Dead whose / meaning is complete" (46). Hemans becomes white, with the "whiteness" of the Savior's "innocence o'er all her / garments, flowing" (47).

Silence and anonymity may emerge as high virtues in the poetry of Dickinson's female contemporaries but not without, as in Dickinson's poetry, the counterpoint of poetry that laments the unexpressed. In "Riches I hold in light esteem"[10] the poet scorns fame. But the unsaid is continually a presence in Emily Brontë's poetry. She voices two sentiments about speaking over and over: it is too late to speak, and one cannot or must not speak. Her poems claim that "It is too late to call thee now" (A 13, 135) or that "I'll not weep that thou art going to leave me" (A 10, 136). "Grief that would not weep" (F 2, 47), and "secret pleasure, secret tears" (J 252, 11) lay mute. Or, something *might* have been said:

> Wildly rushed the mountain spring
> . . . How invincible its roar
> Had its waters won the shore.
>
> (E13, 43)

But the waters do not reach the shore. The unexpressed even hides beneath women who do speak:

> . . . .
> With that sweet look and lively tone,
> And bright eye shining all the day,
> They could not see, at midnight lone
> How she would weep the time away.
>
> (E 19, 106)

The strain against muteness, the denial of voice, and the regret of silence link all these poems. The water does not reach the shore; the tears are not shed; the voice *does not tell* how "she" really feels in either grief or joy. The unsaid haunts an unfinished poem:

> I would have touched the heavenly key
> That spoke alike of bliss and thee;
> I would have woke the entrancing song.
> But its words died upon my tongue;
> And then I knew that entheal strain
> Could never speak of joy again;
> and then I felt . . . [unfinished.]
>
> (D 6, 38)

Somewhere, beyond the speaker's grasp, language does exist that can
speak: the "heavenly key / That spoke alike of bliss and thee," the "en-
trancing song" and the "entheal strain." The poem mourns the speaker's
aphasia; even as she says, "And then I felt," the poem lapses into its final
silence. The lament of the unexpressed does not idealize silence; it reveals
silence as loss.

Even more conventional poets such as Jackson and Browning cannot
insist on silence forever. Female writers of the nineteenth century may
have been encouraged by contemporary ideology to praise silence; de-
spite ideology, it would seem that any writer knew the price of muteness.
Poems and poets may best be anonymous, according to Helen Hunt
Jackson, but she also mourns the unsaid. In "The Song He Never Wrote"
the poet's unsung song escapes him; secrets, echoes, and obscure pulses
suggest it, but he never writes it. He dies, and eternal life does not
compensate for his failure on earth:

> . . . .
> "Why did I halt, and weakly tremble?"
> Even in heaven the memory smote,—
> "Fool to be dumb, and to dissemble!
> Alas for the song I never wrote!"
>
> (255–56)

This concludes Jackson's 1892 collection of poems, on a note of anxiety
that is *not* relieved with a homily on the superiority of heavenly silence.

Browning's poem "The Poet's Vow" narrates a tale that dramatically
illustrates the dangers of silence. The poet gives up his wife for the sky
and earth, claiming that "your silences shall a love express / More deep"
than the voice of child or woman (15). He lives out his vow of solitude,
while his wife pines away. She resorts to dramatic strategy in order to
speak to him: she will die and have herself delivered on his doorstep with
a scroll. Her message details may kinds of failed speech: she has prayed
for him with "bursting sob," with "silent lips," and even while she
seemed to sleep. But now "The corpse's tongue is still." The scroll
challenges him to cry out, cursing him, the narrator points out, by "the
dead's silentness" (19). The grief-stricken poet howls at last and then kills
himself; the moral of the story is that all of humankind must weep
together. This strange, convoluted story demonstrates the cost of mute-
ness. The silence breaks only with a terrible message: a dead woman with
a scroll. Speaking, at last, kills the poet. Both the poet and his wife are

players in the plot of silence; we might consider them two parts of one concern: poet's voice, women's silence, and the incompatibility of the two. Here the poet is named male, and the one who prods him to speak is female. But she accomplishes this only by the example of absolute, final silence. Oddly, she almost outdoes her husband as poet by presenting the "scroll"—both the message on the paper and her*self* as scroll—that makes him both speak and die. The implications are disturbing: Must women immolate themselves to speak to the poet, as a poet?

When the self cannot speak, sheer Gothic horror results in Mary Elizabeth Coleridge's poem "The Other Side of a Mirror":

> I sat before my glass one day,
> And conjured up a vision bare,
> Unlike the aspects glad and gay,
> That erst were found reflected there—
> The vision of a woman, wild
> With more than womanly despair.
> . . . .
> Her lips were open—not a sound
> Came through the parted lines of red.
> Whate'er it was, the hideous wound
> In silence and in secret bled.
> No sigh relieved her speechless woe,
> She had no voice to speak her dread.[11]

The mirror woman reveals the wound of silence that others can hide—hideous, red, and bleeding: "her lips were open." The absence of voice emerges as a gaping, secret wound—a portrayal of silence in the language of female sexuality. Dickinson's volcanic "lips that never lie— / Whose hissing coral part—and shut" (Poem 601) speak the same language. In both Dickinson's and Coleridge's poems the parted lips oppose the rest of mankind in some monumental way. Coleridge's red wound reveals "What once no man on earth could guess"; Dickinson's coral volcano destroys the work of civilized man as "Cities—ooze away—." These oppositions suggest that the woman's voice, if presented to an audience, sweeps away the world created by men: there is no context for what women might say, in cities or on earth. If there is no context, does an audience even exist? To be responsive listeners must understand what they hear. We often hear it said that Dickinson "shunned an audience." But perhaps it cannot truly be said that she had much of one, in her time, ready to understand the language of a red wound, or the language of a volcano, in the work of a female speaker.

Strange dramas sometimes oppose a red wound with some state of whiteness in the poems of Dickinson and her female contemporaries. Blood and wounds connote language and sexuality; white virtue denies sexuality and sometimes language. White power takes women beyond the pale; they speak by a supernatural voice, or they speak the superior renounced language of silence. The mystery and severity of these oppositions—red wound, white language, red voice, white silence— further underscore the deep dilemma of female writers caught some- where between speaking and the absence of audience.

Coleridge's red wound finds its voice in the imaginative realm of "The White Women." A solution to the dilemma of speaking surfaces in the imaginative realm of white words, or the "language of snow," un- troubled by red wounds or volcanic lips. In "The White Women" Cole- ridge finds this netherland:

> Where dwell the lovely, wild white women folk,
>   Moral to man?
> They never bowed their necks beneath the yoke,
> They dwelt alone when the first morning broke
>   And Time began.
>
> Taller they are than man, and very fair,
>   Their cheeks are pale,
> At sight of them the tiger in his lair.
> The falcon hanging in the azure air,
>   The eagles quail.
>
> The deadly shafts their nervous hands let fly
>   Are stronger than our strongest—in their form
> Larger, more beauteous, carved amazingly,
> And when they fight, the wild white women cry
>   The war-cry of the storm.
>
> Their words are not as ours. If man might go
>   Among the waves of Ocean when they break
> And hear them—hear the language of the snow
> Falling in torrents—he might also know
>   The tongue they speak.

Pure are they as the light; they never sinned,
    But when the rays of the eternal fire
Kindle the West, their tresses they unbind
And fling their girdles to the Western wind,
    Swept by desire.

Lo, maidens to the maidens then are born,
    Strong children of the maidens and the breeze,
Dreams are not—in the glory of the morn,
Seen through the gates of ivory and horn—
    More fair than these.

And none may find their dwelling. In the shade
    Primeval of the forest oaks they hide.
One of our race, lost in an awful glade,
Saw with his human eyes a wild white maid,
    And gazing, died.

                            (213)

Only *if* a man can hear the "language of snow / Falling in torrents" will he be an audience for what the white women have to say. These are the women "swept by desire," not the ones at home sweeping the hearth. They are not subordinate to men; they are warriors; they speak their own tongue; they are free from sin; they do not need men for procreation. Is this how far women must go in order to speak? And how does one hear the language of waves or snow? Like Coleridge's mirror woman and Dickinson's volcano, the white women challenge men: a man dies merely from looking at one. The depiction of a landscape in which women have power, and can speak, requires a leap and a realm beyond the given. As in Dickinson's praise of inaudible voices and syllable-less seas, the concept of perfect language verges on silence. The extremity of this idealization of power and white silence may again point to an absence of context for women's language and women's sexuality.

This strain is evident in Elizabeth Barrett Browning's nervous odes to George Sand. In "To George Sand: A Desire" she first portrays the novelist as an androgynous ideal: a "large-brained woman and a large-hearted man" (103). But the poem tries to endow her with "stainless fame," implying that Sand's defiance of sexual convention was too radical a heresy. The woman who dared to name herself—"self-called George Sand"—is in need of some cleaning up, some whitening up, according to

Browning. Out of Sand's warring soul and senses Browning would raise her up, "white as wings of swan." She hopes Sand could join angels and become a "pure" genius "sanctified from blame." Fame, if granted, must be "stainless." Browning would transform the hideous red wound of Coleridge's mirror woman to the blameless white swan. But what was Sand's offense? Was her voice, somehow, not pure, too red?

"To George Sand—A Recognition" (103) also struggles with Sand's sexuality. Browning insists that Sand is "True genius, *but* true woman." Despite the poet-fire, Sand's language is only "a woman's voice forlorn." In the better life, on the heavenly shore, God could "unsex" Sand. If Sand's ideal must not have sex, conventions of sexuality must pose deep problems for the female writer—genius *but* woman. Sand burned white in "a poet-fire," but the red "woman-heart" still beat in the flame. Again, the woman who speaks as a poet will be caught between white words and the red truth—a troubled position.

Susan Gubar points to the identification of sexuality with speaking in two poems by Christina Rossetti: "Rossetti's speaker on the doorstep of 'The Convent Threshold' feels caught between sexuality and chastity. Choosing to become a nun because there is mysterious 'blood' between her lover and herself, she looks down to see her lily feet 'soiled with mud, / with *scarlet* mud *which tells a tale'* [my emphasis]. The same identification of bleeding with telling or singing appears in the vision of the suffering woman poet in 'From House to Home.' "[12] If telling is equated with bleeding and bleeding is evidence of female sexuality, it may be that the act of telling is fraught with all the anxiety of female sexuality. Gubar comments that "the female body has been feared for its power to articulate itself" (246)—feared by men and perhaps also by women with the power of articulation. In this context Dickinson's repeated advice that it is best "not to tell" may be the sentiment of a female writer who, consciously or not, sees speaking as self-revelation of sexuality. This anxiety may translate to poems that insist on silence or to poems that speak in volcanoes. Having an audience may mean that the revelation of sexuality will be understood. For Dickinson and her female poet contemporaries language and sexuality were fraught by schisms and silence. Language was not simply spermatic or the "firmfibred meat." It required something else—a leap to snow language, a struggle between silence and speaking, a conflict between white perfection or a fearsome red articulation. Thus, a revelation of sexuality would mean trouble. There could be many reasons to "shun an audience" for the female poet. Listeners might not understand the white language. And, if the red language slipped out, they would know too much.

Reading two of Dickinson's more mysterious poems in the context of her female contemporaries suggests why Dickinson's own oppositions of red and white resonate so deeply. These poems are among those that make some of Dickinson's boldest claims of authority and voice, in some of her boldest terms. Each opposes an inferior red state with an ascendent white state. The actual meaning of white states can only be inferred from the rest of the poems' images; they are never named or defined. Even then "white election" and "white heat" remain somewhat obscure. If these poems have a subtext on sexuality, it is not surprising that their central images would be so elusive.

"Dare you see a Soul *at the White Heat*" challenges the reader to see what the poem's enlightened speaker sees:

Dare you see a Soul *at the White Heat?*
Then crouch within the door—
Red—is the Fire's common tint—
But when the vivid Ore
Has vanquished Flame's conditions
It quivers from the Forge
Without a color, but the light
Of unanointed Blaze.
Least Village has its Blacksmith
Whose Anvil's even ring
Stand symbol for the finer Forge
That soundless tugs—within—
Refining these impatient Ores
With Hammer, and with Blaze
Until the Designated Light
Repudiate the Forge—

(Poem 365)

This poem can be read as a delineation of the poetic process; the red fire, blacksmith, and anvil produce the superior, created white light. For Dickinson, ambivalent speaker, this is a daring poem: it defines the life of the poet. This statement, however, is almost hidden within the poem's imagery. It could as well be read as a discussion of the progress of the soul, or simply of the blacksmith's art. The oppositions of red states and white states parallel those poems that oppose silence with speaking. Red "is the fire's common tint—," like the everyday, mortal, cheap language of babblers and haranguers. The better light, and the better language, is defined by absence and silence; when the flame dies the light "without a color" produces the "finer Forge" that "soundless tugs—within." The assertion that the soundless, white state excels the common tint of fire echoes Dickinson's claims that the inaudible or the unsaid ranks above the spoken. The white light is so superior that it is even able to "Repudiate" its "Forge." The base red fire recalls Coleridge's red wound, the volcanic lips, and the blood on the white shoes of telling. The pure light of mute language echoes Coleridge's white women of snow language or Browning's transformed Sand as white swan. Here the red state represents some kind of prison that must be overcome if the white light is to be forged, perhaps the prison of mortal language or mortal body. To "mortal body" we might add *female* body—and all its incumbent terrors for female speakers.

"Mine—by the Right of the White Election!" names the red states that must be escaped as "Scarlet prison":

> Mine—by the Right of the White Election!
> Mine—by the Royal Seal!
> Mine—by the Sign in the Scarlet prison—
> Bars—cannot conceal!
>
> Mine—here—in Vision—and in Veto!
> Mine—by the Grave's Repeal—
> Titled—Confirmed—
> Delirious Charter!
> Mine—long as Ages steal!

(Poem 528)

This is one of Dickinson's most exclamatory, emphatic works—a poem that seizes not poverty or absence but, rather, possession. Whatever the speaker declares to be "Mine!" however, is claimed by right of several enigmatic terms: *white election, royal seal, scarlet prison, grave's repeal*. The poem could be read as the soul's claim as it climbs to the white election of heaven. But it can also be read as a wild affirmation of self, which chooses its own kind of ascendancy by its own terms. This can be both intoxicating and perilous: the speaker gains a "Delirious Charter."

"White Election," if an elevation of self, suggests ascendance of absence or willed renunciation. It is a renunciation, however, that elevates the speaker *over* the scarlet prison, which we might view as the prison house of language and sexuality. The speaker wins her title by the "sign" in the scarlet prison, despite bars.

White election is for those who can find the sign or the word in the red wound. The poem echoes the claims of "Dare you see a *Soul at the White Heat*": the seer, the artist, the speaker, finds the true light out of the red forge. Must the scarlet prison, however, be repudiated, or vetoed? Must language, when linked with sexuality, be seen as a prison? The poet claims that white heat or white election are only possible once sexuality has been "escaped" or renounced. We remember that the speaker of "I cannot live with You" gives up a relationship with another for a life of "that White Sustenance / Despair" (Poem 640). This kind of ascendancy poses a severe test for the female speaker. Sexuality must be denied. If sexuality is associated with *telling,* the renunciation of sexuality could well lead to trouble with speaking. The poet of the delirious white election can speak, but perhaps she will speak only slant, disguised, masked, or will speak poems that elude an audience.

When a circus passed Emily Dickinson's house the poet of the white election wrote, "still I feel the red in my mind" (L 318). This curious statement, read in the context of Dickinson's and other female writers' debates on silence, is highly charged. A passing circus produces "red" in the mind. The circus itself connotes lives not lived and worlds unseen. More exotic and transient than the everyday world, it has what Dickinson called "foreignhood." It offers a ticket to the irrational, preconscious, and sexual; it enacts feats of life and death in absurd trappings. *Red* could represent a variety of felt desires for all the circus suggests; one might jump on a trapeze, dismiss the houses of solid towns, and witness Borneo or Timbuctoo. To feel red in the mind may be to feel the desire to *speak* of desire; Dickinson did, very obliquely, in this letter. If experiencing red in the mind brought forth the irrational, preconscious, and sexual, it is likely that our poet of the white heat, the white election, and white despair could not stay there very long. Red in the mind would be as alarming as the brain that giggles endlessly; red speaks the wrong way. It betrays the speaker. It is its own kind of prison, perhaps the prison of desire that cannot be enacted or articulated.

To romance silent language could be the art of those who experience desire as prison. If sexuality becomes associated with *telling,* it is impossible to speak directly unless the speaker is prepared to reveal her sexuality as she reveals herself. For Emerson and Whitman, for example, speaking as a manly man was more euphoric: one could proclaim spermatic language or celebrate the firmfibred meat of the poet. Sexuality and self could be asserted in one breath. To censor one's sexuality as one writes imposes quite a different demand on language: words become the "curtains" of impediment that Whitman complained of, or disguises for desire. Poetry becomes an occasion not to seek and woo an audience but, instead, to avoid an audience. To be understood by an audience might not be confirmation of one's gender and sexuality but, rather, a disjunct, incoherent, disturbing experience of becoming "unsexed," as Elizabeth Barrett Browning hoped for George Sand in the better world. For Dickinson to describe "red in the mind," with or without an audience, was an important step in finding an audience who could recognize the importance of breaking through "white despair" without unsexing the poet.

NOTES

1. Emily Dickinson, Poem 1472, *The Complete Poems of Emily Dickinson,* ed. Thomas H. Johnson (Boston and Toronto: Little, Brown, 1960), 623. All subsequent references are to this edition.
2. Thomas Wentworth Higginson, Letter to Mrs. Thomas (Mary Channing) Higginson, 16 August 1870 (L 342a), in *The Letters of Emily Dickinson,* ed. Thomas H. Johnson (Cambridge: Harvard University Press, 1958), 474.
3. See David Porter, *Dickinson: The Modern Idiom* (Cambridge: Harvard University Press, 1981), 5, 140, 184.
4. William Wordsworth, "Preface to Lyrical Ballads" (1800), in *The Prelude,* ed. Carlos Baker (New York: Holt, Rinehart, and Winston, 1954), 14–15. All subsequent references are to this edition.
5. Ralph Waldo Emerson, "The Poet," *Essays and Letters* (New York: Library of America, 1983), 448.
6. Walt Whitman, "Preface to 1855 Edition of 'Leaves of Grass,' " in *Complete Poetry and Selected Prose by Walt Whitman,* ed. James E. Miller, Jr. (Cambridge: Riverside Press, 1959), 417–18. All subsequent references are to this edition.
7. Ralph Waldo Emerson, *The Journals and Miscellaneous Notebooks of Ralph Waldo Emerson,* vol 7: *1838–1842,* ed. A. W. Plumstead and Harrison Hayford, Journal F2 (1841) (Cambridge: Belknap Press of Harvard University, 1969), 547.
8. Elizabeth Barrett Browning, *The Complete Poetical Works of Ms. Browning* (Boston: Houghton Mifflin, 1900), 197. All subsequent references are to this edition.

9. Helen Hunt Jackson, *Poems* (1892; reprint, New York: Arno Press, 1972), 37. All subsequent references are to this edition.

10. Emily Jane Brontë, *The Complete Poems of Emily Jane Brontë,* ed. C. W. Hatfield (New York: Columbia University Press, 1941), 163. All subsequent references are to this edition.

11. Mary Elizabeth Coleridge, *The Collected Poems of Mary Coleridge,* ed. Theresa Whistler (London: Rupert Hart Davis, 1954), 88. All subsequent references are to this edition.

12. Susan Gubar, " 'The Blank Page' and the Issue of Female Creativity," *Critical Inquiry* 8, no. 2 (Winter 1981): 253–54.

Nobody's Business:
Dickinson's Dissolving Audience

Robert Weisbuch

"Before we are women or men, or Jews or Buddhists for that matter, we are people. It's a grammatical necessity: All kinds of people are just that, kinds of people. Common experience precedes difference, or the world disintegrates."

That's what I said. She said, "I don't believe that," and left me a few months later.

It was a typical dialogue of the American 1970s, one that has been played out in the academy as in the home in countless variations over the last two decades. By now, one hopes, the positions taken have become more flexible and more complex, my pretentious "grammatical necessity" notwithstanding. Still, it was and is an argument worthy of devoted pursuit because it concerns the essence of identity while it questions the very notion of "essence" or "substance," that which literally stands under and forms a basis for existence. "Grammar is political, and universality is the apologetics of an oppressing class," she had replied. "And exactly which and whose world of harmonious accord is in danger of falling apart?"

At the time I was not above citing Emily Dickinson for support. The most independent woman in American history, I had replied, never sundered men from the "We" who were often her "I." Indeed, Dickinson seems, at first, aggressively universalist in a manner that upholds a liberal humanist view, but, apart from my rhetorical need at the time, she is universalist at last in a more complicated way that belongs to a radical Romanticism and to herself. Like Hawthorne, Dickinson can be read with an almost anachronistic comfort as she creates an audience of shared feeling, but the closer she is read the more the experience challenges the reader's commonplace identity. In distinguishing what I will call a domestic and a sublime universality, I want to reverse the procedure of the poems, which typically spiral out in their concerns, to begin from a comforting distance and then circle in to the challenge Dickinson sets for a reader's selfhood.

The plural *we* occurs 542 times in nearly 300 Dickinson poems, and its tacit claim goes against class or gender divisions as definitive. Her *we* most often means "all of us, as human beings," and, speaking of *us,* there are just over 200 occasions of that word as well.[1] Sometimes the collectivizing plural expresses a psychological rule, as in two of many poems concerning the mind's necessary defenses against what she elsewhere calls "a pain so utter— / It would swallow substance up—" (599):[2] "We dream—it is good we are dreaming— / It would hurt us—were we awake" (531); "A doubt if it be Us / Assists the staggering Mind" (859). At other times the plural states a law of perception: "We see—Comparatively" (534). As often, the law is set outside the collective self, by existence: "For each ecstatic instant / We must an anguish pay" (125). Such usages are all-inclusive and in a way that draws attention to their scope, for the categories (psychological, epistemological, cosmological) I just employed will not hold, finally. Most often, Dickinson's plurals of humanity refer to intense emotional states that are also claims upon the nature of being. Emotional states and cognitive revelations, so often one in Dickinson's metaphysic of the nerve endings, are both inner events that individuals experience as particularly their own, in the privacy of the self. These silences are made common property, and the common thus is made intimate. The strategy provides a humbling, sometimes harrowing comfort and a huge claim for the cognitive reach and authority of the emotional life.

Of course, we do not need *we* for such universalizing. Hundreds of other poems attest to a commonality of experience. Dickinson's definition poems all participate in the universalizing process. Every time Dickinson defines and vivifies a word by implying a felt experience informing the definition—whether " 'Hope' is the thing with feathers" (254) or "Hope is a subtle Glutton—" (1547), whether " 'Heaven'—is what I cannot reach" (239) or "Paradise is of the option" (1069)—this very naming may tease a dictionary objectivity by insisting on the poet's livid living-out of the word. Dickinson's speaker in these poems is a wounded dialectician whose definitional stance is a tight-lipped pretense for an intensely subjective relation to the word. But the word's abstract status also makes a claim for the poet's experience as typical, normative, shared. Or, again, any time Dickinson invokes parts of a self to ring her changes upon faculty psychology, that self is all selves: "The Brain—is wider than the Sky—" (632); "The Mind lives on the Heart" (1355). A poet who writes, "Subjects hinder talk" (L 397), means to employ the particular to dramatize the pattern. "For Pattern is the Mind bestowed" (1223), and the pattern is one in which "we," all of "us," participate. Dickinson's frequent subject and constant audience is a sermonic or philosophical we, the encompassing and binding act of the minister or metaphysician.

It is crucial to insist that, however much Dickinson in her writing may exhibit qualities attributable, say, to her status as a woman or as a woman in mid- to late-nineteenth-century New England or as an upper-class person in that milieu or as an unmarried woman or as a half-disaffected Protestant, her clear goal is to discourage such limitary determinants. Her effort is to bind the reader—the good old universalized reader, freed from her or his selfish identity—to the poem.

Dickinson's ideal is the "stopless" life (463), and she seems to have spent a part of the summer of 1862 thinking about what she could not stop for: "Perhaps you smile at me," she wrote to Higginson. "I could not stop for that—My Business is circumference—" (L 268); "Perhaps the whole United States are laughing at me too!" she tells Dr. and Mrs. Holland in an adjacent letter. "I can't stop for that. My business is to love," she writes, and then, comparing herself to a bird nobody hears, "My business is to sing" (L 269). Circumference, the testing of what the feeling brain can and cannot incorporate, is the same "business" as loving and singing, and they stop neither for ridicule or politics (faintly suggested by the naming of the nation and often stressed in her self-mocking ignorance of current events). "The Missing All—prevented Me / From missing minor Things," she claims, citing "Sun's extinction" as one such event

> not so large that I
> Could lift my forehead from my work
> For Curiosity.
>
> (985)

The goal is to recover the "Missing All," if only in that postmortem afterlife of "Costumeless Consciousness" (1454), and that final goal removes the particular dress of gender, race, class, personal or historical age. No one is exempt from such undressing, not even Deity, as the Antitype itself becomes nothing more than typical (though this also makes the

typical grand): "One Crucifixion is recorded—only—," Dickinson re-
marks of Christ, then brusquely sets Him aside, noting "There's newer—
nearer Crucifixion / Than That" (553).

Having established this insistence on the common and shared experi-
encing of peak moments, the poet's implication of an all-of-us, one then
might construct an argument for Dickinson as an especially enthusiastic
and traditional humanist. But this would be a true argument only acciden-
tally and rotten at its neoconservative core for two reasons, the second of
which provides the challenge to selfhood that most complicates any char-
acterization of Dickinson and audience.

But, first, one should note that Dickinson's universality has less to
do with an aristocratic ignoring of class than with a Whitmanesque de-
mocracy that would refuse class (and, at times, as in the poem cited
earlier on Crucifixion, even Deity) its privilege. Her "we" or "I" as
being-in-the-world chimes with Whitman's individual-en-masse, Walt,
minus Walt's nationally representative aspect. And, when social sympa-
thies get expressed, they are inevitably for the spurned, who as often as
not is the poem's speaker. This makes for an argument against seeing
Dickinson as a poetic conservative, one who could be invoked against a
sociological poetics. Her ahistoricism is an almost, for at times her "I" or
"we" is not in fact everyone so much as anyone worth anything (and thus
including the reader if she or he would fare well in the poem). For
instance, this first stanza:

> The lonesome for they know not What—
> The Eastern Exiles—be—
> Who strayed beyond the Amber line
> Some madder Holiday—. . . .
>
>   (262)

Those who went beyond the sun ("the Amber line"), beyond the natural
world and the limits of the consciousness experienced in it, clearly are not
reported-upon strangers to the poem's speaker. They and she and any
reader who would be part of the club form a group for whom existence
has been illuminated and decimated by loss, by an unnameable paradise
revoked: "And ever since—the purple Moat / They strive to climb—in
vain—."

In many other poems this moment of ecstasy followed by revocation
is existential law, universal; here it is a special pain belonging to the

metaphysically lonesome, and it implies an aristocracy of pain that would
exclude the shallow. But beyond this there are enemies lurking in the
poems, a "they" sometimes poised against this less-inclusive "I" or "we."
Their acts are those of an upper-class establishment that sponsors a repres-
sive decorum:

> They shut me up in Prose—
> As when a little Girl
> They put me in the Closet—
> Because they liked me still.
>
> (613)

Or again: "Much Madness is divinest Sense—" and "Much Sense—the
starkest madness" but " 'Tis the Majority / In this, as All, prevail—," and
the Dickinsonian dissenter is by them "handled with a Chain—" (435).
The enemy "they" are elsewhere named "Soft—Cherubic Creatures,"
those "Gentlewomen," "Brittle" ladies who are "ashamed" of "freckled
Human Nature" and of whom "Redemption" is reciprocally "ashamed"
(401). Closer to the center of power and the center of blinding confor-
mity, the enemies are ministers of a sanguine, ultimately sacrilegious
confidence in the afterlife who make "Much gesture from the Pulpit" but
whose "Narcotics" yet "cannot still the Tooth" of a doubt that signifies
real faith and "That nibbles at the soul—" (501). The Dickinsonian minor-
ity opts out: "I'm ceded / I've stopped being Theirs—" in relation to the
"They" who "dropped upon my face" the baptismal "name" (508).

The Protestant clergy of New England and the social matrix that
supports and extends from it creates a Blakean Nobodaddy as its God: if
He is " 'Heavenly Father' " and yet " 'We are Dust,' " as one poem
reasons (1461), then if we are created in our "Father's" image, He be-
comes something of a dust-daddy. His earthly surrogates, Official New
England, repeat the words without hearing them, and that officialdom in
turn creates a society of people Dickinson refuses to know. To Higgin-
son's charge of her " 'shunning Men and Women,' " Dickinson re-
sponds, "they talk of Hallowed things aloud—and embarrass my Dog—
He and I don't object to them, if they'll exist their side" (L 271). But
Dickinson does object, and in objecting she politicizes her reader, though
her Progressive party's platform is the spacious (to some, specious) one
of a general Romanticism: divine madness, silence, intensity, doubt, and
sympathy.

The second and most important reason that we must not subscribe fully to the notion of a comfortingly traditional Dickinson in the realm of reader response has a basis less cultural than ontological. With Dickinson we must ask, finally, not who but what is her audience. Her "we" is less obedient to any humanist tradition than it is part of an exposing of the myth of ego identity. Ego identity is as deep a fiction as exists in the West, to the extent that we can barely discuss it as a fiction at all. "We" cannot think without an "I." Yet much as Dickinson not only admits individual identity but espouses its utmost intensity ("I like a look of Agony, / Because I know it's true—" [241]), that intensity tends to obliterate identity into floating qualities, as the very phrasing of the poem just cited suggests. Dickinson's questioning of a hardened individuality as tragically limiting is part of an American Romantic attempt to challenge the bland assurance of the first-person pronoun and of certainties of personal boundary. I want to argue that it places Dickinson with her generation and that it profoundly affects anything we can say about the relation of the poems to a reader. For that reader, as the usual "I," simply does not exist for her in any conventional way.

The challenging of a commonplace selfhood can range from the nihilistic to the neutral to the celebratory, and often in the same writer. In Melville's novel *The Confidence Man* it is impossible to determine whether there exists one or several title characters or whether the title character numbers no less than the American populace or humanity through all history, and this is largely very bad news. Yet in *Moby-Dick* the ambiguous status of Ishmael, as he wavers inconsistently between limited character-narrator and all-seeing author, or between biblical type and Woody Allen, is not tragedy making so much as it is problematizing and even ultimately salutary: Ishmael's ontology is multiple just as his perceptions are. The voice of Emerson's "Experience" is at once panicky and oppressively laconic as it speaks of "an optical illusion about every person we meet." They "seem alive" yet are, after all, only endless repetitions of this or that temperament, dead allegories. Warming to zero, Emerson murmurs, "Let us treat the men and women well; treat them as if they were real; perhaps they are." Still, "There is no power of expansion in men."[3] And yet in earlier essays such as "Circles" selfhood is not denied as merely a mechanical repetition of temperament but, rather, as a limiting bounds to be transgressed into ecstasy: "There are no fixtures to men, if we appeal to consciousness," he writes there. "People wish to be settled; only so far as they are unsettled is there any hope for them."[4] But there is hope here as there is not in "Experience." And, while it is tempting to argue that the American Romantics begin with a happy denial of the ego to sponsor the "flying perfect" only to end by denying the ego with utmost pessimism as a false claim for integrity, it is after "Experience" that Emerson writes *Representative Men,* in which each great historical hero is but a splinter of a central humanity left to the future for full realization.

There, as often elsewhere, Emerson is a jokey biographer. Given his distrust of history as a guide, he dissolves concrete people and events into invisible and permanent qualities. Plato, for instance, becomes "The Unity of Asia and the detail of Europe," and, while the great hero is found "drawing all men by fascination" to him, "I find him greater when he can abolish himself and all heroes, . . . destroying individualism."[5] Yet again elsewhere Emerson fears that he cannot restrain his amplitude sufficiently to form a self. In a letter he asks Samuel Gray Ward for "a girding belt, that I not glide away into a stream or a gas, and decrease in infinite diffusion,"[6] just as Thoreau describes himself to Harrison Blake as "A mere collection of atoms" and as a "spiritual football."[7] Yet the Thoreau who departs for Walden on 4 July, like the Thoreau in "Walking" whose westward hike represents the whole westward movement of world and national history, is a self larger than any individual ego. He is the American exemplar, just as the Walt of Whitman's "Song of Myself" is a more strident claimant of a representative national personality. And yet again, within five years, in "As I Ebb'd," Whitman will confess that "before all my insolent poems the real ME still stands untouched, untold, altogether unreached." His failure makes him something less even than an ordinary self as he falls "helpless upon the sand," one with the "straw, sands, fragments" of the ocean debris.[8] Yet this is hardly the end of Whitman's oracular persona, as the "eternal float of solution" in "Crossing Brooklyn Ferry" that identifies self with ocean, not its leavings, makes numerous later appearances as well.[9]

The point to this fast survey is not merely inconsistency. It is, rather, to argue that Dickinson's peers employ the everyday first-person as a takeoff point. Whether the destination is a mourning of illusion or a celebration of capacity, the unsettling of the "I," an insistence on its provisional character (however masked by habit and deep ideology), is a near-constant. And the unsettling of the authorial self is passed along to the reader. In any reading experience the "I" that settles into the chair is not quite the "I" that gets generated in a reading experience in which one's pressing affairs are put aside for that period of imaginative athletics wrongly termed "leisure." But my claim is that the reader of American Romantic literature faces a particular disturbance of the usual "I" in that these writers not only state the fragility of that "I" but also construct and foreground techniques that demand a reader's departure from usual modes of understanding: stories that don't tell in any usually chronological way; symbols that do not aid understanding but constitute the only path to it; genres (each of which calls forth a kind of knowing) improbably combined in such a way that each is made partial and the totality is rendered unreachable by the kind of belief each would sponsor; and poems that even appear to the eye strange upon the page, as Whitman's and Dickinson's do.

Dickinson differs in some regards from her fellows. She has a healthy if intermittent respect for the ordinary "I" and its common pleasures. I quoted earlier some poems in which psychological repression is grudgingly espoused as a necessity for survival. Certainly, there are times when she will get impatient with "The Brain, within its groove" that "Runs evenly—and true—" (556): "If your nerve deny you—," she commands in one poem, "Go above your Nerve—" (292); "Peril as a Possession / 'Tis Good to bear" in another (1678); in a third, balm is bomb, as

> A Bomb upon the Ceiling
> Is an improving thing—
> It keeps the nerves progressive
> Conjecture flourishing.
>
> (1128)

"I lived on Dread—," one speaker proudly proclaims, terming "Other Impetus" as "numb—and Vitalless—" (770). Yet, while Dickinson may celebrate the "lightning" aspect of existence regardless of its shock ("But I would not exchange the Bolt / For all the rest of Life—" [1581]), elsewhere she advises approaching it "With Insulators—and a Glove—" (630). That is, Dickinson worries less than the other American Romantics about a failure of vitality and more about its capacity to overwhelm "the Daily mind" (1323).

Even so, while Dickinson never dismisses thoughtlessly the common pleasures of the common self, she does tend, more often than not, to dismiss them and it, finally. This is because she is in every way aware of the daily mind's instability. Should "a Splinter swerve—," that grooved brain is suddenly flooded (556). The self appears secure and stable, but that is only because "On my volcano grows the Grass / A meditative spot," while, meanwhile, "How red the Fire rocks below— / How insecure the sod" (1677). Dickinson must give final acknowledgment to the disruption of the conventional self because that disruption leads to the truer thing, in this poem literally a sub-stance, which is volcanic. Or again, "If ever the lid gets off my head / And lets the brain away," this will show "the world—if the world be looking on—" simply "how far from home / It is possible for sense to live." And the dislocated brain's new and always locale has a name: "The soul there—all the time" (1727). In the first pages of this essay I was emphasizing those aspects of the poetry conforming to that lesser though important side of Dickinson that is in its way wonderfully sociable and loving, fully respectful of the common life, the side that picks the flowers for friends and creates a "we" that encourages a sharing of joys and disasters. But there is a disruptive Dickinson, too, whose love is shown in unsettling a reader, and the rest of this essay is devoted to that self-challenger.

We might begin by asking what makes the poems appear so oddly on the page, and the most obvious answer is the dashes. They connote an epistolary informality perhaps, but also a nervous rush, thus crisis. They suggest as well a poet not only putting the world together but also putting her self together, phrase by phrase. And they force the reader to do the same, to put together meaning in such a way that it is constantly undergoing revision. I can provide an example by arguing with my esteemed coeditor. Elsewhere in this volume, as Martin Orzeck is discussing Dickinson's penchant for renunciation, he quotes a poem (745) that begins:

> Renunciation—is a piercing Virtue—
> The letting go
> A Presence—for an Expectation—
> Not now—

In this poem comparing renunciation to the self-blinding of Oedipus, Orzeck sensibly reads the fourth line as a restatement of lines 2 and 3: "Not now—" is a summing-up of what it means to let go a present good for the hope of attaining something better that the accepting of the present good would not allow. And if the poem stopped there—indeed, when the reader does stop momentarily there—this is exactly right. But, picking up with that line, consider the subsequent several:

> Not now—
> The putting out of Eyes—
> Just Sunrise—
> Lest Day—
> Day's Great Progenitor—
> Outvie

Now the fourth line does not complete by summing up the first three but leads, instead, into the next thought, which provides exactly the opposite meaning: sunrise is more spectacular than the common light of day that follows upon it, and so sometimes we had best accept the present good, as it may "outvie" whatever is to succeed it. As the next lines state that

> Renunciation—is the Choosing
> Against itself—
> Itself to justify
> Unto itself—,

that is, sometimes we must renounce renunciation itself and accept an available good lest our renunciatory ethic become an insensible fetish, I would wish to claim that this reading of the fourth line is more nearly correct: Not now, I'm not going to perform this renunciatory act now.

My point, however, is that Dickinson's point reverses in midcourse—that the line changes meaning after it has brought us to a valuing of the courage of renunciation. This is not merely misdirection, a trick upon the reader. Rather, it is rethinking in the act, a demand upon the reader, and here it allows both for the valuing of an ethic Dickinson predominantly practiced and a warning against its uncritical practice. Meanwhile, like that "Bomb upon the Ceiling," it keeps the reader's "nerves progressive," her or his "Conjecture flourishing." If "The Soul should always stand ajar" (1055), ready to admit of a new idea or the revision of a vision, this poem opens the reader's soul just so.

What the dashes example in small occurs as well in the larger movements of Dickinson's poems. Earlier I quoted the beginning of "The Brain—is wider than the Sky—" (632), which stakes a claim for the mind's capacity to encompass and go beyond nature. In the second stanza the brain is also "deeper than the sea—," absorbing it as "Sponges" can absorb "Buckets," and reimaging but not altering the claim of the first stanza. The third stanza differs crucially:

> The Brain is just the weight of God—
> For—Heft them—Pound for Pound—
> And they will differ—if they do—
> As Syllable from Sound.

The Brain is now compared to Deity or spirit, and at first it may seem that the claim is being extended. In fact, the claim is being severely limited, for there is an absolute difference between the heft of weight between syllable, the brain, and sound, the spirit or God. Sound is weightless; syllable is material and thus weighted, however slightly. The difference is minute but absolute, and mind falls short of the comprehension of God. With its syntax parallel to the first two stanzas, the third stanza constitutes something of a trap for the reader, but this seems to me a misnaming of Dickinson's intention. Rather, it exposes the speaker's egotistic wish and its denial. The poet is learning—here a harsh lesson on her human limits—as she speaks. The poem does not record a prior experience but, rather, creates that experience, and the speaker's very being changes in its course. The reader must become a quickchange artist as well.

But I began this section by noting the strangeness of the poems' appearances on the printed page, and I want to return to "Renunciation— is a piercing Virtue—" to note another oddity. This poem is remarkable on the page for all the white space around it, with several two-word lines and one of one word, and that points to another of the reader's shocks— that spareness of language that makes Dickinson one of the most elliptical writers in English and earns her plaudits in those cultures in which haiku is a tradition. Her ellipses demand a concentrated attention and tend to guarantee the dismissal of the daily world that surrounds the reader; they demand, that is, a participatory effort beyond the norm of the poetry of Dickinson's time and create a rigorous democracy of meaning making.

The last three lines of this poem qualify the notion that renunciation must be renounced by stating when that is the right action:

> When larger function—
> Make that appear—
> Smaller—that Covered Vision—Here—

(745)

By my reading of the poem, the paraphrase would be: We must choose against renunciation when the present good is so fine or large that it makes a smaller good of covering our vision. The phrase "that Covered Vision" would mean renunciation itself, which covers vision by having us close our eyes to the sunrise in the hope that a more spectacular light would follow, an expectation not to be fulfilled. But, if one is reading the poem as in praise of renunciation, the paraphrasing of the lines would be: When some larger expectation makes the present thing viewed, which is only a covered vision, smaller. I read "covered" as referring to the act of covering one's eyes, but it also could be read as referring to that which is viewed as covered, or Neoplatonically second-rate. Again, I think my reading correct, but again, too, the point is that, if it is so, it is so after quite a struggle. And what I deem a misreading is so nearly an alternative reading that the full meaning of the poem must include the poet's very healthy respect for renunciation, even if on this occasion she chooses for the presence over the expectation. Dickinson's poems are not reader friendly in the conventional ways, though, like calisthenics, they may have the reader's health in mind. And the reader's health consists in keeping the nerves progressive, the understanding ajar, and the nerves of sentiment and the understanding of cognition everywhere intertwined.

There is a greater ellipsis, though, at the very center of Dickinson's poetic strategy, and it most greatly challenges the reader's stability. It is a quality I once termed "scenelessness," a graceless word meant to suggest that Dickinson's poems only pretend to locate an occasion for themselves and tell a story, when, in fact, any posited scene is quickly revealed to be illustrative and multisuggestive. The tens of poems about bees and flowers are finally not horticultural, and the hundreds of poems on death and dying often concern experiences within our lives well described by the pun on *devastating*. They dramatize "The dying multifold—without / The Respite to be dead" (1013) as if each such emotional experience is indeed a death. And, just as Dickinson's

scenelessness mocks the mimetic, kids occasion, so her narratives are
less stories than parables. I recall a colleague's angry response to my
reading of the poem that begins:

> I started early—Took my Dog—
> And visited the Sea—
> The Mermaids in the Basement
> Came out to look at me— . . .

(520)

I argued that this is a poem about a visit to the experiential unknowns,
unspecified but including the wilder fantasies of the mind. The poet
chooses to visit these outskirts of consciousness and libido, but she finds
the tide suddenly out of control, threatening to swamp her, and she runs
back to "the Solid Town—," which implies something like common
sense, the brain within its groove. As the tide, personified as a rapacious
suitor, withdraws but does so "bowing—with a Mighty look—," this
suggested to me that his defeat is only temporary and that he is implying,
like the Southern sheriff in the old Dodge automobile ads, "I'm gonna
getcha," if only next time. And that, in turn, implies just what we said
earlier—that, while Dickinson credits a survival instinct, her chief value
is for risk. She will visit that ocean of life again. My colleague found all of
this pretentious and cried, "This is just a poem about a girl and her dog
visiting the seashore." The problem with that argument, of course, is
that mermaids don't really exist and flood tides have rarely been seen to
bow. Dickinson appeals to narrative conventions precisely in order to
overthrow them, and the conventional readerly self is evoked to be over-
thrown. My colleague would have had a particularly difficult time with
some of the death poems, such as "I heard a Fly buzz—when I died—"
(465), for there any literal reading of the poem renders the very speaker of
it an impossibility.

All of Dickinson's poems offer the reader a fill-in-the-blanks test,
and, once you get the pattern right, the number of correct specific an-
swers is infinite. That is, her reader, freed from a particular subject to
bring any number of her or his experiences that fit the pattern to partici-
pate in the poem's design, experiences an intimacy without egotism. The
poems are, in a sense, an autobiography not of Dickinson but of the
reader, and yet, finally, this reader is remade beyond the limits of per-
sonal experience, the bounds of ego.

I can illustrate this principle by indulging in my own autobiographical process with a particular poem:

Did the Harebell loose her girdle
To the lover Bee
Would the Bee the Harebell *hallow*
Much as formerly?

Did the "Paradise"—persuaded—
Yield her moat of pearl—
Would the Eden *be* an Eden,
Or the Earl—an *Earl?*

(213)

We move from a backyard garden to the Garden, Eden, via a medieval moat, which is also a feminine yielding. The fear that the bee will no longer honor or value the flower once it consummates its desire becomes in the second stanza a fear that reaching paradise, intimacy with the Godhead, might similarly reduce its value.

As I read through the poem, I am reminded of mothers warning their daughters not to "give in" to the desires of boys, and a series of 1950s movies come to mind. I am also reminded, more personally, of how badly, when I was a teenager, I desired a little television set in my bedroom and how, after two years of pleading, the television was granted, only to be taken by me very quickly *for* granted and to go virtually unused shortly thereafter. Now this is not a poem about either of those middle-class phenomena, though "lover Bee" certainly places it in closer proximity to the mother-warned teenage girl, but it is fine for a reader to indulge any such analogies in order to get at the pattern. Indeed, my memory of an acquisition I desired and then spurned upon receipt may be the more useful, as it has nothing to do with the poem's particular images and thus suggests the scope of the law the poem provides—that only by a failure to achieve the sought-after good does that good remain worthy of the achieving. This law works its way in the poem through sex and religion, and I suppose my old Magnavox can exist somewhere within that spectrum. Other readers might think of a courtship and marriage or passing a bar exam or ordering a dinner or who knows what, as long as the memory is of an event in which a fulfilled desire caused the loss of desire. From whatever personal beginning all readers end by staring at a horrible law of loss through gain. Dickinson invites the personal memory but then employs it to surround it and, finally, obliterate it as something in-itself, so that we (and by now it is a "we") arrive at an appreciation for the entire pattern, otherwise a dry intellected rule, with all emotion excited.

This intimate universality enacts a carrying of the reader's self beyond that self, and my anecdotal tone here should not betray the audacity of Dickinson's shock tactics in challenging the reader's habitual individuality. I want, finally, to consider Dickinson in the poems as just such a transported reader and to consider the effect of the poet-made-reader on the actual, or "outside," reader of those poems.

Dickinson's aesthetic of reception is expressed in a lexicon of physical violence or violation meant to dramatize how beneficently destructive poetry is of the common understanding. That common understanding to her is less natural than a fearful self-blinkering: in a poem beginning, "We never know how high we are / Till we are asked to rise" (1176), the human capacity for "rising to an occasion" has "Our statures touch the skies—." But this only exposes the degree to which we curtail our statures at all other times:

> The Heroism we recite
> Would be a normal thing
> Did not ourselves the Cubits warp
> For fear to be a King—

This refusal to be great, godlike, out of a clearly baseless fear is what makes Dickinson's aesthetic lexicon of destruction benevolent. But reading does demand, at least metaphorically, the dismantling of the body. Dickinson described to Higginson her aesthetic in just such a way: "If I read a book [and] it makes my whole body so cold no fire ever can warm me I know *that* is poetry. If I feel physically as if the top of my head were taken off, I know *that* is poetry. These are the only way I know it. Is there any other way" (L 342a). "Danger—deepens Sum—" (807), one poem concludes; an authentic act of reading must be dangerous to identity. "A *Wounded* Deer—leaps Highest—" (165), and the reader must be riven if the leap is to be achieved. Right reading for Dickinson is a matter of courage, for language in itself is immortally powerful: "A Word made Flesh is seldom / And tremblingly partook," and "Each one of us" tastes this forbidden "food" to the extent of "our specific strength" (1651). In that same poem "A Word that breathes distinctly / Has not the power to die," while in another poem "A Word dropped careless on a Page," if infected, may cause us to

> inhale Despair
> At distances of Centuries
> From the Malaria—.
>
> (1261)

Dickinson described her own words as the determinedly intense march of a horse, explaining to Higginson that her inexact rhyming and other poetical niceties were "Bells, whose jingling cooled my Tramp" (L 265).

    Yet the body-threatening power of language is itself secondary to the power of inner experience and, thus, to the power of reading.

> Could mortal lip divine
> The undeveloped Freight
> Of a delivered Syllable
> 'Twould crumble with the weight.
>
> (1409)

And reading is just such an attempt to develop the freight of that syllable, for "The Poets light but Lamps—," and while, mortal, they "Themselves—go out—," their words go out in another sense, outward, as the lamps will

> Inhere as do the Suns—
> Each Age a Lens
> Disseminating their
> Circumference—.
>
> (883)

The reader's courage completes and expands the poem, making the poet immortal, even as the "mortal lip" may "crumble with the weight."

    Now all of this constitutes Dickinson writing about reading and may seem very much less to the point than the actual effects of reading her. But her explicit commentary upon reading carries a special importance, because I want to argue that, in a less exact manner, the persona of the poems is almost inevitably a reader. This preference for reaction as against its initiation is stated openly in "I would not paint—a picture—" (505), in which the speaker would prefer to be the viewer of that picture rather than the painter:

> I'd rather be the One
> Its bright impossibility
> To dwell—delicious—on— . . .

In this paean to the power of response Dickinson finally pulls back from that extreme claim for reading to wish for the status of both poet and listener at once: "Had I the Art to stun myself / With Bolts of Melody!" This self-dichotomizing, in which the poem's speaker is the reactive part of the self stunned by a more active part of the self, typifies a poet who elsewhere writes:

> One need not be a Chamber—to be Haunted—
> One need not be a House—
> The Brain has Corridors—surpassing
> Material Place—.
>
> (670)

One aspect of the self can stun or haunt another, and so in this internalized drama Dickinson can be stunning poet and stunned reader both. But she is also and always, more metaphorically, the poet *as* reader, in the sense that the Dickinson persona is profoundly reactive. I can explain this best by citing another self-dichotomizing poem:

> Presentiment—is that long Shadow—on the Lawn—
> Indicative that Suns go down—
>
> The Notice to the startled Grass
> That Darkness—is about to pass—.
>
> (764)

Notice here that the active part of the self, presentiment, anticipation of an apparently dreaded event in this case, is itself reactive, for the event that creates the presentiment is never mentioned. Yet the emotion of presentiment is the active partner to a more reactive one, "the startled

Grass," the less intellectual, more immediately emotional aspect of self that is affected. We have a doubled innerness in this poem, or we might say that the internal—presentiment—is treated as if it is an external property in relation to something still more immediately internal, the startled nerve endings. And, while such dense innerness may not be so readily apparent in all the poems, in most the speaker listens; that is, the speaker dramatizes an inner, thus readerly, reaction to an unnamed and (in a sense) less important outer cause. Something happens to her—we do not usually know what, for she does not wish to obscure "internal difference, / Where the Meanings, are—" (258). The poem is the drama of the internal difference and its meanings, and this is thus a readerly writing. Given that, what happens to the persona constitutes instructions for reading not only texts but also life.

Further, to read well, texts or life, is to die. It is to go beyond the limits of the corporeal self, much less "the Daily mind" (1323). Again, any harrowing or/and ecstatic experience is analogous in this always-analogizing poet to death, with its promise and its danger and its un-knowability, and the reading of poetry is just such an experience. As we consider the totality of Dickinson's poetry and, marking its many self-contradictions, note nonetheless that the final opting is for removing the gloves and grasping with naked hands the bolt of life lightning, this is simultaneously Dickinson's instruction to the reader: "If your Nerve, deny you— / Go above your Nerve—" (292).

But to where does one journey "above your Nerve"? And who is the reader once there? A last poem tells us that as well:

> I'm Nobody! Who are you?
> Are you—Nobody—Too?
> Then there's a pair of us?
> Don't tell! they'd advertise—you know!
>
> How dreary—to be—Somebody!
> How public—like a Frog—
> To tell one's name—the livelong June—
> To an admiring Bog!
>
> (288)

Often classified with "Publication—is the Auction / Of the Mind of Man" (709) as Dickinson's defense against seeking recognition—she described to Higginson any attempt to get her work published as "foreign to my thought, as Firmament to Fin—" (L 265), though that claim is disputed in some essays in this volume—this poem means more than that. Certainly, it comments on being a "nobody" in the colloquial sense and affirms what she wrote to Higginson in that same letter: "If fame belonged to me, I could not escape her—if she did not, the longest day would pass me on the chase— . . ." But *Nobody* here may mean as well "no-body" or at least suggest the refusal of fixed identity in preference for the soul ajar. The poem opens with a statement of introduction that both undermines itself and the self then seeks to confirm the new acquaintance, the reader within the poem, in this same un-identity. The problem with being Somebody, not just a well-known person but a consistent ego, is stasis, mechanical repetition, just as Emerson complains of in "Experience": the unendingly same croakings of a frog to a bog full of admirers, whose admiration depends on the Somebody's cowardly resistance to change. June may be a pleasant month, but a "livelong," lifelong June makes even a Californian wish for a change of season. The protean ego espoused by the Nobody state is furiously dynamic, "on the chase," unending in the different sense of reaching no finality. "Immortality contented / Were Anomaly" (1036), and the self must imitate spirit to become "This limitless Hyperbole" (1482).

The reader of this readerly writer in turn must imitate her self. "Peril as a Possession / 'Tis Good to bear," and the most terrible and best peril is the dispossession of the Somebody self. When Dickinson wrote that "Subjects hinder talk!" she meant, by "subjects," topics, but she might as well have meant the subject self of the froglike "I." As for whom, I began with a grammatical injunction, and I end with a truer one. There is no reader of Dickinson; there is only the reading. The noun must become a verb.

NOTES

1. Figures derive from *A Concordance to the Poems of Emily Dickinson*, ed. S. P. Rosenbaum (Ithaca: Cornell University Press, 1964), which is keyed to Thomas H. Johnson's three-volume variorum edition.
2. The poems are reprinted in accordance with the editor's choice of variants in the one-volume edition, *The Poems of Emily Dickinson*, ed. Thomas H. Johnson (Boston: Little, Brown, 1960). References to this text appear in the essay by poem number. Letters in the essay are quoted from *The Letters of Emily*

Dickinson, ed. Thomas H. Johnson and Theodora Ward, 3 vols. (Cambridge: Belknap Press of Harvard University Press, 1958). References to this edition appear in the text (as "L").

3. Ralph Waldo Emerson, "Experience," in *The Collected Works,* ed. Alfred R. Ferguson and Jean Ferguson Carr (Cambridge: Harvard University Press, 1983), 3:27–49.

4. Ralph Waldo Emerson, "Circles," in *Collected Works,* 2:182.

5. Ralph Waldo Emerson, *Representative Men,* in *The Complete Works,* ed. Edward Waldo Emerson, 12 vols. (Boston and New York: Houghton Mifflin, 1903–4), 4:53 and 23.

6. Ralph Waldo Emerson, *Letters from Ralph Waldo Emerson to a Friend,* ed. Charles Eliot Norton (Boston and New York: Houghton Mifflin, 1899), 35–36.

7. Henry David Thoreau, *The Correspondence,* ed. Walter Harding and Carl Bode (New York: New York University Press, 1958), 302.

8. Walt Whitman, "As I Ebb'd," in *Leaves of Grass, 1860 Facsimile Edition,* ed. Roy Harvey Pearce (Ithaca and London: Cornell University Press, 1961), 195–99. The quoted passages are from sections 5 and 16.

9. Walt Whitman, "Crossing Brooklyn Ferry," in *Leaves of Grass,* Norton Critical Edition, ed. Sculley Bradley and Harold W. Blodgett (New York: Norton, 1973), 164, l. 107.

Dickinson's Figure of Address

Virginia Jackson

Lyric Media

In his preface to the first publication of Dickinson's poems in 1890 Higginson began by warning his readers that "the verses of Emily Dickinson belong emphatically to what Emerson long since called 'the Poetry of the Portfolio,'—something produced absolutely without the thought of publication, and solely by way of expression of the writer's own mind." Dickinson herself could not be "persuaded to print," Higginson wrote, because, although the daughter of "the leading lawyer of Amherst," she "habitually concealed her mind, like her person, from all but a very few friends . . . she was as invisible to the world as if she had dwelt in a nunnery." The Dickinson that Higginson thus introduced is "emphatically," "absolutely," "solely" private, a creature of privilege (one of her own favorite words), a law unto herself. Modern readers have often complained of Higginson's apologetic presentation of the poet whose fame would so far outstrip his own, and many have sought to qualify his notion of Dickinson's isolation. Higginson's placement of Dickinson's audience has gone largely unchallenged, however, and it is worth asking why we have been so content to stay in the position he bequeathed to us. What his introduction made sure of was that those first readers of the poems in "print" knew that what they were being allowed to read was not intended to be read by *them*. To this admonition the response in the 1890s was immediate and popular interest: Dickinson's *Poems* became a sensation, a best-seller, a "fad."[1] If the notion of a published privacy—a privacy that circulates—has proven immensely attractive ever since, perhaps this is because we still share with that first public the assumption that Dickinson's privileged self-address entitles her to the definition of lyric poet in its purest form.

Nowhere is the definition of lyric poetry as privacy gone public more striking than in the publisher's advertisement for the second volume of the *Poems* in 1894 (Buckingham, 387). Beside several citations from reviews proclaiming Dickinson's "original genius," Roberts Brothers chose to include this perplexing notice:

> Here surely is the record of a soul that suffered from isolation, and the stress of dumb emotion, and the desire to make itself understood by means of a voice so long unused that the sound was strange even to her own ears. —*Literary World*
>
> 16mo, cloth, $1.25 each; white and gold, $1.50 each;
> two volumes in one, $2.00

How could such a comment be expected to sell books? The publisher's motive becomes even more difficult to assign when we take into account the context of this citation, for it is drawn from Dickinson's first bad review. Reacting against Dickinson's sudden popularity in 1890, the reviewer for Boston's *Literary World* compared Dickinson to the first deaf-mute to be educated, called her "a case of arrested development," and commended "this strange book of verse—with its sober, old-maidenly binding, on which is a silver Indian pipe, half fungus, half flower—to pitying and kindly regard" (Buckingham, 48). The publisher, having reduced the price of the first edition of the *Poems,* seems to have anticipated what is only clear now in retrospect: even this extremity of condescension merely exaggerated the appetite of the reading public. The "old-maidenly" pathos of Dickinson's isolation (here notably, as in Higginson's preface, transferred from person to book) answered to an idea that what the poetic voice registered *was* "the record of a soul that suffered" from an exemplary self-enclosure. The reviewer's comment on the book's ornament ("half fungus, half flower") also slips curiously across the border between writer and text, and, while it is certainly meant to sound disparaging, it partakes as well of the idea that darkness and deprivation produce a lyric beauty.

This sort of transference from person to text to symbol of poetic inspiration goes on frequently in the early reviews and always in the interest of opposing a valued and implicitly feminized lyric quality to public convention. "It is a rare thing in these days of universal print to find a poet who is averse to seeing his or her work before the public," wrote a reviewer for the *Boston Daily Traveller*. "The freedom and fullness of verse written only as expression of the inward thought, without heed of criticism or regard for praise, has a charm as indefinable as the song of a wild bird that sings out of the fullness of its heart" (Buckingham, 23). Wittingly or unwittingly, the reviewer was glossing his own echo of Higginson by echoing Shelley's classic description of the poet as "a nightingale, who sits in darkness and sings to cheer its own solitude with sweet sounds; his auditors are as men entranced by the melody of an unseen musician, who feel that they are moved and softened, yet know not whence or why."[2] Entranced by Higginson's revelation of the invisibility of the source, the readers to whom Dickinson's first editor addressed her poems responded by understanding that his portrait of a wealthy white woman shut up in her house made Dickinson the perfect figure of the lyric poet.[3]

In order to grasp in detail the elements of Higginson's Dickinson that established her as such an apt candidate for the role of lyric poet par excellence, we would need to pursue more of the reception history than the present context allows. What I want to pursue here, instead, is the structure of address supposed by the definition of Dickinson's as a private—and therefore transcendent—lyric voice. If her old-maidenly strangeness, her nunlike privacy, worked (and still works) to make her poetry seem to readers like the melody of Shelley's "unseen musician," this must be because from this moment—the moment that Dickinson's writing was published and received as lyric poetry—devolves a history of reading a particular structure of address into the poems. This structure is one in which saying "I" can stand for saying "you," in which the poet's solitude stands in for the solitude of the individual reader—a self-address so absolute that every self can identify it as his own. The fact that it was *her* own seems in effect to have made Dickinson a clearer mirror for the poetics of the single ego. Already consigned to the private sphere by reason of gender (and kept comfortably there by benefit of class), Dickinson could represent in person and in poem (the two so quickly becoming indistinguishable) the prerogative of the private individual—namely, the privilege to gain public power by means of a well-protected self-sufficiency.[4] The ease with which *I* can become *you, she* becomes *he,* and the private self is coined as public property in a poetics of individualism was aptly exemplified by William Dean Howells's influential literary championship of Dickinson in her first year of publication: "The strange *Poems of Emily Dickinson* we think will form something of an intrinsic experience with the understanding reader of them," Howells began. Just how "intrinsic" that experience was for Howells he reveals at the end of his essay: "This poetry is as characteristic of our life as our business enterprise, our political turmoil, our demagogism, our millionarism" (Buckingham, 64). The poetry Higginson was so careful to cast "emphatically" as the "expression of the writer's own mind" immediately became the expression of the reader's own identity. What Howells so explicitly says—and he says it not just for himself but for each of "us"—is "Emily Dickinson, *c'est moi.*" It is as much as to say, as has so often been said since and in so many ways, "Emily Dickinson, *c'est le moi.*"

To say that in remaining closed upon herself Dickinson managed to represent *the* self and therefore to become "characteristic of *our* life" is to trace in her poetry the syllogistic logic of address that dominates post-Romantic theories of lyric reading. Put simply, that logic converts the isolated "I" into the universal "we" by bypassing the mediation of any particular "you." This bypass or evasion serves the purpose of satisfying what Herbert Tucker has recently called "the thirst for intersubjective confirmation of the self, which has made the overhearing of a persona our principal means of understanding a poem."[5] The key term here is *overhearing:* the "intersubjective confirmation of the self" performed by a reading of lyric based upon the identity between poet and reader must be achieved by denying to the poem any intersubjective economy of its own. On this view in order to have an audience the lyric must not have one. The paradox is audible in Shelley's 1821 "Defence" and is fixed into definition by John Stuart Mill in 1833 in a moment that Tucker self-consciously echoes. "Eloquence is *heard,* poetry is *overheard,*" Mill writes. "Eloquence supposes an audience; the peculiarity of poetry appears to us to lie in the poet's utter unconsciousness of a listener. Poetry is feeling confessing itself to itself, in moments of solitude."[6] In order to overhear such a radically internalized solitude, the reader is supposed to partake of a parallel—that is, identical—seclusion. Mill's figure for this parallelism is striking: lyric "song," he writes, "has always seemed to us like the lament of a prisoner in a solitary cell, ourselves listening, unseen in the next" (*Essays,* 14). Cell to cell, one prisoner to another, this form of address is sustained by the pathos of solitary confinement—but who or what has imposed the sentence? When, in 1957, Northrop Frye repeated without alteration Mill's version of lyric as "preeminently the utterance that is overheard," he went so far as to say that there is "no word for the audience of the lyric" because "the poet, so to speak, turns his back on his listeners."[7] In Frye's repetition of Mill "the lament of the prisoner" has become the individual poet's choice; the poet "turns his back" on a real, historical audience in order to create ("so to speak") a fictive one. In Frye's words "the lyric poet normally pretends to be talking to himself or to someone else: a spirit of nature, a Muse . . . a personal friend, a lover, a god, a personified abstraction, or a natural object" (249). As the range of Frye's list suggests, by not addressing anyone in particular the poet "pretends" to address everything in general—to achieve a form of transcendentally apostrophic address. But Mill's prison scene poses questions that haunt Frye's modern lyric inwardness: Why should the poet pretend? What are the conditions of such isolation? Is all lyric, then, imaginary address? Is there no difference between an apostrophe to a natural object and an intimation to a personal friend? Does the poet choose to turn his or her back, or is he or she somehow constrained to do so—by history, by circumstance, or by the very theory of reading that defines lyric address as the subject's self-address, as not directed toward any specific destination and therefore universally applicable to objects of imagination, objects of tradition, objects of desire, objects of worship, objects of thought, and objects of perception alike?

Dickinson's poetry and the last century's reading of Dickinson's poetry take up the questions implicit in this general and selective view of lyric theory in ways that might redeem them from rhetorical circularity. As we shall see, the poems often situate themselves on the border between constraint and choice, self and other, actual address and its mimesis, history and fiction, reference to the particular and allegory of the universal. In effect, the poems thematize the very issues that preoccupy post-Romantic theories of the lyric. And, as Higginson and his contemporaries were the first to notice, the poet herself made literal the seclusion of the lyric self in its solitary cell. Those readers were also the first to read that literal confinement back into metaphor, so that the listeners in the next cell become Mill's "ourselves." The metaphor that supports such a reading is *the* lyric metaphor: the figure of the speaking voice. If we think of the lyric as "the lament of a prisoner in a solitary cell," then we must position ourselves as readers who are hearers "unseen." The metaphor of voice bridges the otherwise incommutable distance between one "solitary cell" and another, between two otherwise mutually exclusive individuals. Most important, it does so by claiming to transcend the historical circumstances of those individuals, by placing "us" in the same metaphorical moment with the poet/prisoner ("listening . . . in the next" solitude).

In the pages that follow I would like to suggest another way of placing ourselves in relation to Dickinson's structures of address. Rather than consider the lyric "I" as a "speaker," or, as Tucker puts it, a "persona" who talks to herself and so speaks for all of us, I want to examine what happens when Dickinson's writing directly addresses a "you," when that writing attempts to turn toward rather than away from a specific audience. In turning from "I" to "you," and from the metaphor of voice to the act of writing, Dickinson's poems may trace an economy of reading very different than the one that Higginson and his contemporaries imagined: a circuit of exchange in which the subjective self-address of the speaker is replaced by the intersubjective practice of the writer, in which the poet's seclusion might be mediated by something other than ourselves.

"You—there—I—here—"

The way in which I address you depends upon where you are. If you are very near, I can whisper. If you are across the table, I can speak. If you are upstairs or just outside, I can shout. If you are too distant to hear (even to overhear) my voice, I can write. And in the illusion peculiar to written address, the condition of your absence (the condition of my writing) conjures a presence more intimate than the whisper—more intimate, that is, than the metaphor of the voice, of a speaking presence, would allow.[8] Dickinson acknowledges this property of writing often in her letters, as when she writes to Susan Gilbert that,

> as I sit here Susie, alone with the winds and you, I have the old *king feeling* even more than before, for I know not even the *cracker man* will invade *this* solitude, this Sweet Sabbath of our's.[9]

As Dickinson writes, "*this* solitude" becomes an intersubjective space in which the deictics *here* and *this* can point away from what it is to be alone toward a moment in which, in writing, the writer is "alone with." As Dickinson's emphasis suggests, it is the page itself that offers a communion that displaces in that moment what earlier in the letter she has called "*their* meeting." Their meeting takes place in church; our meeting takes place in "the church within our hearts." And, as she writes, the transmutation of church building to mutual sympathetic investment comes to depend upon the very transit that both threatens and enables such investment "within." Within a sublime solitude ("the old *king feeling*") uncompromised by public commerce (the comical "*cracker man*") Dickinson's letter goes on to imagine a private commerce that does not oppose privacy to community or inside to outside but, instead, makes the first term inclusive of the second, turning the terms of solitude inside out. This reversal of the normal order (the order in which the public space would include the private, outside would contain inside) takes place not through a logic of identity but, rather, by means of the difference that is the very medium of written address:

> I mourn this morning, Susie, that I have no sweet sunset to gild a page for *you,* nor any bay so blue—not even a chamber way up in the sky, as your's is, to give me thoughts of heaven, which *I* would give to you. You know how I must write you, down, down, in the terrestrial; no sunset here, no stars; not even a bit of *twilight* which I may poeticize—and send you! Yet Susie, there will be romance in the letter's ride to you—think of the hills and the dales, and the rivers it will pass over, and the drivers and conductors who will hurry it on to you; and wont that make a poem such as can ne'er be written?

What the movement of this letter makes explicit—and I want to maintain that it is very much what is implicit in the movement of several of Dickinson's poems that take the direction and destination of address as their subject—is that "*this* solitude" in which I am not alone but "alone with" has everything to do with the material circumstances of writing and little to do with what that writing will be taken (figuratively) to represent. Representation as mimesis, especially in the ideal terms that "I may poeticize," would be inevitably elegiac (in Dickinson's pun, "I mourn this morning"'s distance from the "sweet sunset" of which Susan may have written). Rather than send a metaphorical "here" there, Dickinson asks her reader to imagine the "romance in the letter's ride"—that is, to retrace the deferral of the letter that Susan now holds in her hands. From Dickinson's hand through the hands of "the drivers and conductors" to Susan's hand, the letter becomes "a poem such as can ne'er be written." It does so, paradoxically, because, rather than "poeticize" the celestial, it remains "down, down, in the terrestrial" within an economy of hands, hills, dales, rivers, drivers, conductors, and literal letters instead of within an idealized universe of gilded pages, "thoughts of heaven," sunset, stars, "a bit of *twilight*." The intimacy established in the physical exchange of the letter, the intimacy that makes of its transfer a "romance," is a privacy encompassing the public circle already inscribed upon it with the writer's admission of what makes *"this* solitude" of the written page something "of ours." What writer and reader mutually possess is not identical solitudes (my sunset like your sunset, my stars like your stars, my "little chamber way up in the sky, as your's is") but the letter itself. That letter substantiates the otherwise purely metaphorical relation between writer and reader. It embodies the separation between their two bodies. But, since it is not a metaphor, this third, literal body is also always insufficient, radically contingent. As Dickinson writes at the end of her letter:

> Susie, what shall I do—there is'nt room enough; not *half* enough, to hold what I was going to say. Wont you tell the man who makes sheets of paper, that I hav'nt the *slightest respect* for him!

The epistolary convention of complaining that one's time to write has run out has turned here to a mock protest against the page that will not "hold what I was going to say." What the page does hold, however, is what Susan holds and is (thanks, nevertheless, to "the man who makes sheets of paper" and, like the "drivers and conductors," adds another pair of hands to the letter's history) held within it. The object of address has become its subject, as the letter has implicated everyone "outside" the writer's solitude within the "sheets of paper" that hold not "what I was going to say" but only what can be written, read, held.

Just as the letter to Susan allows Dickinson to displace the plane geography of here and there, outside and inside, with the more complex discursive field available to reading and writing, the poems of direct address often begin in a pathos of distance or isolation that they then revise by revising the very conditions of address, its premises. Poem 640, "I cannot live with You—," takes up the question of rhetorical premises (i.e., predication) quite literally and has thus become one of the poems most often read as testimony of Dickinson's literal seclusion. If, however, "I cannot live with You—" tells us, as Cynthia Griffin Wolff has suggested, "more about Emily Dickinson herself than any other single work," it is remarkable that it should say "I" by saying "you" so often (more often than does any other poem in Dickinson's corpus).[10] As Sharon Cameron has written, "We must scrutinize the poem carefully to see how renunciation can be so resonant with the presence of what has been given up":[11]

I cannot live with You—
It would be Life—
And Life is over there—
Behind the Shelf

The Sexton keeps the Key to—
Putting up
Our Life—His Porcelain—
Like a Cup—

Discarded of the Housewife—
Quaint—or Broke—
A newer Sevres pleases—
Old Ones crack—[12]

These lines are indeed resonant with the presence of what is absent, though perhaps this is because it is not the object of address—the phenomenal "You" her- or himself—that is here renounced but, instead, a figure for "you" (the first of what will be a series of such figures) that is considered and found wanting. What is strategically renounced, in other words, is not the presence of the other but the way in which figurative language works to replace that other with an illusion of presence that would mean the other's death. It is this illusion that the poem tries hard not to forget. The results of forgetting are enacted in these first stanzas in the oddly extended initial comparison of "Our Life" to "a Cup / Discarded of the Housewife—" and locked away by the "Sexton." When what "would be Life"—that is, the full presence that would cancel language, that would make writing unnecessary—leaves "Our" hands, it becomes reified into figure. In Dickinson's stunningly contracted line the passage from redundant presence to figurative absence is a matter of shifting pronouns: "Our Life—His Porcelain—." Like the "*cracker man*" and "the man who makes sheets of paper" in Dickinson's letter to Susan, the Sexton who "keeps the Key" seems at first an agent of invasion and constraint, the representative of the (notably masculine) public world imposing his law upon "Our Life." But what a Sexton does, we recall, is, according to Dickinson's dictionary, "to take care of the vessels, vestments, &c., belonging to the church."[13] For the Sexton sacramental symbols are *things* ("Our Life—His Porcelain—") and so can be handled "Like a Cup," valued or devalued ("Discarded") according to the hands they fall into. The Sexton does not stand for what separates "I" from "You," for a public law

to which "Our [private] Life" is opposed; rather, what the Sexton repre-
sents is the transformation of "Our Life" into figure. Once that figure is
introduced the simile takes over, intensifying the sense of referential insta-
bility signaled by the change in pronouns and by the apparently arbitrary
little narrative of the "Housewife." The Sexton and the Housewife are
thus the antitypes to the "drivers and conductors" of Dickinson's letter:
they take the figure of the "cup" literally, and, forgetting that it *is* a figure
(as are they), they have the potential of delivering it into the wrong hands.

But whose are the right hands? If "Life is over there—" when it
becomes a metaphor, where is it if it does not? Is there any alternative to
the privative fatality of figuration? These are questions that the poem
backs away from in the third stanza to ask over and over with an urgency
bordering on obsession. Before considering the litany of responses that
make up the body of the poem, we may better understand what is at
stake in the apparent opposition between Life as full presence and Life as
figure by placing it beside an analogous difference in another poem from
the same period (about 1862) and written on the same stationery as is
Poem 640. "I think To Live—" (Poem 646) begins in very much the same
way as does "I cannot live with You—" but seems tellingly unable to
move beyond its beginning:

> I think To Live—may be a *Bliss
> To those *who dare to try—
> Beyond my limit to conceive—
> My lip—to testify—
>
> I think the Heart I former wore
> Could widen—till to me
> The Other, like the little Bank
> Appear—unto the Sea—
>
> I think the Days—could every one
> In Ordination stand—
> And Majesty—be easier—
> Than an inferior kind—
>
> No numb alarm—lest Difference come—
> No Goblin—on the Bloom—
> No *start in Apprehension's Ear,
> No *Bankruptcy—no Doom—

But Certainties of *Sun—
*Midsummer—in the Mind—
A steadfast South—upon the Soul—
Her Polar *time—behind—

The Vision—pondered long—
So *plausible becomes
That I esteem the fiction—*real—
The *Real—fictitious seems—

How bountiful the Dream—
What Plenty—it would be—
Had all my Life *but been Mistake
Just *rectified—in Thee

*Life *allowed *click *Sepulchre—
Wilderness *Noon *Meridian *Night *tangible—
positive *true *Truth *been one *bleak *qualified—

The first line of this poem, especially in the variant version, echoes directly the tautology that launches Poem 640: "I think To Live—may be a *Bliss *Life." (Because the variants are important to attend to here, please note that I have, at the risk of legibility [as I explain at more length in n. 12], included them beside the superscribed asterisks that stand in for Dickinson's x marks in the manuscripts.) As Mary Jo Salter has recently suggested, Dickinson's variants "may have represented to her either revisions or . . . overtones: that is, each well-chosen alternative was at least as right as any other, and possibly most beautiful when held in mind with the other(s), like a chord."[14] I would only add to Salter's important point that, if we are to attend to the words that crowd the bottom of the second page of the manuscript of "I think To Live—" as "overtones" rather than revisions, we should do so not by overhearing them as polyphony but by reading them as polygraphy. As Dickinson put it in a letter to Higginson, "A Pen has so many inflections and a Voice but one" (L 470). Perhaps so many inflections of the pen riddle the page of "I think To Live—" because to inflect (literally, to bend; to turn from a direct line or course) that initial tautology is the poem's problem. What "I think To Live—may be a *Bliss *Life" and "I cannot live with You— / It would be Life—" share as redundant propositions is the implication that, were the possi-

bility of presence not foreclosed, all one could say would be "Life—
Life—Life—Life—Life" over and over in a blissful stutter. Put another
way, the desire that informs these poems is the desire that they need
not be written.

But the poems are written, of course, and so inflected with a desire
that diverts the stutter with which they begin by almost ending. Given
this predicament, the poems proceed in a direction that is anything but
linear. Loop by stanzaic loop, the quatrains of "I think To Live—" turn
back upon that opening line as if locked by the Sexton's key within its
syntax. The stanzas assume the burden of defining an infinitive that the
first stanza has already defined as indefinable: "Beyond my limit to
conceive— / My lip—to testify—."[15] What the rest of the poem bears
witness to is the attempt to write the unsayable, to inflect an ideally
uninflected—experience? sense-certainty? *Life,* as the term appears in
these poems, is an ontological absolute. "Had we the first intimation of
the Definition of Life," Dickinson wrote to Elizabeth Holland, "the calm-
est of us would be Lunatics!" (L 492). Not being able (or refusing) to
define *what* it is, the poem goes on to decline *where* Life "may be" if "it
would be." That proleptic *may be* places the stanzas that follow in the
perspective of anticipation, so that what "may be" would be conceivable
only in terms of what was: "the Heart I former wore," "an inferior kind"
of time. This entanglement of anticipation and retroaction predicated in
the first three stanzas by the repetition of "I think" gives way in the
fourth stanza to another anaphora: "No . . . / No . . . / No . . . /
No . . . no . . . ." We could read the retrograde progression from the
third to the fourth stanzas as a (failing) attempt to extricate thinking from
the temporal trap in which the grammatical structure of the poem has
thinking locked. In those first stanzas "Difference" has already come; the
"*start *click in Apprehension's Ear" has already been registered. The
"click" (of the key?) in the variant interrupts the first several stanzas'
grasp (apprehension) of what it "may be" "To Live" and marks their
suspicion (apprehensiveness) that that *what* is ungraspable in language.
When the fifth stanza then seeks to deny the denial of the fourth, its
"Certainties" are made less certain by the differential (i.e., linguistic)
framework that they claim to transcend. While the alliteration and subtle
assonance of the lines strive to give the impression of sameness (an im-
pression located in the acoustic affects: "Certainties . . . Sun" / "Midsum-
mer . . . Mind" / "steadfast South . . . Soul"), "Sun," "Midsummer,"
and "South" are themselves only articulable in their difference from the

"Polar time—behind—." The poem, still enmeshed in the tragic temporality of a retroactive anticipation, cannot name the place beyond this predicament until its last two spare monosyllables: "in Thee." The figure of address is revealed in the end to have been the "what" that the poem has anticipated all along. In Helen McNeil's reading, " 'Thee' is whatever would give the mind whatever the mind desires."[16]

At the end of "I think To Live—" the deferred designation of *Thee* is not, however, merely the vehicle of desire's fulfillment; *Thee* is the name *of* desire, its unlocatable location. Or perhaps we should say its suspended location, for it is in the end at the dead center of the chiasmus between "the fiction—*real—*true" and "The *Real *Truth—fictitious." When desire's prolepsis "so *plausible *tangible—*positive becomes" that desire "seems" answerable, its object is canceled by the rhetorical crossroads at which that object is sublated in *seems*. That suspension is, in effect, a refusal to sublimate *Thee* by apprehending the other in figure—that is, to forget that its plausibility would be an effect of the apostrophe that the poem defers until its last line. At the end of the poem *Thee* is the term for the horizon (Dickinson would say "circumference") of figurative language itself. And, in what I will suggest is a crucial and crucially tentative way, the limit beyond which we can no longer locate the object of the poem's address is, in the Latin roots of each of the variants, inflected by the figure of the hand that reaches rather than of the voice that speaks: *plausible* (to clap with the hands), *tangible* (to touch with the hands), *positive* (to place with the hands). The apostrophe that works retroactively to bring the object of address into the poem is qualified by its position at the edge of the poem's temporal grasp. Captive of neither the Imaginary "Other" self of the second and third stanzas nor of the Symbolic register of stanzas 4 through 6, *Thee* is in the position that Lacan came to name "the Real": that point on the horizon of language that sets desire (or language-as-desire) in motion but which language (or the subject constructed from it) cannot (in order to keep desiring) apprehend.[17]

What this reading of "I think To Live—" allows us to understand about the anxiety of the first lines of "I cannot live with You—" is that that anxiety stems not only from the distance that separates *I* from *You* but also from the consequences of the apostrophe that separation invokes. While "I think To Live—" defers its apostrophe until its last word (so that, in effect, the apostrophe cannot become a prosopopoeia, cannot attribute to *Thee* a face, a figure), "I cannot live with You—" begins with the problem of keeping *You* in the Real, outside its own apostrophe's reach.[18] That reach, as the poem demonstrates at length (at fifty lines, this is one of Dickinson's longest poems) is extensive: it encompasses this life, death, afterlife, heaven, hell, memory, the self:

> I could not die—with You—
> For One must wait
> To shut the Other's Gaze down—
> You—could not—
>
> And I—Could I stand by
> And see You—freeze—
> Without my Right of Frost—
> Death's privilege?
>
> Nor could I rise—with You—
> Because Your Face
> Would put out Jesus'—
> That New Grace
>
> Glow plain—and foreign
> On my homesick Eye—
> Except that You than He
> Shone closer by—
>
> They'd judge Us—How—
> For You—served Heaven—You know,
> Or sought to—
> I could not—
>
> Because You saturated Sight—
> And I had no more Eyes
> For sordid *excellence *consequence
> As Paradise

As Cameron suggests, this "catechism is one of renunciation" (78), but it is important to notice that what is renounced at each stage of this cate-chism is a face-to-face encounter with "You." In other words, what is renounced is the performative affect of apostrophe, the trope that brings *You* into the moment of speech. In the fourth and fifth stanzas that renun-ciation turns on the moment of death (as "I could not die—with You—" follows almost by catechistic rote upon the first line, save for the graphic stutter of the hyphen), or the moment a nineteenth-century reader would recognize as the death vigil. Whether one shuts "the Other's Gaze down—" or "I stand by / And see You—freeze—," the emphasis is on envisioning an encounter that the poem does not want to envision, not only because doing so would be an admission of mortality but also because seeing the other's face would mean turning "You" into a fiction. That fiction would allow address to transcend the material circumstances of separation, as the abrupt and seamless transition from physical death to life after death insists. If the poem were to admit such transcendence (and this is, after all, the historical moment of Elizabeth Phelps's *The Gates Ajar,* the popular novel in which reunion after death is carried on in vivid, even domestic detail and to which the last stanza of the poem may contain an allusion), "Your Face / Would put out Jesus.' "[19] But by not imagining its own apostrophe as transcendent, the poem does not give a "Face" to *You*; what it does, instead, is to tally the consequences if it were to do so. The complexity of this conditional temporality is very much like that of "I think To Live—," and it has, understandably, confused a reader as perceptive as Cameron. "Interestingly enough," Cameron writes, "what prohibits union seems to be the fact that it has already occurred. . . . For although 'Because Your Face / Would put out Jesus'—' seems suppositional, two stanzas later the event is echoed, and located not in the future at all, but rather in the past:

> Because You saturated Sight—
> And I had no more Eyes
> For sordid excellence
> As Paradise."

(80)

The problem with this reading is the assumption that the slip into the past tense constitutes the ninth stanza as an "event." As in the first stanzas, in which "Our Life" becomes "his Porcelain" when the figure is taken literally, the shift from the sixth quatrain's *Would* to the seventh stanza's *Shone* happens at the point at which the poem, for the moment, enters into its own fiction. Not incidentally, "I esteem the fiction—*real *true" at the very moment that the poem turns back upon the I's "Eye," and the effect of that turn is blinding. In the fictive vision that the figure of apostrophe would make plausible, the illusion of a full presence would blind the I/Eye to the fact that "Your Face" would be an illusion, an affect of performative utterance (the variant for the "excellence" of the figure's therefore ironically "sordid" Paradise is "consequence"). To mistake the performative dimension of apostrophe for a statement of historical presence would be to become the Sexton, for to imagine that "over there" is already here is to make sure that "You" will dissolve into figment. As Dickinson wrote in an earlier poem, "You see I cannot see—your lifetime—" (Poem 253), the representation of desire's object threatens to take the place of that object itself:

> Too vague—the face—
> My own—so patient—covers—
> Too far—the strength—
> My timidness enfolds—
> Haunting the Heart—
> Like her translated faces—
> Teazing the want—
> It—only—can suffice!

When the ninth stanza of "I cannot live with You—" enters into the past tense of ideal union *as if* that union had already occurred, the "translated faces" of desire tease the poem momentarily out of thought. If the poem ended here, we could say that apostrophe had worked its charm. But the three stanzas that issue from this moment deny apostrophe its due, and, in so renouncing the "saturated Sight" of figure, they must find a way out of its "Haunting" and "Teazing" logic. They must reach toward, in other words, what "only—can suffice" without appropriating the object in a rhetorical illusion of sufficiency. They must give "You" a figure that is not a "translated face."[20]

As in "I think To Live—," in which the inflections of the pen bear witness to what is "Beyond my limit to conceive— / My lip to testify—," the concluding movement of "I cannot live with You—" sustains an address to a "You" positioned just beyond the poem's (or apostrophe's) limit. Stanzas 10 and 11 withdraw from the fictive moment of absolute insight to reassert the fallacy of an identity between self and other, here and there. Thus, the penultimate stanza sums the danger of a figurative logic of self-projection:

> And were You—saved—
> And I—condemned to be
> Where You were not—
> That self—were Hell to Me—

This last line is inflected with two important literary echoes: Satan's "I Myself am Hell" and Heathcliff's Satanic address to the dead Catherine. The allusion to *Paradise Lost* has often been noticed, but it has not been noticed that Dickinson's Milton has been mediated here by Brontë's Miltonic hero, who, "condemned to be" where Catherine is not, invokes her presence in his own tormented apostrophe, an invocation that grows directly from the question "Where is she?":

> Not *there*—not in heaven—not perished—where? Oh! . . . Catherine Earnshaw, may you not rest, as long as I am living! . . . Be with me always—take any form—drive me mad! Only *do* not leave me in this abyss, where I cannot find you! Oh, God! it is unutterable! I *cannot* live without my life! I *cannot* live without my soul![21]

Heathcliff, master of the egotistical sublime that he is, keeps Catherine with him and "Not *there*" in the very form of his address to her. In the novel the performative force of his utterance actually works: Catherine stays, one of desire's "translated faces." If the pathetic tug beneath the statement "I cannot live with You— / It would be Life—" has been all along "I *cannot* live without my life," that pathos is finally qualified (or "rectified") by the allusion to *Wuthering Heights* and Brontë's ambivalent portrait of her hero's fantastic act of identification through invocation. The concluding stanza of Dickinson's poem suggests an alternative to the sort of romantic selfhood that Heathcliff—and especially Heathcliff's use of the figure of apostrophe—represents.[22]

That alternative is sketched in lines that offer an appropriately tentative version of a form of address that would not be an act of appropriation:

> So We must meet apart—
> You there—I—here—
> With just the Door ajar
> That Oceans are—and Prayer—
> And that White Sustenance—*privilege *exercise
> Despair—

These lines are remarkable for what they do not say. They do not say, with Heathcliff, "Be with me always." They do not locate the invoked "You" within the self; they do not claim that your *there* has been transmuted (or, in Dickinson's better word, translated) into my *here*. In other words, the lines recognize the threat inherent in the figure of apostrophic

address; they register the way in which "this figure," as Jonathan Culler
has written, "which seems to establish relations between self and other
can in fact be read as an act of radical interiorization and solipsism."[23] The
sort of diplomatically erotic "relations" that Dickinson's poem imagines
at its close are predicated upon the rejection of such solipsism: "You"
remain "there—I—," stranded between hyphens, remain "here." And, as
Griffin Wolff has suggested, "what sense can there be in the lines 'So We
must meet apart— / You there—I—here—,' unless 'here' refers to the
very page on which the poem is printed?" (423). What sense, indeed. If
the directly referential function of *here* persuades us that what the deictic
points to is the page we hold in our hands (but not exactly *that* page, of
course, once the poem "is printed" and many pages are delivered into
many hands), what would the referential function of *there* be? Griffin
Wolff's solution—that " 'We,' reader and poet, do indeed 'meet,' but
only 'apart,' through the mediating auspices of the Voice and the verse"—
ignores the problem that the extended final stanza is the solution to. "The
Voice and the verse," the poem's apostrophic structure, "can in fact be
read," as Culler puts it, "as an act of radical interiorization and solipsism."
What I would prefer to read in the stanza's extra two lines is an alternative
to the metaphor of the voice of the poet speaking to herself "here" in the
poem we are reading. What we are reading is not a voice (or a "Voice"). It
is, as Griffin Wolff herself points out, a page. The difference seems impor-
tant in a poem so preoccupied with the effects of the very figure of
opening one's mouth to say "O," to say "You." Whatever "that White
Sustenance *exercise *privilege" may be taken to be, it is manifestly
silent. In fact, as a metaphor for "Despair," "that White Sustenance,"
positioned on the threshold of *there* and *here, I* and *You,* seems strangely
silenced in much the same way that *Despair* is said to be in another poem
that attempts to define the term:

> The difference between Despair
> And Fear—is like the One
> Between the instant of a Wreck—
> And when the Wreck has been—
>
> The Mind is smooth—no Motion—
> Contented as the Eye
> Upon the Forehead of a Bust—
> That knows—it cannot see—

(Poem 305)

Unlike the "saturated Sight" of the fiction apostrophic address attempts, the "Eye"/I of Despair "knows—it cannot see—." In Dickinson's pun that *Eye* is "contented": substantive, contained, capacious in its loss. The word's etymon links it to *Sustenance* as "the Forehead of a Bust" is linked to "White Sustenance" by the muteness of its physical substance. That White Sustenance, like the white page on which she writes, is all that is left to the poem's I if the transcendence of figurative address is refused. The poem's *I* and *You* are sustained by that page in the sense that they are both (as pronouns) borne by it and (as subjects) hold it as they write and read, but, compared to the imagined vision of Paradise, the slight weight of a page is small compensation. It is, in fact, no compensation at all in the Emersonian sense of an ideal reciprocity, in which, as Emerson wrote, "the copula is hidden."[24] The page rather sustains (holds up from under) the tenuous connection between *I* and *You* by materializing that copula, a relation as difficult to read as is the grammatical copula of the poem's last lines.

For in some subtle and disturbing sense the White Sustenance of the page is as blank as is the gaze of the statue—of a figure of a figure. The (agrammatical) placement of *are,* on which the catachretic series of metaphors of the last lines depends, makes the identity between "that White Sustenance—*exercise *privilege / Despair—" and the page much more difficult to hold in mind than the simile that I have just ventured can admit. On the basis of this single and singularly awkward copula, "the Door ajar," a metaphor of place that would stabilize the relation of *there* and *here,* gives way to *Oceans,* a much less stable figure of place, and then to *Prayer,* a metaphysical displacement of presence. "Prayer is the little implement," Dickinson wrote,

> Through which Men reach
> Where Presence—is denied them.
> They fling their Speech
>
> By means of it—in God's Ear—
>
> (Poem 437)

Such an ironic apostrophe, a futile "exercise," a pathetic "privilege," presses rather desperately against the "White" page that is itself the trace of apostrophe's ambition. Not I, not you, not here, not there, not this, but "that"—if "White Sustenance" is a figure for the page, then it is a figure without a face. It is the historical, as opposed to the fictive, material of address.

That address's capacity to mediate—to join *I* and *You* as subjects precisely by keeping the pronouns "apart"—depends, of course, on its successful passage from self to other. To return to the terms of Dickinson's letter to Susan, "the letter's ride to You—" is what allows reading to take place at all. My placement of Dickinson's poem in the context of that early letter to which I would like now to return is not (my reader will have noticed) accidental: as is well known but often forgotten when we read the published volumes of the poems, Dickinson enclosed most of the poems that were read in her lifetime within her correspondence. Martha Nell Smith has urged that we regard that correspondence as Dickinson's "own method of publication."[25] Certainly, there are good reasons for reconsidering the affiliations between the letters and the poems: not only did she send poems in and as letters; write poems about letters and letters about poems; dispatch poems with flowers, bread, fruit, photographs, and books (even, once, a dead bee); but many of the manuscripts that have survived (especially from the later period) were written on the insides of envelopes or on the reverse of her own epistolary drafts or others' letters. One poem, which David Porter describes, was "written in the space around a postage stamp with paper arms glued on," another 1876 poem written "on an invitation to a candy pull sent to her twenty-six years earlier."[26] Perhaps even more suggestive is the fact that the fascicles, or handmade books that Higginson had in mind when he wrote of her "Portfolio," were copied onto letter paper (the same paper, in many cases, that she used for correspondence). Given the gesture that I am borrowing from the letter to Susan and reading back into the ending of "I cannot live with You—," the literal materials of Dickinson's writing acquire a new romance that is still to be written. Beside the historical circulation of the poems *as* correspondence, then, we might want to place the historical materials of Dickinson's written address, materials that readers of the poems in "print" cannot, of course, hold.[27] I would like to turn, in closing, to the question of what Dickinson's present audience *can* hold—to the sustenance, as it were, of our reading, to our place as recipients of what in an oft-quoted poem Dickinson called her "letter to the World," a letter "committed," as Dickinson wrote in a suggestive pun, "To Hands I cannot see—" (Poem 441).

Although Dickinson's specifically written forms of address mediate between self and other in a much more directed (Dickinson might say "plausible") way than does the metaphor of lyric voice, as the tentativeness (and desperation) of the conclusion of "I cannot live with You—"

suggests, in being more specific than the figure of the transcendentally individual voice, the medium of the page is also less sure of its destination. Though a letter or a poem to Susan might imply the historical Susan as its ideal reader, the letters and poems that have come into our hands have, in their passage, implicated us as readers as well. Rather than stand as voyeurs identified with a privileged lyric *or* excluded from a private communication, we need to take account of the way in which a third position has been built into Dickinson's structures of address. Poem 1664, "I did not reach Thee," anticipates—both thematically and in the textual history of its transmission—with an eerie clarity the difficulty of coming to terms with our historical predicament as twentieth-century readers of Dickinson. The temporal confusion that we have noticed in "I think To Live—" and "I cannot live with You—" also informs this poem, but this time it is the time of reading itself that proves difficult if not impossible to locate:

> I did not reach Thee
> But my feet slip nearer every day
> Three Rivers and a Hill to cross
> One Desert and a Sea
> I shall not count the journey one
> When I am telling thee.

Like the opening stanzas of Poem 640 and Poem 646, this stanza opens by closing a possibility to which it must then attempt a different approach. But how can one approach a destination that has already been canceled as destination? How can one get from here to there when (to paraphrase Gertrude Stein) there is no there there? The second line's assertion that "My feet slip nearer every day" is logically baffling in its apparently willful denial of the situation that the first line has already stated as fact. In slipping from past to present tense, the line is not progressing but backing up—or, in Robert Weisbuch's phrase for such moves in Dickinson's poems, the poem is "retreating forward."[28] It does so in order to recount in the fictive present a time the sixth line explicitly identifies as the time of "telling," an encounter that can take place "When" I reach what "I did not reach." As in "I think To Live—," the line between history and fiction is here a treacherous one to tread, and yet for four more stanzas it is literally the line that the "I" does tread, her poetic "feet" (in Dickinson's usage, almost always a pun on metric writing) traversing

"Three Rivers and a Hill . . . / One Desert and a Sea." The poem's geography is reminiscent of "the hills and the dales, and the rivers" that Dickinson imagined in the early letter to Susan as the "romance in the letter's ride to you—." In the letter, we recall, Dickinson compares that romance to "a poem such as can ne'er be written." Such a poem, however, was written: it is what we now have as Poem 1664—although, in more than one sense, the poem slipped near its destination.

The text of "Poem 1664" is available to us only by virtue of a transcript made by Susan herself. There is no manuscript version of this poem in Emily Dickinson's hand; the hand from which the published poem was taken is Susan's.[29] If the hand-to-hand economy of written correspondence is to mediate our future reception of Dickinson's poems (as I have been arguing that both the historical form and figurative content of Dickinson's writing suggest that it should), then another message sent to Susan acquires an uncanny sense for us: "for the Woman whom I prefer," Dickinson wrote, "Here is Festival—Where my Hands are cut, Her fingers will be found inside—" (L 288).[30] Removed from the "Festival" of Dickinson's "Here," from the time and place of her writing, not the preferred reader of the poems but the readers those poems defer, future critics of Emily Dickinson would do well to notice that there are more than two pairs of hands complicit in this startling figure of address. Reading Emily Dickinson here and now, ours are the unseen hands most deeply "committed": they are doing the cutting. At a moment when contemporary literary theoretical debates turn on the problem of whether a literary text always reaches its destination or whether it has always already gone astray, it is worth returning to Dickinson's forms of address with an eye to the way in which they have anticipated both alternatives and to the corrective they offer retroactively to Higginson's still influential version of Dickinson's writing as privileged self-address.[31] At least it is time that we cut more carefully, that we learned to tell the difference.

NOTES

1. The recent volume entitled *Emily Dickinson's Reception in the 1890s: A Documentary History,* ed. Willis J. Buckingham (Pittsburgh: University of Pittsburgh Press, 1990), finally makes the enthusiasm of the immediate reception of Dickinson's poems evident to modern readers. The collection is especially important, for, as Buckingham notes, "twentieth-century Dickinson criti-

cism, in many ways, has been a history of mis-characterizing the nineteenth-century reception (as mostly unfavorable) for the purpose of writing against it" (xii). I would only add that that "purpose" is informed by a modern interest in exaggerating Dickinson's isolation from her own historical moment, an isolation that makes it easier for us to place her in our own.

2. Percy Bysshe Shelley, "A Defence of Poetry," in *Romantic Critical Essays,* ed. David Bromwich (Cambridge: Cambridge University Press, 1987), 223. It is important to note that, when taken out of context, Shelley's figure of the poet as nightingale can (and has) become a cliché that the argument of Shelley's essay actually works against. Rather than an impression of unmediated voice, what the poem gives to the reader, according to Shelley, is, as Bromwich reads the "Defence," "only the text of the poem [which] remains as a positive trace or inscription. Its sense may vanish with the mortality of the author. But its power may revive nevertheless, under a different and unfamiliar aspect, at the coming of later authors and readers who find that the traces concern them after all" (213).

3. For a related "account of the relation, for [Dickinson], of privacy to the genre of lyric poetry," see Christopher Benfey, *Emily Dickinson and the Problem of Others* (Amherst: University of Massachusetts Press, 1984), 29–62. While Benfey's concerns parallel my own, he ends by emphasizing, rather than qualifying, the self-enclosure of the poems: what Dickinson "requires above all," Benfey writes, "is that something about her, or *in* her, remain hidden from the view of others. It is the terrible exposure of existence that appalls her" (62). My emphasis rests, instead, on what Dickinson's poems of direct address *do* "ex-pose," or place outside the self.

4. For a discussion of the relation between domestic self-enclosure and the development of American individualism, see Gillian Brown, *Domestic Individualism: Imagining Self in Nineteenth-Century America* (Berkeley: University of California Press, 1990). Brown's premise in this book, "that nineteenth-century American individualism takes on its peculiarly 'individualistic' properties as domesticity inflects it with values of interiority, privacy, and psychology" (1), is very suggestive for a reading of Dickinson that would take into account the specifically domestic (and thus gendered) cast of Dickinson's seclusion.

5. Herbert F. Tucker, "Dramatic Monologue and the Overhearing of Lyric," in *Lyric Poetry: Beyond New Criticism,* ed. Chaviva Hosek and Patricia Parker (Ithaca and London: Cornell University Press, 1985), 242.

6. John Stuart Mill, "What Is Poetry?" in *Essays on Poetry,* ed. F. Parvin Sharpless (Columbia: University of South Carolina Press, 1976), 12.

7. Northrop Frye, *Anatomy of Criticism* (Princeton: Princeton University Press, 1957), 249–50. While Frye is quoting Mill, it is important to note as well that his emphasis on the poet's own agency in "turning his back on his audience" is mediated by the modernist aesthetics of Joyce (whom he quotes) and, implicitly, Eliot.

8. This introduction to Dickinson's version of what Derrida has named "the scene of writing" could be read as a reductive gloss on that idea in *The Post*

Card: From Socrates to Freud and Beyond, trans. Alan Bass (Chicago and London: University of Chicago Press, 1987). For a related (though very different) understanding of the importance of the scene of writing in American literature, see Michael Fried, *Realism, Writing, Disfiguration* (Chicago and London: University of Chicago Press, 1987), esp. 93–161.

9. Emily Dickinson, *The Letters of Emily Dickinson,* ed. Thomas Johnson and Theodora Ward (Cambridge: Belknap Press of Harvard University Press, 1958), L 77 (hereafter cited in the text by letter number).

10. Cynthia Griffin Wolff, *Emily Dickinson* (New York: Alfred A. Knopf, 1986), 419. There are, to be precise, thirteen instances of the pronoun *you* in Poem 640, as against ten instances of *I.*

11. Sharon Cameron, *Lyric Time: Dickinson and the Limits of Genre* (Baltimore and London: Johns Hopkins University Press, 1979), 78.

12. My citations of Dickinson's poems will follow the three-volume edition of *The Poems of Emily Dickinson,* ed. Thomas H. Johnson (Cambridge and London: Belknap Press of Harvard University Press, 1955), but I will incorporate into Johnson's edition the placement of the variants as they appear in *The Manuscript Books of Emily Dickinson,* ed. R. W. Franklin (Cambridge and London: Belknap Press of Harvard University Press, 1981). I have modified the placement of the variants in the Johnson edition in order to emphasize the difficulty of choosing between them or of determining from them the poet's choices. The choice made by Johnson was to print the manuscript without variants as a complete poem and then to key the variants by line number beneath what he called "the poet's own preferred text." This procedure certainly makes the poem easier for us to read, but it designates as "preferred" a text that is closed upon itself (recluse-like) in a way that the manuscript version decidedly is not. For a discussion of the role of the variants in the interpretation of Dickinson's poems, see Cristanne Miller, *Emily Dickinson: A Poet's Grammar* (Cambridge and London: Harvard University Press, 1987), 46–49. Sharon Cameron's recent book *Choosing Not Choosing: Dickinson's Fascicles* (Chicago and London: University of Chicago Press, 1992) is the first full-length study of Dickinson's variant practice. Because, as Cameron puts it, "the variants extend the text's identity in ways that make it seem potentially limitless" (6), it should also be noticed that any interpretive use of the variants will also put into question the poem's legibility as such. As R. W. Franklin pointed out in 1967 (arguing in the opposite direction), from a poem such as "Those fair— fictitious People" (Poem 499), which "exists in a semi-final draft with twenty-six suggestions that fit eleven places in the poem . . . 7680 poems are possible—not versions but, according to our critical principles, poems" (*The Editing of Emily Dickinson: A Reconsideration* [Madison: University of Wisconsin Press, 1967], 142). My suggestion is that this conclusion should indeed lead to a reconsideration not only of Dickinson's practice but especially of "our critical principles."

13. Dickinson's dictionary was the 1841 edition of Noah Webster's *American*

Dictionary of the English Language (Springfield, Mass.: George and Charles Merriam).

14. Mary Jo Salter, "Puns and Accordions: Emily Dickinson and the Unsaid," in *Yale Review* 79, no. 2 (Winter 1990): 194.

15. While Johnson prints "To Live" in the three-volume edition of the *Poems* with the initial letters capitalized (as the words appear in the manuscript), in the much more often read single volume of *The Complete Poems of Emily Dickinson* (ed. Thomas H. Johnson [Boston and Toronto: Little, Brown, 1960]) he prints the phrase as "to Live." That slip of the pen (or the press) effectively cancels what I take to be the poem's emphasis on the infinitive itself (and on the vastly underestimated play of the letter itself in Dickinson's poetry as a whole).

16. Helen McNeil, *Emily Dickinson* (New York: Virago/Pantheon, 1986), 19. McNeil's reading of Dickinson also argues that Dickinson is "a woman who writes rather than speaks," and her emphasis is informed (as mine is) by Derrida's interest in the "becoming literary of the literal" (*Writing and Difference,* trans. Alan Bass [Chicago and London: University of Chicago Press, 1978], 230). I depart from her only in emphasizing what happens to the literal once it passes on, taking up where she leaves off when she writes that Dickinson's poems "now survive as unaddressed gifts" (181). For a relevant discussion of Dickinson's treatment of her audience as participants in a gift economy, see Maragaret Dickie, *Lyric Contingencies: Emily Dickinson and Wallace Stevens* (Philadelphia: University of Pennsylvania Press, 1991).

17. This schematic version of the function of the Real in Lacanian theory should be referred to Lacan's *Le séminaire XX: encore* (Paris: Seuil, 1975). A translation of the seminar appears as chapter 6 of *Feminine Sexuality: Jacques Lacan and the École Freudienne,* eds. Juliet Mitchell and Jacqueline Rose (New York: Pantheon Books, 1982). For a discussion of the temporality peculiar to the interrelation between the Real, the Symbolic, and the Imaginary, see Jane Gallop, *Reading Lacan* (Ithaca and London: Cornell University Press, 1985), 74–92. For an extended (and brilliant) application of Lacanian theory to Dickinson's poetry, see Mary Loeffelholz, *Dickinson and the Boundaries of Feminist Theory* (Urbana and Chicago: University of Illinois Press, 1991).

18. On the implication of prosopopoeia within the figure of apostrophe, see Paul de Man, "Anthropomorphism and Trope in the Lyric," *The Rhetoric of Romanticism* (New York: Columbia University Press, 1984), 239–62.

19. For an interesting discussion of the relevance of both the moment of death in American nineteenth-century culture and Phelps's novel to Dickinson's poetry, see Barton Levi St. Armand, *Emily Dickinson and Her Culture* (Cambridge: Cambridge University Press, 1984), 39–78 and 117–52.

20. By suspending the question of the "face" that Dickinson may imagine for the addressee, it will also be noticed that I am suspending the question of the reader's gender. In the poems that I am reading here, that gender seems to me strategically (rather than accidentally) indeterminate precisely because the face is not envisioned. For a reading of Dickinson's poems of address that

emphasizes different poems in which the reader may be gendered, see Karen Oakes, "Welcome and Beware: The Reader and Emily Dickinson's Figurative Language," in *ESQ: A Journal of the American Renaissance* 34, no. 3 (1988): 181–206.

21. Emily Brontë, *Wuthering Heights* (1847; reprint, Boston: Houghton Mifflin, 1956), 143. In a late letter to Elizabeth Holland, Dickinson half-quotes Heathcliff's exclamation, revising it into a somewhat perverse congratulation on the birth of a first grandchild (Katrina Holland Van Wagenen): "say with 'Heathcliff' to little Katrina—'Oh Cathie—Cathie!' " (L 866).

22. For an important discussion of Dickinson's departure from the masculine romantic sublime, for which Brontë's Heathcliff may stand as model, see Joanne Feit Diehl, *Dickinson and the Romantic Imagination* (Princeton: Princeton University Press, 1981); and *Women Poets and the American Sublime* (Bloomington and Indianapolis: Indiana University Press, 1990).

23. Jonathan Culler, "Apostrophe," *The Pursuit of Signs: Semiotics, Literature, Deconstruction* (Ithaca and London: Cornell University Press, 1981), 146.

24. Ralph Waldo Emerson, "Fate," in *Selections from Ralph Waldo Emerson,* ed. Stephen E. Whicher (Boston: Houghton Mifflin, 1957), 347.

25. Martha Nell Smith, *Rowing in Eden: Rereading Emily Dickinson* (Austin: University of Texas Press, 1992), 16. See also Cristanne Miller's discussion of Dickinson's "Letters to the World," in *A Poet's Grammar,* 1–19.

26. David Porter, *Dickinson: The Modern Idiom* (Cambridge and London: Harvard University Press, 1981), 82.

27. As Jerome J. McGann has suggested in his book *The Textual Condition* (Princeton: Princeton University Press, 1991), "The full significance of Dickinson's writing will begin to appear when we explicate in detail the importance of the different papers that she used, her famous 'fascicles,' her scripts and their conventions of punctuation and page layout" (87). The work that McGann prescribes is beginning to be done: see Susan Howe's essay on Dickinson in *Sulfur* 28 (1991): 134–55; and Nell Smith's *Rowing in Eden.* For a discussion of the relevance of the material conditions in (and on) which script is produced, see Jonathan Goldberg, *Writing Matter: From the Hands of the English Renaissance* (Stanford: Stanford University Press, 1990).

28. Robert Weisbuch, *Emily Dickinson's Poetry* (Chicago and London: University of Chicago Press, 1972), 177.

29. According to appendix 11 of the three-volume Johnson edition of the *Poems,* sixty-one of Dickinson's extant poems derive from transcripts made by Susan Gilbert. Another fifty-three poems derive from transcripts made by Mabel Loomis Todd. The edition involved in the transcriptions is impossible to determine, as the autograph copies are now lost.

30. See also L 272, to Samuel Bowles: "Sue gave me the paper, to write on—so when the writing tires you—play it is Her . . .—for have not the Clovers, *names,* to the Bees?"

31. I refer here to the now well-known debate between Lacan and Derrida, which centers on Lacan's claim, at the end of his seminar on Poe's "The

Purloined Letter," that "The sender, we tell you, receives from the receiver his own message in reverse form. Thus it is that what the 'purloined letter,' nay, the 'letter in sufferance' means is that a letter always arrives at its destination" (trans. Jeffrey Mehlman, *Yale French Studies* 48 [1972]: 72). Derrida's argument appears in "The Purveyor of Truth," trans. Willis Domingo et al., *Yale French Studies* 52 (1975), and is reprinted and extended in *The Post Card*. The form of my allusion to this debate echoes that of Joel Fineman in "Shakespeare's *Will:* The Temporality of Rape," in *Representations* 20 (1987): 69 and 75. I borrow the form of Fineman's response in order also to borrow his powerful answer to both Lacan and Derrida: "Literary letters *always* arrive at their destination precisely because they *always* go astray." In the context of Dickinson's writing we might say that, once that writing went "astray" in 1890, it was destined to arrive—here, now—as literature.

Reading Seductions: Dickinson, Rhetoric, and the Male Reader

R. McClure Smith

In the summer of 1851 the twenty-year-old Emily Dickinson attended a performance by the popular Swedish singer Jenny Lind and concluded, with typical directness, that she would "rather have a Yankee." Immediately following Dickinson's expression of national pride, however, is her interesting speculation on the possible reason for Lind's popular acclaim, an astute perception that the singer's popularity was not explicable solely in terms of her musical talent. Dickinson noted, in a letter to a female friend, that the positive response of the audience was the result of a spontaneous affection for Lind herself: "How we all loved Jenny Lind, but not accustomed oft to her manner of singing did'nt fancy *that* so well as we did *her*." In fact, Dickinson was so taken by the appeal of the artist over the art that she repeated this point: "*Herself*, and not her music, was what we seemed to love—she has an air of *exile* in her mild blue eyes, and a something sweet and touching in her native accent which charms her many friends."[1]

Dickinson's consistent use of the collective pronoun in this letter is a testament to her equally close observation of the response of Lind's immediate audience. Indeed, she goes on to catalog, with hyperbolic amusement, her father's specific reactions to the "show":

> Father sat all the evening looking *mad*, and *silly*, and yet so much amused you would have *died* a laughing—when the performers bowed, he said "Good evening Sir"—and when they retired, "very well—that will do," it was'nt *sarcasm* exactly, nor it was'nt *disdain*, it was infinitely funnier than either of those virtues, as if old Abraham had come to see the show, and thought it was all very well, but a little excess of *Monkey!*

That Dickinson should express a particular interest in the response of the audience to the show is hardly surprising. Not only does she express in her poetry an absorbing interest in the capacity of a poem to render its effects on a reader,[2] but the Dickinson philosophy of controlled reader response is perhaps most perfectly expressed in Poem 1206:

> The Show is not the Show
> But they that go—
> Menagerie to me
> My Neighbor be—
> Fair Play—
> Both went to see—[3]

The speaker is not so much a viewer as a voyeur. Uninterested in the performance itself, her primary fascination is with the reactions of the audience to that performance. Indeed, for her, the peripheral show put on by the viewers supersedes anything the actual show can produce. The better entertainment is the viewing of the uninhibited and therefore genuine reaction of one's "Neighbor" to the "Show." The original display is of interest only as the catalyst for another. Significantly, the uninhibited response of the audience, that more significant theatrical presentation, is a consequence of its ignorance: these are observers who, little suspecting that they are simultaneously observed, are momentarily exposed by the very fact of their viewing.

"The Show is not the Show" can be considered a neat summation of a Dickinson aesthetic of reception that assumes what is of interest is not the response but, rather, the attitude assumed by the responders and that the reading is less valuable than the subsequent exposure of the readers in the course of their analyses. As such, it can serve as useful textual confirmation of my own suggestion that insight into Dickinson's poetry comes not merely through penetrating analysis and explication of the poetry itself but also through an analysis of the wild, strange "menagerie" of responses to that poetry and that the examination of Dickinson's poetic necessitates a parallel study of its various *affects* as those affects are manifested in critical readers. To that end this study is a brief reading of Dickinson's critics, or, more precisely, a reading *of* reading. The focus has been narrowed to Dickinson's male critical readers for two reasons. First, I draw a series of parallels between the psychoanalytic and the critical dialectic. Obviously, the peculiar Freudian romance—the male analyst reading (and being simultaneously read) by a female analysand—can more precisely demarcate the critical scene of reading established between Dickinson's poetic text and a specifically male reader. Second, as Dickinson herself discovered when observing her father's response to Jenny Lind's performance, there is often substantial entertainment in viewing the uninhibited response of a male critic to a female "performer," especially when the success of her performance is inextricably linked to her personal appeal.

Dickinson's poetry is especially interesting because it seems designed to elicit a "menagerie" of responses from a targeted reader. The manipulation of that reader by the poem is, paradoxically, facilitated by the poem's exaggerated offering to the reader of the possibility of its own manipulation. For example, Poem 738 is a poetic offering insofar as it is possible to imagine that the poem's speaker is the poem itself directly interpellating its typical reader:

> You said that I "was Great"—one Day—
> Then "Great" it be—if that please Thee—
> Or Small—or any size at all—
> Nay—I'm the size suit Thee—
>
> Tall—like the Stag—would that?
> Or lower—like the Wren—
> Or other heights of Other Ones
> I've seen?
>
> Tell which—it's dull to guess—
> And I must be Rhinoceros
> Or Mouse
> At once—for Thee—
>
> So say—if Queen it be—
> Or Page—please Thee—
> I'm that—or nought—
> Or other thing—if other thing there be—
> With just this Stipulus—
> I suit Thee—

(Poem 738)

The poem assumes that it will be what the male reader chooses to make it, responsive to his every whim. This is generally true of Dickinson's canon: her poems can suit the desire of their readers perfectly. In this case whether a reader attempts to interpret this poem as representing the voice of Dickinson discussing her varied personae ("If Queen it be") or, my own pun-determined choice, a representation of language speaking itself ("Or Page—please Thee") ar *anything* else at all ("Or other thing—if other thing there be—") is ultimately all the same. The fact that the speaker (and poem) offers the possibility that she (and it) can be made absolutely malleable to the desire of its addressee (and reader) is all that matters. My own refashioning of the poem—the interpretation of it as a self-reflexive poetic allegory—is simply a suitable example of how the speaker's "Stipulus" ensures her poem's successful initial engagement with a reader's interpretive desire.

Sometimes we would be wise to take the speaker of a Dickinson poem at her word. I assume that the stunning conclusion to Poem 505 is not ironic but, rather, an accurate representation of Dickinson's aesthetic stance:

> Nor would I be a Poet—
> It's finer—own the Ear—
> Enamored—impotent—content—
> The License to revere,
> A privilege so awful
> What would the Dower be,
> Had I the Art to stun myself
> With Bolts of Melody!

This would be a far from ironic statement coming from a poet whose central strategy is reader directed. Indeed, it might be argued that the rendering "Enamored—impotent—content—" precisely demarcates the specific affects of a Dickinson poem on its reader. Of course, syntactic ambiguity is often the cause of an initial reader enamoration, and this poem is no exception to its own rule: the phrase "it's finer—own the Ear—" is a finely tuned ambiguity. Is it better to be the reader (who owns that receptive ear) of the poem? Or is it better to be the author (who owns and therefore controls the receptive ear *of another*) of that poem? The ear that is most frequently "owned" by the Dickinson poem is that of its critical reader. And, if we can imagine the speaker of Poem 1496 as *the poem itself,* then we listen to the voice of a language aware of its being regarded as an object of a specifically male critical desire:

All that I do
Is in review
To his enamored mind
I know his eye
Where e'er I ply
Is pushing close behind

Crucial to the Dickinson strategy of enamoration is one of the most common themes of her poetry: her notion that the best pleasure is an experience of loss. For Dickinson that pleasure is usually defined as the awareness of a distance between desire and its goal; the act of desiring is, in itself, unsurpassable and infinitely more delightful than the consummation that could accommodate it. The phraseology may change from poem to poem, but the implication is always the same: that "Delight is as the flight—" (Poem 257); that " 'Heaven'—is what I cannot reach!" (Poem 239); that "Spices fly / In the Receipt—It was the Distance— / Was Savory—" (Poem 439); that "Impossibility, like Wine / Exhilirates the Man / Who tastes it; possibility / Is flavorless—" (Poem 838); that "Who never lost, are unprepared / A Coronet to find!" (Poem 73); that "Not of detention is Fruition— / Shudder to attain" (Poem 1315). As "Within its reach, though yet ungrasped" is "Desire's perfect Goal—" (Poem 1430), the narrators of the poems revel in the "sumptuous Destitution" (Poem 1382) that is an "ecstatic limit / Of unobtained Delight" (Poem 1209). Frequently, the poems are miniature studies of this pleasure paradox, vignettes of joyous deprivation. That the fragility of momentary possession is a value in itself, that "Danger—deepens Sum—" (Poem 807) is the repeated refrain. Desire defines pleasure, and, since desire is always process, whether one strives to possess or suffers the insecurity of temporary possession, true pleasure can never be stasis. Pleasure must assume the dynamism of the desire that constitutes it.

Central to Dickinson's poetics, therefore, is a psychodynamics of desire in which desire is cultivated as an end in itself, in which the ultimate aesthetic pleasure is realized through the frictional frustration that dilates the interval of anticipation that precedes interpretation. The intensity of desire is sufficient to render any eventual satisfaction a virtual anticlimax, for, while the satisfaction of attainment is finite, the motor of desire is infinite, involving process. The postponement of satisfaction and the distance of the object of desire are therefore the prerequisites for the eventual realization of an intensely exquisite longing, the state of perpetual deferral that is being a desiring subject. The consequence of the absolute centrality of this process of desire is that the poetry, the repeated exploration and mapping of the psychic space of frustration that opens between desire and an unattainable goal, is equally the most continually restless of pleasures for the subject who reads.

The most detailed discussion of this paradoxical poetics of desire is Richard Wilbur's brilliant essay "Sumptuous Destitution." Wilbur discusses Dickinson's "economy of desire" solely as the expression of an aesthetic philosophy, which interests Wilbur, himself a poet, as being a truth of art and therefore far from peculiar to his precursor. Dickinson's is not a personal philosophy per se; what she discovered was "that the soul has an infinite hunger, a hunger to possess all things . . . the creature of appetite pursues satisfaction, and strives to possess the object in itself; it cannot imagine the vaster economy of desire, in which the pain of abstinence is justified by moments of infinite joy."[4] This reduction of Dickinson's poetics through generalization is misleading precisely because the calculated postponement of satisfaction has ramifications beyond the poet's philosophic theorizing. It is also implicit in the writing of her poetic text, in her strategic approach to a reader. "Sumptuous destitution" is the *practice* of the poetry to the extent that the poems are the exemplification of Dickinson's aesthetic philosophy *in action*. The central tenet of this philosophy is that interpretive frustration, and a consequently provoked desire for meaning, is preferable to an easy hermeneutic possession, and that frustration of the reader's desire—both the narrative desire to reach an ending and the hermeneutic desire to penetrate a meaning—is simultaneously the pleasurable stimulus of it. In other words, to understand the full implications of Dickinson's aesthetic philosophy we need to take into consideration the effects of her "frustrating" poetry on its reader. If "True Poems flee" (Poem 1472), then what does that mean for a reader who is a "creature of appetite" seeking "satisfaction" and "possession"? If "consummation" is "the hurry of fools" (L 922), then what if the purpose of Dickinson's poetry is to educate the reader in the "vaster economy of desire" that is non-consummation, a lesson taught through a sophisticated syntactic playing on the reader's "hunger"? And what if that hunger extends beyond the appetite for knowledge? In other words, what if Dickinson's poems are most importantly vivid explorations of the psychodynamics of their *readers'* desires?

The psychodynamics of desire is, of course, the primary study of contemporary psychoanalysis. Since the business of both psychoanalysis and literary criticism is the interpretation that deals with a crisis in signification, the most valuable analogy between them concerns the nature of reading. Shoshana Felman's discussion of the significance of the Lacanian reading of Freud for textual interpretation is valuable here, in particular her observation that for Lacan "Freud's discovery of the unconscious is the outcome of his reading in the hysterical discourse of the Other his own unconscious."[5] It was while listening to "hysteric" discourse that Freud "read" there was an unconscious, for he was implicated in his patients' discourse and directly affected by what they told him. Felman observes that this discovery has significant implications for the psychoanalytic critic of literature because it suggests that

> the activity of reading is not just the analyst's, it is also the analysand's: interpreting is what takes place *on both sides* of the analytic situation. The unconscious, in Lacan's eyes, is not simply the object of psychoanalytical investigation, but its subject. The unconscious, in other words, is not simply *that which must be read* but also, and perhaps primarily, *that which reads*. The unconscious is a reader. What this implies most radically is that whoever reads, interprets out of his own unconscious, is an analysand, even when the interpreting is done from the position of the analyst.[6]

For Felman the psychoanalytic approach to literature is far more usefully textual than biographical. While the reading situation can still be assimilated to the psychoanalytic situation, the poet is now far more than simply the analysand on the couch. In fact, the status of the poet is not merely that of the patient but also that of the analyst, for, if "unconscious desire proceeds by interpretation," then the converse is equally true— that "interpretation proceeds by unconscious desire." As Felman observes, Lacan's foregrounding of the analytic dialectic—the fact that, since interpretation always takes place within a transferential situation of reading, the interpreter is both analyst and analysand—has tremendous implications for a literary critic who is in the place of the psychoanalyst in the "relation of interpretation" but in the place of the patient in the "relation of transference."

Readers of Dickinson's poetry are particularly susceptible to becoming patients in the relation of transference. I have already observed that Dickinson's poetic discourse does not merely discuss but is also predicated upon a condition of deferral in which gratification continually recedes before attainable grasp. This poetic discourse not only sustains its reader in the often uncomfortable state of *being a desiring subject* but also, as a result of its notorious linguistic opacities, this discourse eventually forces a confrontation with the process of reading that may be not unlike making sense out of unconscious material. The syntax of Dickinson's poetic texts introduces disruptions into the habitual process of reading poetry that produce and reveal feelings of inadequacy and vulnerability in her readers, and it may well be that those syntactically impacted poems put their readers through an experience of reading analogous to psychoanalysis.

Psychoanalysis is essentially a study of how a rhetorical seduction may be conducted by means of interpretation, of how the actual interlocutions of the psychoanalytic encounter—the analyst and the analysand interacting in the dialectic relationship that is the talking cure—imply or actualize a verbal seduction of sorts. That specific psychoanalytic seduction is usually called "transference." Interestingly, Dickinson's readers have notoriously attempted to interpret her texts in terms of scenes of "seduction," either factual, fictional, or rhetorical. William Shurr has recently given more credence to the theory that Dickinson's "relationship" with the Reverend Charles Wadsworth resulted in her being "seduced and abandoned, and that such an event had something to do with the poetry"; Cynthia Griffin Wolff has suggested that the poetry "might best be read against a purely literary model, the novel of seduction"; Suzanne Juhasz has argued that her letters effect a strategic "rhetorical seduction" of their reader; and Karl Keller has found in her poetry both the bold assertiveness of a "crude seductress" *and* a "daring virgin inviting seduction, foreplay and penetration."[7] Similarly, Dickinson's use of the lyric as an apparently confessional mode—telling tales of seduction through the grammar of a textual body and the self-reflexivity of an intrusive "I"—has led John Cody to diagnose her as the quintessential hysteric, a diagnosis disputed by David Porter's suggestion that it is Dickinson's poetic discourse that is symptomatically hysterical.[8] As we will see, this prevalent critical desire to identify and validate a scene of seduction in relation to Dickinson's poetry, or to attempt to manipulate the poet (and/or her discourse) into an analytic situation of seduction, may well itself be symptomatic, the ostensible figure of the potential seduction of the critical analyst as desiring subject by the grammar of Dickinson's textual body.[9]

But before I begin my examination of the uncanny effects contingent on male critical readings of the "body" of Dickinson's poetry, I want to emphasize that the analysis of the rhetorical seduction of male critics by that poetry is not simply a study of the sexism implicit in so many critical readings of the poet. The extent of overtly sexist Dickinson criticism has been ably documented by others.[10] I believe that the extensive sexism in Dickinson studies is merely reflective of a larger gender dynamic that occurs in the hermeneutic space between the male reader and the poems in the act of interpretation. What we find in male critical readings of Dickinson's poetic text is something more revelatory than a careless chauvinism.

The male literary critic's strange attraction to Dickinson, itself the subject of *this* analysis, is partly the consequence of Dickinson's particular susceptibility to an easy critical appropriation, an appropriation that can be directly related to the fact of her gender. In that context perhaps the most prophetic statement ever made by a critic of Dickinson was A. C. Ward's observation of 1932 that "the supposed enigmatic personality of Emily Dickinson will no doubt make her the victim of literary body-snatchers throughout successive generations."[11] Successive generations of Dickinson critics have indeed proven to be particularly adept "body-snatchers," seizing the "body" of her poems (the corpus, if you will) for their own, often dubious, critical purposes. Indeed, if there has been one staple of Dickinson criticism, it has been that very confusion of the body of work with the physical body of the poet. A critical reading of an individual poem is always liable to slip into a critical analysis of the Dickinson life: as a frustrated woman; as a woman crippled by dysfunctional family relationships; as a woman trapped within her own self-made signifying system; as a woman uncovering new sources of power from the heart of an apparent powerlessness.[12] In this way the posthumous life of Dickinson's art has always proven inseparable from the posthumous art of her life. The movement from poetry to poet and the inability of readers to separate the physical and textual body is, however, not so much evidence of their failure as it is of the success of Dickinson's designs upon the reader. That the desire for the substance, or body, of Dickinson should be a transformation of the desire for a sexual body, and that her readers should display that specific confusion, seems to have been the intention of the rhetorical fusion of textuality, sexuality, and eschatology through which she sought to make her word flesh.

The "sexist" approach to Dickinson's poetry is most evident in early New Critical readings. Unlike the psychoanalytic approach to literature, in which Freudian or Lacanian sexism is often implicit, there would appear to be nothing intrinsically sexist in the reading method of a New Criticism whose aspiration to scientific objectivity and emphasis on textual form would seem to mitigate against any overt sexism. Since blatant sexism is evident in New Critics' readings of Dickinson, we must assume that the criticism of that earlier era, less sensitive to issues of gender, was simply more careless in its subjective expressiveness. Rereading that criticism should not make the contemporary critic more complacent in his or her own self-congratulatory righteousness; the sexism of the postmodernist age, like all of its other manifestations of subjectivity, is merely more self-aware and, therefore, more covertly and carefully expressed. The value of reading the male New Critics is that they present us with a more honest portrait of Dickinson's male reader than their circumspect successors.

The exemplary portrait of that New Critical male reader might well be of a man who regarded a female poet as fundamentally *other*. This is apparent, for instance, in the commentary of R. P. Blackmur, who apparently found it difficult to think of Dickinson in human terms. At first she is feline: "It sometimes seems as if in her work a cat came at us speaking English." Later Blackmur decides that, if Dickinson is a cat, she is certainly not a fully grown one, her work revealing "the playful ambiguity of a kitten being a tiger." But, if at times she is nothing more than a paper tiger, on other occasions Dickinson has a more significant bite: "It is as if she got . . . the sense of vampirage which is usually only a possible accompaniment of relation."[13] Blackmur's discussion of Dickinson is often only barely contained within the framework of the human: whenever he has recourse to metaphor, the subject of his analysis invariably evokes an extrahuman analogy. The emphasis on Dickinson's otherness in Blackmur's criticism is at least partly due to his heightened awareness of her as a woman. That sense of otherness is not merely a consequence of the dearth of female poets in the critic's experience (although that is possibly explanation enough) but also evidence of a poetic strategy whose single most important component is a subtle emphasis on the writer's gender and, consequently, on her otherness in relation to a male reader. And, while individual New Critics disagreed on the value of the poetry, there was consensus on the personality of the poet. Allen Tate found in Dickinson's poetry a power emanating from the frustrations of a deprived woman, or, more precisely, "a dominating spinster whose every sweetness must have been formidable."[14] The nature of Dickinson's frustration is more explicitly examined by others. John Crowe Ransom remarked that Dickinson did not have "her own romance, enabling her to fulfill herself like any other woman," and David Higgins chronicled the aesthetic consequences of this frustration: "Emily's inability to fulfill herself in marriage may account for the subject matter and number of poems she wrote."[15]

Consistent in these approaches is the assumption that Dickinson's art is a mapping of her personal frustration. That conclusion is, of course, evidence of a critical failure to hold the poet separate from the poetry. But it also emerges from a genuine sense of frustration somehow *realized* through the critical reading of the poetry. If we consider the affective cultivation of a sense of frustration in the reader as a deliberate rhetorical practise, as evidence of Dickinson's aesthetic theory of sumptuous destitution in action, then that frustration is, of course, far from representative of the poet's state of mind. On the contrary, that frustration is the reader's (and who has not had a frustrated reading experience with a Dickinson poem?). Therefore, the critical assertion that Dickinson was herself unfulfilled or frustrated may be a projection of the reader onto the poet and the impetus of that projection traced to the reader's unsatisfactory reading experience of the poems.

The possibility of that frustrative overlap suggests that there is either an inappropriate critical distance achieved between the male critic and the Dickinson poem initially or an appropriate critical distance that duly collapses in the course of his reading of that poem. The comments of Blackmur, Tate, and Higgins suggest that the collapse of objectivity is inevitable when the critic's approach to any poem is already predetermined by an attitude toward the female poet, partly predetermined in turn by an attitude toward women in general. Indeed, one apparent problem for the male Dickinson critic is his potentially falling in love with the poet. In Robert Hillyer's observation of 1922 on the slow spreading of the Dickinson cult—"year by year knowledge of the secret spreads, as friend whispers to friend and confides the inimitable poet to a new lover"[16]—we can see how falling in love with the poet, falling in love with the poetry, being a poetry lover, or being a lover can become somewhat confused. It was to Archibald MacLeish's credit that he was willing to admit that *"most of us* are half in love with this dead girl."[17]

Falling in love with Emily Dickinson produces many of the typical symptoms of the experience: a certain losing of equilibrium and of sure-footed judgment; the forfeiture of a sense of objective distance and a consequent submerging of the subject in the other; and, most of all, the inadvertent betrayal of the self. Perhaps the most evident symptom of this process of critical "falling in love" is a studied protectiveness toward the poet. This protectiveness, often manifesting itself as a tender male gallantry, is an effect of the intimate Dickinson voice—the vehicle for an address that often suggests a direct personal relationship with her reader. A resultant feeling of protectiveness toward the poet is as apparent in the most sophisticated poststructuralist critic as it is in a "common" reader, who, it must be said, has always been ready to acknowledge such feelings as an integral part of reading Dickinson. It is when that sense of a unique personal communication metamorphoses into a feeling, on the critic's part, of intuitively personal comprehension that we find a peculiar self-righteous elitism from which the common reader is immune. The sense of intuitive personal relation with the poet can produce a stunningly patronizing mode of address in the male critic. For example, when David Higgins discusses Dickinson's potential relationship with the "Master," he does so in these words: "Did Emily or did she not have sexual relations with her master? Almost certainly she did not . . . her accounts of the crucial event indicate that 'Master' only held her on his knee: intimacy enough for Emily."[18] Higgins here provides us with a superb example of the unconscious irony implicit in the patronizing male critical approach to Dickinson: the tone of a critic's approach to his subject ("intimacy enough for Emily") can mimic the event described by his prose. This is also the temptation that Dickinson invariably offers to her male critics— to become, momentarily, Master.

That strange mélange of critical protectiveness and personal connect-edness is evident in many of Dickinson's early critics, not all of them male. For example, George Whicher's observation of 1930—that "her poetry is not the formal mask of a personality, but a living face vibrant with expressiveness. . . . Though many looking into the well of her being have seen only the distorted image of their own desires, a free mind may discern beneath the surface her true form and substance"—to a degree echoes Ella Gilbert Ives's 1907 comment that "in life she was arrogantly shy of a public that now shares her innermost confidence, and touches with rude or hallowed finger the flesh of her sensitive poetry; the soul of it, happily only the sympathetic can reach."[19] The interaction of a critical sympathy and an elitist protectiveness produces a strangely defensive appreciation of the poet's art. Allan Tate's comment of 1932 that the poetry is "a magnificent personal confession" but "in its self-revelation, its honesty, almost obscene" and Edmund Blunden's observation of 1930 that "passions like hers are not for immodest circulations" would seem, at first, to suggest that these critics find something potentially immodest in the *content* of the poetry.[20] But perhaps it would be more precise to locate the "immodesty" they find in the naive reader's potential interaction with the poem—hence, the critical assertions that Dickinson can be easily misread by an audience liable to find her "immodestly" circulating. It is the interaction between the Dickinson poem and its reader that demands a proper critical regulation. This is not a surprising conclusion if we review the previous critical comments and ask: What makes a personal confession become *obscene?* What kind of poetry can be read in an *immodest* manner? What does it mean to *touch the flesh* of a poetry that has a living face? What kind of poetry can mirror the *distorted image* of its reader's *desire?* The vocabulary of this criticism makes its own case for the necessary policing of such a suggestively stimulating sensuous art.[21]

Perhaps what makes Dickinson's verses so peculiarly uncomfortable for their male reader is best articulated by that *Boston Herald* reviewer of the 1890 first edition, who felt that "to turn over the pages . . . is to feel as if committing an intrusion, so direct and so forcible are many of its utterances. . . . There is a peculiarly penetrating quality about these scraps of verse [that] fill one with the delight of a new possession."[22] While it is the critic who is intrusive, it is the verses that are penetrating. That is nothing if not a strange penetration, for it is a penetration *of* the reader that "fills" him, in turn, with the delight of a new possession. To penetrate the verses is to be penetrated by them, while to be possessed by them is the prerequisite for possession of them. Reading the poems calls into question notions of appropriation and ownership, particularly, given the evidence of the critic's vocabulary, the sexual appropriation that is often the approximation of aesthetic ownership.

Interestingly, and presumably not coincidentally, a similarly peculiar critical vocabulary emerges from discussions of Dickinson's radical poetic irregularity: this lexicon invariably focuses on the problem of the "attractiveness" of Dickinson's form. Nineteenth-century critics, bemused by Dickinson's experimental poetics, inevitably concluded, given the century's poetic norm, that "her modeling is almost fatally defective" and that "neglect of form involves the sacrifice of an element of positive attractiveness."[23] Surprisingly, later critics, even in coming to praise the experimental complexity of her poetics, maintain the vocabulary of their predecessors in describing that "form." That fatally defective, and therefore unattractive, sense of form becomes a *fatale* attractiveness to the extent that Yvor Winters could say in 1938 that "her popularity has been mainly due to her vices."[24] The assimilation of the unattractive form can be seen as far back as 1923 in Martin Armstrong's comment that "these imperfections come to seem things appropriate and attractive, just as an imperfection of accent or awkwardness of gesture becomes an added charm in a charming personality."[25] This is the sentiment echoed a year later by Conrad Aiken in his observation that "Miss Dickinson's singular perversity, her lapses and tyrannies . . . become a positive charm," leading to "our complete surrender to her highly individual gift, and to the singular, sharp beauty, present everywhere, of her personality."[26] Again, this is a succinct demonstration of the apparent inability of critics to keep the personality of the poetry separate from their reading of the personality of the poet, and it is equally apparent whenever twentieth-century critics have recourse to descriptive metaphor when dealing with Dickinson's unique style: Aiken's comment of the 1930s that he was impressed by the "spinsterly angularity of the mode" and Geoffrey Hartman's 1980 observation that Dickinson criticism "has to confront an elliptical and chaste mode of expression . . . the danger is not fatty degeneration but lean degeneration: a powerful, appealing anorexia" are evidence of an apparently consistent biographical reading of poetic form.[27] Indeed, the critical shift from Dickinson's poetry being metaphorically recontextualized as the work of a twentieth-century anorectic as opposed to a nineteenth-century spinster is fascinating enough to be worthy of a separate study.

It would seem that, no matter the circumstances of the historical reading, Dickinson's strange attractiveness to her critical analysts is inextricably connected to her attractiveness as a woman. In his perceptive 1891 review of the first edition of the poems William Dean Howells makes this provocative statement: "The strange poems . . . we think will form something like an intrinsic experience with the understanding reader of them"[28] A review of the criticism of Dickinson's poetry since then would seem to suggest that the intrinsic experience was one of seductive attractiveness for which Aiken's comment—"the colors tease, the thought entices, but the meaning escapes"—is emblematic.[29] Even more interesting is how often the reader's description of his interaction with the poem, an interaction involving that element of teasing attractiveness, suggests an intense physical proximity to the poem. Thus, Howells's own intrinsic experience of the love poems was that they were of "the same piercingly introspective cast as those differently named. The same force of imagination is in them; in them, as in the rest, touch often becomes clutch." Maurice Thompson's reading experience is even more vividly metaphorically suggestive: "It gives one a thrill of vexation to be trifled with just on the horizon of what appears about to turn out to be a fine lyrical discovery. . . . A large part of the fascination of verse like this is generated by the friction of disappointment on delight. You are charmed with the thought and fretted by the lapses from intelligible expression."[30] Similarly, R. P. Blackmur's negative comparison of Dickinson with Dante is also suggestively physical; in Dante "immortality is so much more enlivening than in Dickinson that a different part of our being quivers in response to it."[31] This, of course, raises the interesting question of which "part of our being" *does* quiver in response to Dickinson. Without being overly flippant, I would suggest that Dickinson's *is* a poetics of quivering being, and the analyses of these critics provide compelling evidence that extended contact with the poetry of Dickinson reproduces, in the critic, a metaphorical vocabulary of tactile, physical contact. In effect, knowing the poetry is knowing the poet. It must be doubtful if even Whitman generated the range of critical vocabulary that Dickinson has in this study: *charmed, fascination, touch, thrill, half in love with, entices, tease, trifled with, lapses, defective modeling, anorexic, imperfections, unattractive, spinsterly, immodest, flesh, vulgar, obscene, vices, perversity, vampirage.*

Perhaps it should therefore not be surprising that contemporary male critics often express a foreboding insight, normally in marginal asides, into the dangers of personal revelation, of the implication of self in their reading process. We can see this in John Cody's pondering whether readers "may recognize in the poetry some of their own anxieties and reservations" and his observation, while discussing the misreadings Dickinson elicits, that sometimes "the psychological atmosphere of the poem has repelled the critic before he could come to grips with the message." Cody concedes that he is himself vulnerable to just such a response, when he notes that "the convulsions of the spirit found in Emily Dickinson's poems are only the culminating manifestation of processes incipient in all

of us . . . most of us who read her poems recognize ourselves in them"[32]
Cody, a practicing psychoanalyst, is only too aware that an analysand can
be a potential seducer. Elsewhere he interprets Dickinson's rhetorical
tactics in her dealings with T. W. Higginson as an example of her "repeat-
edly seducing him into submitting his self-important and inept literary
advice." Small wonder, therefore, that he feels it necessary to reject out of
hand any notion that the nature of his own study is "seducing one's
attention away from a proper regard for literary values through an inquisi-
tiveness about personalia."[33] Throughout Cody's analytic text the avoid-
ance of a possible seduction by the subject of his analysis is palpably
evident. This resistance to Dickinson's text (and thereby to Dickinson
herself) is perhaps most evident in his tendency to portray her in the
most unappealing physical terms imaginable.[34] This is not the place to
indulge in a full-scale analysis of Cody's *analysis* of Dickinson, despite the
fact that, as an analyst in an inevitably countertransferential situation, he
leaves himself open to precisely that reading, but it is worth noticing
that, just as it was for so many of the New Critics, an identifiable *frustra-
tion* seems to be the key to Cody's interpretation of Dickinson's life and
work: his exposition of that personal frustration is heavily dependent
upon the assumption that her "insatiable love needs and their frustration
saturate the poetry and the letters."[35]

Alternatively, David Porter's poststructuralist focus on the poet's
language leads him to identify frustration as a quality of the poetry itself:
"There is frustration in the poems, an obscure agitation that often does
not break through into consciousness." Porter's study of the apparent
autonomy and self-reflexivity of Dickinson's language concentrates on
the linguistic strategies of poems that give the reader "the constant possi-
bility of slipping off the ledge of the familiar. . . . Readers get taken to
the edge and must look over." This unsettling sense of being on the brink
of comprehension, of poems that "agitate without ever quite bringing
issues to clear articulation," is central to Porter's definition of modernity.
The modern is precisely this agitating teasing quality of withholding:
"This . . . is a modern poem because it gives enough to engage but
withholds all the rest."[36] For Porter what makes Dickinson an exemplary
modernist is the fact that she foregrounds modernism's strategy of seman-
tic teasing. To some extent, then, Dickinson's linguistic strategy, the
syntactic engagement that is simultaneously a withholding, is Porter's
contemporary version of the frustration paradigm that we have seen in
other of Dickinson's male critics.

So, it is with some inevitability that Porter's specific focus on Dickinson's "frustrating" language becomes also a focus on her corporeal self. For, while he asserts that Dickinson did not establish a "designed body of completed work" and that her idiom "cannot be a model for a body of work or a body of knowledge," he does believe that her language had an "autogenous energy that worked deliberately to create its own corporeality."[37] And it is to the language of the poetry as seductive body that Porter reacts, often ambiguously. If, at one point, "her devouring language grips and startles," at another it is found "trembling with nervousness and need."[38] Since Dickinson's is a poetic language both shy and aggressive, coy and direct, it is only with difficulty that Porter can reconcile the apparently paradoxical processes of poems that simultaneously draw from and overpower the reader: "Her parables are propelled by a need that overpowers us. They embarrass us by drawing from us with their enactment of need." Thus, while it is Dickinson herself who "courts" allegories of visitation "with indecent glee," it is her poems that evince "what one must call brilliant impurity." If, frustratingly, "instead of proceeding by the reasonableness of syntax or the obligations of representation, her poems dart and posture," it is only to be expected that "the list of her deviations would be the recitation of the body of her poetry."[39] Commenting on the difficulties of reading a particular Dickinson poem, Porter observes that "cumulative weirdness of this sort impedes habitualization . . . preventing us from sliding off poems with easy gratification." What Porter's phenomenological critical vocabulary identifies in Dickinson is a readerly frustration almost palpably physical: "In short, a reader emerges from the most empathetic and pleasurable immersion in the body of poetry quite unable to report its order of knowledge or perception."[40]

Yet Porter seems only too aware of the dangers of the subjective reading to which other Dickinson critics have proven so readily susceptible. Of an earlier critic he notes, "Winters discovered in this woman of surpassing linguistic power, as other critics have, what he wanted to find in the first place." More important, he also recognizes just what produces that subjective reading: it is the effect upon the individual reader of a language that is a "void of mystery that changes its appearance as the reader's various approaches create this or that origin." Porter's significant comment on those various approaches, and the battery of purely subjective inferences that they bring to bear on her poems, is also a perceptive summation of the history of Dickinson criticism:

"Dickinson's ambiguity, indefiniteness, and lack of reference create mystery that invites, indeed traps, readers into sexual speculation of a predictable and even self-revelatory kind."[41]

The criticism of Karl Keller, in its willingness to accept that invitation, simply marks the self-reflexive postmodern turning upon itself of a timeless critical technique of "reading" Dickinson.[42] Keller consciously embraces transferential seduction and thus effectively circumvents the interpretive frustration produced when "her life, like her poetry, seduces without offering complete satisfaction." The calculated outrageousness of his celebration of the "polymorphous perverse" in Dickinson that provides for her reader "a little naughtiness, a little nastiness, a little playfulness, a little freakishness, a spectacle"; his characterization of her as a "lovely, lost vamp," who, undergoing a "conflict between hormones and integrity . . . whored often enough to make one wonder which was primary with her"; his assertions that she is "as much of a poetic voyeur as Whitman" and "manages to make Freud trite"; and his memorable speculation that it is "not hard to imagine her . . . as a performer of some sort, or as a hooker"[43] are evidence of a memorable seduction *of* and *by* the poetry. Significantly, Keller does not simply assume that "Emily Dickinson is a great tease" but also that this system of teasing should be necessarily reproduced by the critic; his own critical intention is to "play with what I—teased—know about Emily Dickinson . . . a tease of my own, to see what life a subject may yet yield." This is substantially more than the mental "teasing out" of a subject for clarity's sake. Keller's critical reading is itself an elaborate teasing; not only is it thoroughly playful in its outrageousness; it also plays with the reader, is something of a joke, a spoof, a tease. When Keller observes that "my own teases here explore some possibilities for enjoying her critically by talking about her in a substantially different way,"[44] he is merely making explicit what has been implicit in so many previous male critical readings of the poet. Keller's reading of Dickinson is ultimately shocking only in its honesty.

Dickinson's male readers, past and present, provide substantial textual evidence that her poetry is frequently read in a situation analogous to the psychoanalytic dialectic. In that dialectic the analyst seeks to imitate lack itself in order to incite an analysand to work with desire. The successful analyst, who mimes the analysand's unsatisfied desire, has no palpable reality in the analytic situation: she or he is the creation of the analysand, essentially an illusion of something not said in the analysand's other.[45] In a similar way the syntactic voids within Dickinson's poetic texts (combined with the suggestively absent details of her incomplete life text) successfully incite her readers to work through a hermeneutic desire that proves self-revelatory. The provocation of subjective reading investments can problematize the supposedly "objective" critical rhetoric of a reader to the extent that there can be a subtle transferential repetition of the poetic text by the commentary that would seek to appropriate it critically.[46] Indeed, the extent of such critical repetitions raises the question of whether there can ever be any interpretive metalanguage suitable for addressing Dickinson's poetry.

Certainly, in the course of a reading of "Dickinson" the critical analyst is implicated in some of the problematics of transference. The peculiar critical vocabulary often employed by Dickinson's male readers is obviously the unconscious expression of a confused conflation of the poet and her text. The rejection of the reader's interpretive "advances" by the syntax of the text is frequently taken as a strangely personal affront, and the failure of an interpretive reading strategy to appropriate the poem satisfactorily can produce—as it frequently did in the New Critics— either a denial or a qualified acceptance of the poetry's merit. The rejection of the reader by the poet or poetry that duly provokes a critical rejection of the poet or poetry by the reader might be considered the useful figuration of those rather more substantial transferential effects elsewhere evident in the male critical text.[47] The most obvious of those effects is the defensive identification of unfulfilled desire as thematically central to Dickinson's poetry when it is actually often the male reader's transferential repetition of the anxiety and frustration produced by, and implicit in, the inhibiting syntax of that poetry. Crucially, however, the cultivation of frustration was, as we have seen, an intrinsic component of the poet's practice of "sumptuous destitution," in which the problematic Dickinson syntax became the rhetorical vehicle for the simultaneous stimulation and deferral of her readers' interpretive desire. Equally significant, the critical male reader may also transfer his own unconscious emotions onto the text. Often this occurs as a negative countertransference, in which an unanalyzed part of the reader becomes implicated in the analysis. The most obvious consequence is that the reading-affects of Dickinson's poetic text prove to be as often akin to love and hate as to meaning; male readers of the poetry have found innumerable ways to express fascination, repulsion, protectiveness, titillation, anger, frustration, and lust in their critical writings. The seduction of the psychoanalytic dialectic often

manifests itself as both affection *and* hostility: Dickinson's male critical
readers merely provide us with a rather thorough demonstration of the
vagaries of transference love.

   There is evidence that Dickinson's poetry can similarly implicate the
interpretive desire of her female readers. Louise Chandler Moulton's
nineteenth-century response, for example, simply parallels that of her
male counterparts, when she finds in the poetry "a fascination, a power, a
vision that enthralls you, and draws you back to it again and again. . . . It
enthralls me, and will not let me go . . . with every page I turn and
return I grow more and more in love. I am half tempted to wish that
while Emily Dickinson lived she had given more of herself to the
world."[48] The assertions of "love" and "half temptation" could have been
produced by any number of Moulton's male contemporaries. Similarly,
contemporary feminist accounts of Dickinson's poetic strategies are
equally liable to assert that Dickinson's poetry "originates in frustration"
or to state that "the experience of having desires that were imperfectly
gratified through her major relationships . . . is the central fact of Emily
Dickinson's life."[49] Contemporary readings that exaggerate Dickinson's
frustration in order to emphasize her entrapment in patriarchal structures
may well simply replicate the reading paradigm of the male New Critics.
Alternatively, the recent feminist criticism that has argued Dickinson's
poetic strategy emphasizes a metonymic intimacy with the reader[50]
would suggest the possibility of a rhetorical countertransference could be
greater in a female reader. Vividly empathetic readings of Dickinson by
Adrienne Rich, Susan Howe, and Camille Paglia demonstrate that this
might well be the case.[51] A detailed analysis of the critical rhetoric uncon-
sciously employed by Dickinson's female readers should be an important
future project for feminist criticism.

   Considering sumptuous destitution a rhetorical practice of Dickin-
son's poetry that stimulates a frustrated desire within her readers would
have significant implications for all contemporary critical readings of
Dickinson. In particular, it would necessitate a long overdue reappraisal
of the psychoanalytic critical approach to the poet. Dickinson has always
seemed the perfect subject for the psychoanalytic method of biography
and criticism. Indeed, John Cody has pointed out that the poet's relation-
ship with her dominating father; her failure to communicate with an
essentially absent, valedictorian mother; her later retreat into self-
imposed reclusion; her often ambiguous sexuality; and, most of all, the
articulate capacity for fantasy evident in her poetry combine to make

Dickinson "the psychoanalysand *par excellence.*"[52] In his problematic study Cody succinctly demonstrates to what degree Dickinson, the analysand, can provide a wealth of material for her critical analyst. While disagreeing with many of Cody's conclusions, I do find myself in agreement with his assertion that Dickinson is the analysand par excellence, at least insofar as the Freudian analysand par excellence is a woman whose "hysterical" discourse can subtly implicate her analyst.[53] Yet, given the fact that it is possible to consider Dickinson's a hysterical discourse (and therefore, by implication, an analytic discourse), a more valid contemporary critical focus would be on the responses of her readers to that discourse. The question of whether Dickinson was in any way pathological would then be supplanted by the question of what it is that makes her art an object of desire for her readers, or, rather, from what the power of her art over those readers derives. Finally, rather than regarding Dickinson as a suitable analysand, as a prime candidate for psychoanalytic study, we might be well advised to consider her to be simultaneously an exemplary, if speculative, psychoanalyst whose own primary study was of her readers. Since it is Dickinson's *text* (and not just the biography of her personal neuroses) that is an analytic case in the history of literary criticism, she might be said to have a literary case history. That literary case history can serve as an important analytic object. In fact, future generations of Dickinson scholars may find that the critical responses of their predecessors to her poetry will prove to be a more valid subject of critical interpretation.[54]

NOTES

1. *The Letters of Emily Dickinson*, ed. Thomas H. Johnson and Theodora Ward, 3 vols. (Cambridge: Harvard University Press, 1958), 46. Hereafter Dickinson's letters are cited in the text according to the numbering in *Letters.*

2. Dickinson's personal "affective" response to poetry is encapsulated in her famous comment to T. W. Higginson: "If I read a book [and] it makes my whole body so cold no fire ever can warm me I know *that* is poetry. If I feel physically as if the top of my head were taken off, I know *that* is poetry. These are the only way I know it. Is there any other way" (L 342a). Significantly, her definition of *genius* was this: "Genius is the ignition of affection—not intellect, as is supposed,—the exaltation of devotion, and in proportion to our capacity for that, is our experience of genius" (L 691). The most thorough study of Dickinson as a poet of the sublime is Gary Lee Stonum, *The Dickinson Sublime* (Madison: University of Wisconsin Press, 1990).

3. Dickinson's poems are identified in the text according to the numbering in *The Poems of Emily Dickinson,* ed. Thomas H. Johnson, 3 vols. (Cambridge: Harvard University Press, 1955).

4. Richard Wilbur, "Sumptuous Destitution," in *Emily Dickinson: A Collection of Critical Essays,* ed. Richard B. Sewall (Englewood Cliffs, N.J.: Prentice-Hall, 1963), 132–33.

5. Shoshana Felman, *Jacques Lacan and the Adventure of Insight* (Cambridge: Harvard University Press, 1987), 23. Throughout this study the influence of Felman is ubiquitous. The linkage of specific linguistic "seduction" and the interlocutions of the psychoanalytic dialectic have become common in literary criticism. See, for example, Felman, *The Literary Speech Act: Don Juan with J. L. Austin, or Seduction in Two Languages,* trans. Catherine Porter (Ithaca: Cornell University Press, 1983); and Jane Gallop, *The Daughter's Seduction: Feminism and Psychoanalysis* (Ithaca: Cornell University Press, 1982). The analogy has been most fully developed in the assumption of contemporary narrative theory that the relationship of narrator to listener is analogous to that of reader and text and that both are instances of psychoanalytic transference. See Ross Chambers, *Story and Situation: Narrative Seduction and the Power of Fiction* (Minneapolis: University of Minnesota Press, 1984); and Peter Brooks, *Reading for the Plot: Design and Intention in Narrative* (New York: Random House, 1985).

6. Felman, *Lancan,* 21–22.

7. William Shurr, *The Marriage of Emily Dickinson: A Study of the Fascicles* (Lexington: University Press of Kentucky, 1983), 189; Cynthia Griffin Wolff, *Emily Dickinson* (New York: Knopf, 1986), 275; Suzanne Juhasz, "Reading Emily Dickinson's Letters," *ESQ* 30 (1984): 171; Karl Keller, *The Only Kangaroo among the Beauty: Emily Dickinson and America* (Baltimore and London: Johns Hopkins University Press, 1979), 25–26.

8. David Porter asserts that Dickinson's is a "language . . . covering hysteria"; that one poem has a "hyperbole that threatens to erupt in hysteria"; that the language of another "seems to be the surface display of a latent hysteria"; and that a third "has no knowledge at all, only hysteria" (*Dickinson: The Modern Idiom* [Cambridge: Harvard University Press, 1981], 79, 112, 163, 207). Porter's powerful analysis of Dickinson's poetics of "the aftermath" can thus be seen to derive from the Freudian assumption that "hysterics suffer mainly from reminiscences."

9. It should be noted that very specific rhetorics of seduction were a major discursive formation of the antebellum period. Cathy Davison has noted the significance of rhetorics of seduction in postrevolutionary and antebellum fiction (*Revolution and the Word: The Rise of the Novel in America* [New York: Oxford University Press, 1986]), and Carroll Smith-Rosenberg has examined the manipulation of rhetorics of seduction by the influential moral-reform movement (*Disorderly Conduct: Visions of Gender in Victorian America, 1830–1870* [New Haven: Yale University Press, 1982]). The immediate consequence of the prevalence of seduction in fictional and reformist rhetorics is a

plethora of seduction narratives as news stories in such local newspapers as the *Springfield Republican,* the *Hampshire and Franklin Express,* and the *Hampshire Gazette* during Dickinson's lifetime.

10. See Adrienne Rich, "Vesuvius at Home: The Power of Emily Dickinson," *Parnassus: Poetry in Review* 5 (1976): 49–74; and Suzanne Juhasz's polemical introduction to the collection *Feminist Critics Read Emily Dickinson,* ed. Suzanne Juhasz (Bloomington: Indiana University Press, 1983).

11. A. C. Ward, "A Major American Poet," in *The Recognition of Emily Dickinson: Selected Criticism since 1890,* ed. Caesar R. Blake and Carlton F. Wells (Ann Arbor: University of Michigan Press; Toronto: Ambassador Books, 1964), 146.

12. The critical positions assumed by John Cody, Cynthia Griffin Wolff, David Porter, and Adrienne Rich, respectively.

13. R. P. Blackmur, "Emily Dickinson's Notation," in Sewall, *Dickinson,* 80, 86, 83.

14. Allen Tate, "Emily Dickinson," in Sewall, *Dickinson,* 19.

15. John Crowe Ransom, "Emily Dickinson: A Poet Restored," in Sewall, *Dickinson,* 97; David Higgins, *Portrait of Emily Dickinson: The Poet and her Prose* (New Brunswick, N.J.: Rutgers University Press, 1967), 86.

16. Robert Hillyer, "Emily Dickinson," in Blake and Wells, *Recognition of Emily Dickinson,* 98.

17. Archibald MacLeish, "The Private World: Poems of Emily Dickinson," in Sewall, *Dickinson,* 160 (my emphasis).

18. Higgins, *Portrait of Emily Dickinson,* 105.

19. George Whicher, "A Centennial Appraisal"; and Ella Gilbert Ives, "Emily Dickinson: Her Poetry, Prose and Personality," both in Blake and Wells, *Recognition of Emily Dickinson,* 139, 71.

20. Tate, "Emily Dickinson," 27; Blunden, "An Unguessed Poetry," in Blake and Wells, *Recognition of Emily Dickinson,* 134. Dickinson's own comment on this phenomenon might well be her observation that "shame is so intrinsic in a strong affection we must all experience Adam's reticence (L 318).

21. T. W. Higginson is, surprisingly, an exception to this rule. He observed of Dickinson that "she interested me more in her—so to speak—unregenerate condition" (qtd. in *Emily Dickinson's Reception in the 1890s: A Documentary History,* ed. Willis J. Buckingham [Pittsburgh: University of Pittsburgh Press, 1989]), 188.

22. "Scraps of Verse from the Pen of Emily Dickinson," in Buckingham, *Dickinson's Reception,* 67.

23. Maurice Thompson, "Miss Dickinson's Poems"; and anonymous *Scribner's Magazine* reviewer, "The Point of View," both in Buckingham, *Dickinson's Reception,* 96, 120.

24. Yvor Winters, "Emily Dickinson and the Limits of Judgment," in Sewall, *Dickinson,* 28.

25. Martin Armstrong, "The Poetry of Emily Dickinson," in Blake and Wells, *Recognition of Emily Dickinson,* 108.

26. Conrad Aiken, "Emily Dickinson," in Sewall, *Dickinson,* 18.

27. Aiken, "Emily Dickinson," 15; Geoffrey Hartman, *Criticism in the Wilderness: The Study of Literature Today* (New Haven and London: Yale University Press, 1980), 130. On the topic of Dickinson and anorexia, see also Heather Kirk Thomas, "Emily Dickinson's 'Renunciation' and Anorexia Nervosa," *American Literature* 60 (1988): 205–25.

28. Howells, "Editor's Study," in Buckingham, *Dickinson's Reception,* 74.

29. Aiken, "Emily Dickinson," 14.

30. Howells, "Editor's Study"; and Thompson, "Miss Dickinson's Poems," both in Buckingham, *Dickinson's Reception,* 77, 96–98.

31. Blackmur, "Emily Dickinson's Notation," 83.

32. John Cody, *After Great Pain: The Inner Life of Emily Dickinson* (Cambridge: Harvard University Press, 1971), 396, 4, 354.

33. Cody, *After Great Pain,* 433, 4.

34. At times Cody's apparent distaste for his subject is vivid. A typical narrative digression, from what he sees as a rape scenario within a poem, describes Dickinson as "a not very attractive, reclusive spinster whom her would-be rapist would scarcely have had occasion even to see, much less lust after." Elsewhere she is described as "loveless, excluded, almost burned out as a poet, and reduced to the status of a queer, hypochondriacal, and depressed old maid" (Cody, *After Great Pain,* 288, 438).

35. Cody, *After Great Pain,* 39.

36. Porter, *Dickinson,* 293, 21, 118, 74.

37. Porter, *Dickinson,* 82, 292, 135.

38. Porter, *Dickinson,* 133, 79. It is worthwhile comparing Porter's twentieth-century response to Dickinson's language with that of one of her nineteenth-century reviewers, John White Chadwick, who commented on "phrases so packed with strangeness, force, suggestion, poems so tremulous with tenderness or so bent under the burden of their mystery, that they shock us with almost intolerable delight or awe" ("Poems by Emily Dickinson," in Buckingham, *Dickinson's Reception,* 63). This response to Dickinson's corporeal language is clearly an ahistorical one.

39. Porter, *Dickinson,* 171, 17, 106, 114, 156.

40. Porter, *Dickinson,* 48, 3.

41. Porter, *Dickinson,* 280, 187, 125. Porter has an interesting discussion of this phenomenon in his first book on Dickinson, in which he observes that the reader,

> lacking precise contextual direction provided by the poem itself, brings to it his casual inferences, and, in effect, is compelled to give symbols a reading rooted in his own experience . . . the verbal equivalent of sfumato, the technique in expressionistic painting whereby information . . . on a canvas is given only piecemeal and thereby necessarily stimulates the imaginative projection of the viewer, who, out of his own experience, supplies the missing contours and, ultimately, the con-

text. (*The Art of Emily Dickinson's Early Poetry* [Cambridge: Harvard University Press, 1966], 99)

42. Indeed, Keller's reading of Dickinson itself takes a markedly postmodern turn in its development from *The Only Kangaroo among the Beauty: Emily Dickinson and America* (Baltimore and London: John Hopkins University Press, 1979) to the experimental format of his essay "Notes on Sleeping with Emily Dickinson" (Juhasz, *Feminist Critics Read Emily Dickinson,* 67–79) four years later. The essay is a series of short confessional fragments, some of the more startling (and perceptive) of which are worthy of complete quotation:

> The poems on sleeping with someone are instructions, I believe, on how to "take" her. When she writes about wild nights, she is not only describing her ecstasy but also instructing us how to react to her, what to expect, what to get. She thus couples with the critic. She thus holds.

> This woman can tease a man. But though she goes far towards the really crazy, she never loses her inhibitions, for then there would be no imagination necessary, no lure. She pulls a man in.

> Emily Dickinson's anticipation of a male readership (her critics, not her cult) nears anxiety. She performs; they analyze. When they perform the poetry, they near anxiety. She then becomes *their* critic.

> She created the space for someone to understand her, enclose her, love her—quite like all the white space around one of her poems. *She* created that white space, I think we have to believe. She lets one in lovingly.

43. Keller, *Only Kangaroo,* 2, 230, 26, 275, 268, 247.
44. Keller, *Only Kangaroo,* 3–4.
45. Dennis Donoghue observes in his review of Sewall's biography that "we hardly see her at all, for she is visible neither in chores nor poems but only in the void beyond them. . . . The void is where there is nothing but absolute desire, and the objects of desire have long since been overwhelmed by its force" (*Times Literary Supplement,* 7 May 1976).
46. Shurr's book is a convenient example of this problem. He worries that, if Dickinson's poetry is "a mere matrix, a form without content, which can give structure and meaning to the unformed experience of the reader," then it is potentially a "matrix for stimulating the subjectivities of each reader." But subjective stimulation is then precisely the narrative Shurr reads in the fascicles: the attraction between Dickinson and Wadsworth "was mutually recognized and sexual stimulation was high." So, while Shurr sees Dickinson's sexual stimulation of *that* privileged reader to an emotional pitch of response as the goal of the (supposedly) mailed fascicles, he comprehensively fails to realize the implications to the assumed perspective of his own

position as another reader of the fascicles. When he asserts that "the narra-
tive core of Emily Dickinson's fascicle poetry is the classic love triangle
involving the married couple and the outsider," he obviously intends his
reader to visualize Dickinson at the apex of a triangle whose base positions
are occupied by the Reverend and Mrs. Wadsworth. But his own assumed
perspective as the critical observer of this relationship recreates the love
triangle with the new base being the "marriage" between Dickinson and
Wadsworth and he himself occupying the apex (Shurr, *Marriage of Emily
Dickinson,* 48–49, 195, 30).

47. In psychoanalysis the "hysterical" discourse of the female analysand can be
characterized as precisely the disorder that puts in question the knowledge of
the male analyst. Martha Noel Evans has observed that the positioning of the
analyst as male and of the analysand as female often has peculiar conse-
quences in the writings of French male analysts. The "hysterics" are charac-
terized as "difficult patients who elicit reactions of hostility, impatience,
anger, exasperation, and sometimes love," while their analyst, "whether
yielding to anger or to desire . . . playing the male role in this romance,
appears to feel undone by the hysteric, who perpetually attempts to dislodge
him from his place as an authority." Evans's description of what occurs when
the analyst is confronted by the hysteric's false seductiveness, false in that she
does not follow through on her original offer of love to the analyst—in
short, that she is a tease—is informative:

> This sequence of seductiveness and withdrawal seems to be particularly
> enraging to male analysts. Desire is first aroused according to the nor-
> mal procedures of female seduction by a woman posing herself as an
> object; but then desire is left unsatisfied by the hysteric's insistence on
> her status as a subject. . . . In these circumstances, analysts say they feel
> undone, impotent or castrated, and their response is to master their
> anger and humiliation by returning the hysteric to object status as an
> item in textual theory. (Martha Noel Evans, "Hysteria and the Seduc-
> tion of Theory," in *Seduction and Theory: Readings in Gender, Representa-
> tion, and Rhetoric,* ed. Dianne Hunter [Chicago: University of Illinois
> Press, 1989], 77–79)

48. Louise Chandler Moulton, "A Very Remarkable Book," in Buckingham,
Dickinson's Reception, 34–37.
49. Vivian Pollack, *Dickinson: The Anxiety of Gender* (Ithaca: Cornell University
Press, 1984), 9, 27.
50. See, for example, Cristanne Miller, *Dickinson: A Poet's Grammar* (Cam-
bridge: Harvard University Press, 1987); and Margaret Homans, "Oh Vision
of Language!': Dickinson's Poems of Love and Death," in Juhasz, *Feminist
Critics Read Emily Dickinson,* 114–33.
51. See Rich, "Vesuvius at Home"; Susan Howe, *My Emily Dickinson* (Berkeley:
North Atlantic Books, 1985); and Camille Paglia, final chapter of *Sexual*

Personae: Art and Decadence from Nefertiti to Emily Dickinson (Yale University Press, 1990).
52. Cody, *After Great Pain,* 6.
53. Cody's psychoanalytic reading of Dickinson first necessitates his manipulation of her into the *position* of psychoanalytical analysand. Thus, Dickinson's lyric poetry is read by Cody as confessional, as a discourse marked by autobiographical disclosure, despite her famous protestation of the fact that the speaker of the poems was a "supposed person." Cody's diagnoses are thus, to say the least, problematic.
54. My thesis that Dickinson's text is an analytic case in the history of literary criticism and that the poet might be said to have a literary case history is, of course, modeled on Shoshana Felman's treatment of Edgar Allan Poe (see Felman, *Jacques Lacan,* 27–51).

Part 2:
Dickinson's Letters to the World

This is my letter to the World
That never wrote to Me—
The simple News that Nature told—
With tender Majesty

—Poem 441

Dickinson's Letters to Abiah Root: Formulating the Reader as "Absentee"

Martin Orzeck

For the listener, who listens in the snow,
And, nothing himself, beholds
Nothing that is not there and the nothing that is.
—Wallace Stevens, "The Snow Man"

I'm Nobody! Who are you?
Are you—Nobody—Too?
Then there's a pair of us!
—Emily Dickinson, Poem 288

Emily Dickinson's early letters seem at times a virtual chronicle of loss, absence, and loneliness. This is not to deny them their many moments of humor and genuine compassion (her letters to Austin during the period are exemplary in this regard), but a predominant emotional strain in the correspondence up to 1862 is anxiety, lest the person written to, absent for the moment, never return. This anxiety is buttressed by a significant pattern of biographical details as well, for just about every important relationship during Dickinson's formative years issued into a sequence of frustration or loss for the developing artist, acquainting her with the perils of intimacy from her adolescence into her early adult years, when she began to document the process in her poetry. Girlhood letters to Austin, Abiah Root, and Jane Humphrey, followed by those to her future sister-in-law Susan Gilbert, all express an obsessive attachment to the departed correspondent, a jealous longing for that person's return, and a compensatory resolution to make language serve as a somewhat poorer substitute for the ecstasy of personal presence.

We should remain circumspect in dealing with these letters and treat them as the valuable rhetorical documents that they are. The early

Dickinson correspondence can provide a vital link in our understanding of the poet's development *as a poet* if we examine what it has to say about the youthful writer's early spiritual concerns, the matters that spoke to the heart for her, and, most particularly, the issues and circumstances generally prompting Emily Dickinson, as a schoolgirl and then as a young woman, to write. What were her communicative needs? Probing her expressed attitudes toward audience in these letters offers us one reliable focus by which we can observe closely and accurately the developing Dickinson rhetoric. Robert Weisbuch is essentially correct when he asserts, "The 'I' of the poems is not Emily Dickinson of Amherst, Massachusetts," and we would be critically naive to assume otherwise.[1] That "I" is a speaker in a poem, a fictional device employed by a skillful artist toward a particular poem's artistic ends. On the other hand, it is equally naive to assume that the links between the poet's early personal life and her mature work are neatly severed and that the poems constitute a separate identity unto themselves with scant connection, if any at all, to a private life lived. A sensible middle ground can be reached if we consider the relationships prior to the poet's period of unprecedented, frenzied literary production in the early 1860s as personally *and* aesthetically formative, the letters of this period serving as a kind of rhetorical workshop, a forum in which Dickinson crafted not only the durable, tough-minded persona that Weisbuch and others have noted but also a sense of audience to which that persona was a necessary response.

By focusing on Dickinson's letters to a single correspondent, we gain the additional advantage of coherence in the development of an exclusive epistolary relationship. Dickinson's letters to Abiah Root are particularly useful in this regard for several reasons. For one thing, there is a substantial number of them (twenty-two) written over a nine-year period of time. Furthermore, Abiah was a close friend (one of the "five," Dickinson's select schoolgirl friends among whom matters of urgency and intimacy were commonly shared) but not a member of the immediate Dickinson family.[2] Thus, the separation that developed between the once close correspondents was not further complicated by any domestic or other relational bonds; it was the natural separation between two people growing in different directions. But, most particularly, these letters are interesting because Emily Dickinson's correspondence with Abiah Root continued into 1854, a scant four years before the poet began sewing her work into packets. Because of the proximity in time between the completion of this essentially epistolary relationship and the commencement of Dickinson's poetic career, we should be able to assert some fresh and useful rhetorical links between these letters and the poems that follow.

Paradoxically, one of the distinguishing characteristics of the reader emerging from Dickinson's early correspondence with Abiah Root is her *absence*. In this sense, we would not be claiming too much for the letters of Dickinson's teen years to suggest that in them she first learned to employ writing as a structured response to the loss, and subsequent absence, of someone close to her. Directed, as just about all of them are, to her brother Austin and to Abiah, the letters of 1845–46 evince a jealous longing for the return of the absent correspondents. Each had recently departed, Austin to Williston Seminary, in nearby Easthampton, and Abiah, having completed her studies at Amherst Academy, to her home in Feeding Hills, near Springfield. It is not unusual in these letters for Dickinson to remark on her reader's absence as the occasion for the writing act. At an early point in their correspondence, for instance, she even playfully projects herself into Abiah's imagined presence: "I can imagine just how you look now. I wonder what you are doing this moment. I have got an idea that you are knitting edging. Are you. Wont you tell me when you answer my letter whether I guessed right."[3] Thus, we can see from the outset that Dickinson conceived of letter writing as an imaginative exercise through which the writer might project herself into the absent one's presence for the duration of her discourse. It is in a similar vein that she remarks to Mary Bowles some fourteen years later: "I have a childish hope to gather all I love together—and sit down, and smile."[4] The futility of her childish dream seems to have been evident to Dickinson from the outset, however, and, as we shall see in the remaining letters to Abiah, the poet learned to compensate for the denied presence through the language addressed to the absent reader, instead.

It is in her fourth letter to Abiah that Dickinson laments, "I long to see you, dear Abiah, and speak to you face to face; but so long as a bodily interview is denied us, we must make letters answer, though it is hard for friends to be separated."[5] What interests us here is Dickinson's sense of the written word mitigating the pangs of longing caused by her reader's absence. By making "letters answer," Dickinson endeavors to render a broken chain of intimacy whole again. Elsewhere in the same letter she alludes to this restorative power of the written word when she recounts her own reading response to Abiah's previous message:

> I was very unwell at the time I received your letter & unable to busy
> myself about anything. Consequently I was down-spirited and I
> give you all the credit of restoring me to health. At any rate, you
> may have your share. It really seemed to give me new life to receive
> your letter, for when I am rather low-spirited nothing seems to cheer
> me so much as a letter from a friend. At every word I read I seemed
> to feel new strength & have now regained my usual health and
> spirits.[6]

Though the sentiments may strike us as commonplace, even for a
fourteen-year-old, the fact that Dickinson is already articulating a sensitiv-
ity to the *affective* capacity of language merits our attention. Furthermore,
her view of language as a precision instrument, the effects of which can
be calibrated "at every word," significantly foreshadows the awe she
later expresses for the power of individual words. Actually, we are not
that far removed here from Dickinson's best-known enunciation of this
theme in her undated Poem 1651, "A Word made Flesh is seldom." When
properly read, individual words can simulate an actual communal pres-
ence by becoming "Flesh," their "very food" sustaining the "low-
spirited" reader to "our specific strength." It becomes the reader's respon-
sibility, then, here as elsewhere in Dickinson's writing, to accept the
potential nourishment, offered "at every word," to the fullest extent that
the receiving consciousness can achieve. In addition to restoring the
"usual health and spirits" to the beleaguered soul, words offer a "new
strength," which an exemplary but absent reader (in this case Dickinson
herself) consumes and internalizes.

All of this suggests a budding literary awareness, which when ma-
ture would continue to attribute enormous value to the claims of lan-
guage upon human consciousness. But, as time passed, prospects for the
kind of linguistic reciprocity cited earlier dimmed between Dickinson
and Abiah, and a sense of estrangement began to enter Dickinson's tone.
As Richard Sewall points out, Abiah "was one of the two girls, in
Amherst or out [no letters to Dickinson's other spiritual confidante,
Abby Wood, are extant], with whom Emily discussed freely the matter
that bore so heavily on all these young people, their spiritual condi-
tion."[7] Thus, it is during her year at Mount Holyoke that Dickinson
began to write to her friend about the inaccessibility of a God, who
would become the most important of all her absent auditors. While
evidence concerning the degree to which Mount Holyoke's highly

charged religious atmosphere affected Dickinson's day-to-day happiness there remains inconclusive, she notes its fervor with interest in one message to Abiah and remarks as well on the gravity the topic of conversion had assumed in her mind: "There is a great deal of religious interest here and many are flocking to the ark of safety. I have not yet given up to the claims of Christ, but trust I am not entirely thoughtless on so important & serious a topic."[8] Placing herself, as she does here, outside "the ark of safety," Dickinson characterizes the spiritual process of conversion as an ambiguous combination of introspection and acquiescence. To reach the true ark of safety, however, it seems one must quest *for* (rather than "flock" to) it. Her obvious pun here shows in seed Dickinson's later scorn for those who would become the "Soft—Cherubic Creatures—" of Poem 401. They, we discover, are the paragons of a sham religion, available to the mob through a mere surrender to "Dimity Convictions." That Dickinson could never bring herself to join such a flock has been discussed by just about everyone who has written extensively on her religious views. What they do not usually discuss, though, is the bearing her refusal had on the development of the poet's conception of audience.

For instance, precisely where does Abiah, the reader in this case, stand in relation to the communal flock? And, perhaps more important, where does she stand in relation to Dickinson's own reluctance to give up "to the claims of Christ?" Dickinson tests the limits of her reader's sympathy in her next letter to Abiah when she voices an even greater urgency with regard to the "all-important subject":

> Father has decided not to send me to Holyoke another year, so this is my *last term*. Can it be possible that I have been here almost a year? It startles me when I really think of the advantages I have had, and I fear I have not improved them as I ought. But many an hour has fled with its report to heaven, and what has been the tale of me? . . . I tremble when I think how soon the weeks and days of this term will all have been spent, and my fate will be sealed, perhaps. I have neglected the *one thing needful* when all were obtaining it, and I may never, never again pass through such a season as was granted us last winter. Abiah, you may be surprised to hear me speak as I do, knowing that I express no interest in the all-important subject, but I am not happy, and I regret that last term, when that golden opportunity was mine, that I did not give up and become a Christian. It is

not now too late, so my friends tell me, so my offended conscience whispers, but it is hard for me to give up the world.[9]

Yet again we see the conversion experience presented as something to be acquiesced in, something surrendered to, when those who have read the poems know that they regularly present the experience as something to be quested after. Nevertheless, Dickinson expresses her disappointment over an opportunity missed and suggests, with characteristic skepticism (note the qualifying *perhaps*), the implausibility of a God who, observing the missed opportunity, will seal her fate forever. Ironically, the passage derives much of its rhetorical appeal from the fact that it is written to a reader who unequivocally *believes* in such a God. That Abiah has apparently achieved "the one thing needful" (she *has* acquiesced) thus creates distance between her and Dickinson, while providing a vital tension to their correspondence.

It is in *Counter-Statement* that Kenneth Burke tells us: "The formal aspects of art appeal in that they exercise formal potentialities of the reader. They enable the mind to follow processes amenable to it."[10] So, too, we might add, should articulations of conventional religious sentiments. What strikes the reader of the quoted passage, however, is its *struggle* with the accepted pattern of religious conversion, and, by expressing that struggle to a reader amenable to the required acquiescence, Dickinson imperils the reader-writer relationship altogether. There is more at stake here than simply a young woman's struggle with giving up "the world" and becoming a Christian. There is the incipient poet enunciating the interior debate of her already "Compound Vision" to a spiritual confidante upon whom she is depending to provide a sympathetic audience. Assuming the importance of the relationship with Abiah in Dickinson's mind (outside of Austin, she may have been the poet's only regular correspondent at this time), we can see that the developing writer has risked a great deal here.

The fact that there followed a five-and-a-half-month gap in the correspondence should strike us as significant, and Dickinson makes Abiah's troubling silence the subject of her next letter. Having now returned home from Mount Holyoke, Dickinson writes the long absent correspondent, questioning whether or not she had been too "presuming" in the intimacy with which she had shared her conflict. Remarking on the time that has passed since her last, unanswered letter, Dickinson voices her anxiety that the bond of their written communication has been broken:

Slowly, very slowly, I came to the conclusion that you had forgotten me, & I tried hard to forget you, but your image still haunts me, and tantalizes me with fond recollections. At our Holyoke Anniversary, I caught one glimpse of your face, & fondly anticipated an interview with you, & a reason for your silence, but when I thought to find you search was vain, for "the bird had flown." Sometimes, I think it was a fancy, think I did not *really* see my old friend, but her spirit, then your well known voice tells me it was not spirit, but yourself, living, that stood within that crowded hall & spoke to me—Why did you not come back that day, and tell me what had sealed your lips toward me? Did my letter never reach you, or did you cooly decide to love me, & write no more? If you love me, & never received my letter—then may you think yourself wronged, and that rightly, but if you dont want to be my friend any longer, say so, & I'll try *once* more to blot you from my memory. Tell me very soon, for suspense is intolerable.[11]

Whether Abiah intended the cut to Dickinson or not is irrelevant at this point. The fact remains that Dickinson perceived the silence as a cut, directly resulting, we can safely assume, from her own sense of a too "presuming" and perhaps too frank confession of her spiritual condition. Yet the crisis elaborated in this passage has less to do with the "all-important subject," finally, than with the problem of an unsympathetic and unresponsive auditor. It is, after all, Abiah's silence that has so haunted the developing poet, who tantalizes herself with "fond recollections" of what she once thought was a bond between sympathetic spirits. The short vignette about the Holyoke anniversary simply serves to confirm Abiah's corporeal existence, but the essential relationship Dickinson has sought to preserve through writing, the link in "that golden chain" of spiritual communion, has "sadly dimmed."

In a sense, then, Dickinson is grappling here with the paradoxical difference between the essence found in absence ("I did not *really* see my old friend, but her spirit") and the impoverishment of that essence by physical presence ("It was no spirit, but yourself, living, that stood within that crowded hall"). Sewall remarks on the uneasiness this apparent contradiction occasioned in the mind of the poet throughout her career, when he says: "Essence, for her, required absence. . . . That she was not happy with this seems clear; absence is a kind of death."[12] Nevertheless, success in the poems of her maturity (and in large measure the conflict they dramatize) stems from Dickinson's need to address this essence in absence while renouncing the physical presence that threatens to diminish it. Dickinson has just begun to recognize the conflict in the October 1848 letter to Abiah Root without really beginning to resolve it, and yet its centrality to her poetic vision cannot be questioned when we consider her paraphrasing of the dilemma in the opening of a poem dated fifteen years later:

> Renunciation—is a piercing Virtue—
> The letting go
> A Presence—for an Expectation—
> Not now—
>
> (Poem 745)

The budding poet was now learning the severe lesson of her vocation, which would require her to renounce (or at least subdue) her interest in the immediate gratification offered by friendship, public interaction, even the pursuit of fame, in order to pursue "an Expectation" measured in absence: "A Presence . . . Not now."

Sewall notes a change in tone in the letters to Abiah *during* the Mount Holyoke period; however, a more significant shift in tone seems to occur after the letter of October 1848.[13] Having failed in the "larger function" of sympathetic audience for Dickinson's interior struggle, Abiah now receives what Sewall has characterized as some of Dickinson's "most daring experiments in style." In fact, what occurs in these half-dozen or so remaining letters is a shift in Dickinson's stance toward her reader as well as in the subject matter she emphasizes. Even when they appear most whimsical, the remaining letters present Dickinson's serious need to summon a presence out of the absence. In this respect they become *about* the reader as absentee.

A letter of January 1850 begins as follows:

> The folks have all gone away—they thought that they left me alone, and contrived things to amuse me should they stay long, and I be lonely. Lonely indeed—they didn't look, and they couldn't have seen if they had, who should bear me company. *Three* here instead of *one*—wouldn't it scare them? A curious trio, part earthly and part spiritual two of us—the other all heaven, and no earth. *God* is sitting here, looking into my very soul to see if I think right tho'ts. Yet I am

not afraid, for I try to be right and good, and he knows every one of my struggles.[14]

Still remaining outside the ark of safety, Dickinson now creates a partially divine communion of her own imagining, one that depends, however, upon a tolerant God, for whom the attempt to be right and good counts, as does every single one of the poet's inner struggles. Into the circle she welcomes her idealized reader: "Then *you* are here . . . and you dont appear to be thinking about anything in particular . . . you seem aware that I'm writing you, and are amused I should think at any such friendly manifestation when you are already present." "But *which* Abiah is present?" we might ask. Certainly not the one who remained unresponsive for six months after hearing an intimate account of her correspondent's spiritual crisis. Although the overriding tone of this letter is whimsical, as I have acknowledged, Dickinson is still formally distancing herself here, in contrast to indulging in the "strange audacity" of her October 1848 letter, which made her "almost wish [she] had been a little more humble not quite so presuming." Consequently, Dickinson addresses herself to a "friendly manifestation" of a "part earthly and part spiritual" Abiah, whom she now dramatizes as being safely "amused" rather than put off by the letter's bantering tone.

Dickinson sustains her comic pose through a virtuoso narrative about a cold that has "come all the way from the Alps," before warning her reader of the potential snares in such "vain imaginings": "They are flowers of speech, they both *make* and *tell* deliberate falsehoods, avoid them as the snake." After this humorous depiction of the function of metaphor (yet another distancing device) Dickinson abruptly shifts her tone and subject matter: "Something besides severe colds, and serpents, and we will try to find *that* something. It cant be a garden, can it, or a strawberry bed, which rather belongs to a garden—nor it cant be a school-house, nor an Attorney at Law. Oh dear I dont know what it is! Love for the absent dont *sound* like it, but try it, and see how it goes."

Despite the playfulness of this letter, its tentative tone reveals a speaker searching for the appropriate stance from which to address a reformulated absentee reader. In the next sentence Dickinson ambivalently seeks to reassert her former intimacy: "I miss you very much indeed, think of you at night when the world's nodding, 'nidnid nodding[']—think of you in the daytime when the cares of the world, and it's toils, and it's continual vexations choke up love for friends in one of our hearts." All of this posturing is suitably friendly, given what has passed in their previous relationship, but it is also less than convincing. It is becoming clear that Dickinson has chosen another path down which the actual "living" Abiah cannot come. And, as for Dickinson ever turning down the path of acquiescence and "flocking to the ark of safety," that is "a Sealed Route," as she later says in Poem 615. Of her new vocation Dickinson seductively inquires: "Would'nt you love to see God's bird, when it first tries it's wing? If you were here I would tell you something—*several* somethings which have happed since you went away, but time, and space, as usual, oppose themselves, and I put my treasures away till 'We *two* meet again.' " Even as she invites the projected reader on her newfound pilgrimage, Dickinson seems to be struggling to observe the distinction between the reader as confidante and the actual Abiah, who has once before proven unresponsive to her spiritual questing. Dickinson closes the letter with the kind of halfhearted, conventional sentiments that even the uncritical schoolgirl might well see through, and she compounds the sentiments by ambivalently offering her orthodox interlocutor a sad alternative:

> If you are thinking soon to go away, and to show your face no more, just inform me—will you—I would have the "long-lingering look" which you cast behind—It would be an invaluable addition to my treasures, and "keep your memory green." "Lord keep all our memories green," and help our affection, and tie "the link that doth us bind" in a tight bow-knot that will keep it from separation, and stop us from growing old—if *that* is impossible—make old age pleasant to us—put it's arms around us kindly, and when we go home—let that home be called *Heaven!*
>
> Your very sincere, and *wicked* friend,
Emily E. Dickinson

Despite her clichéd manner in expressing the sentiment, Dickinson's use of nostalgia within this passage is instructive with regard to her later formulations of audience in the poems. For instance, her words indicate a desire to maintain a functioning image of the beloved friend who *was* as an added component to the treasure that *is*—in this case her poetic calling. But, while acknowledging (and at least implicitly accommodating) Abiah's possible desire to depart, Dickinson insists upon this "long-lingering look" as her means of preserving a presence even in the wake of her friend's absence. This desire serves as a paradigm for the reader-writer relationship in countless Dickinson poems, which concern themselves not so much with winning the sympathy of the would-be friend or lover before her as with articulating the reconstruction of her experience of loss to an engaged listener. As David Porter tells us in *Dickinson: The Modern Idiom:* "Despite the biographers, the elementary experience has little to do with inaccessible lovers. The crucial affair for her, rather, is living after things happen. It is a preoccupation with afterknowledge, with living in the aftermath. The perspective of poem after poem is from afterward, from behind the 'soft Eclipse.' "[15] For Dickinson, then, keeping Abiah's memory green was more of a pragmatic than a sentimental decision. It would become a compound addition to the developing poet's imaginative treasure, both as a lingering reminder of their lost intimacy and as a silent, engaged listener to whom Dickinson could turn and divulge the "afterknowledge" of that loss (and other losses) remembered.

Given the implications of this reformulated presence in absence for Dickinson's artistic freedom, it should hardly surprise us that the remaining letters to Abiah Root are sprinkled with "minor heresies" and filled with talk of a "golden dream," which seems to supersede the "golden chain" of their earlier childhood relationship. Yet Dickinson's eagerness to follow this dream stimulates even further ambivalence toward her reader:

> It's *Friday* my dear Abiah, and that in another week, yet my mission is unfulfilled—and you so sadly neglected, and dont know the reason why. Where do you think I've strayed, and from what new errand returned? I have come from "*to and fro,* and walking up, and down" the same place that Satan hailed from, when God asked him where he'd been, but not to illustrate further I tell you I have been dreaming, dreaming a *golden* dream, with eyes all the while wide open, and I guess it's almost morning, and besides I have been at work, providing the "food that perisheth," scaring the timorous dust, and being obedient, and kind.[16]

Dickinson has been forced to absent herself from her reader, not merely by her domestic "errands" (she later quips in the same paragraph, "God keep me from what they call *households,* except that bright one of 'faith'!") but by a more isolated errand in her own epistemological wilderness. The same journey that has caused her to neglect her friend, however, now compels Dickinson to return and pique Abiah's curiosity outright ("Where do you think I've strayed, and from what new errand returned?"). Once more she seeks to tease the uninitiated reader into a realm of unknown experience, suggesting an immediate connection in the mind of the Amherst poet between her own pursuit of withheld knowledge and her compulsion to tell someone the results of that pursuit. The passage becomes astonishing when viewed through the lens of an early poem in which Dickinson declares:

> Therefore, as One returned, I feel—
> Odd secrets of the line to tell!
> Some Sailor, skirting foreign shores—
> Some pale Reporter, from the awful doors
> Before the Seal!
>
> (Poem 160)

In both letter and poem the implied reader is someone, either unable or unwilling to follow (possibly both), who must remain far this side of "the line" yet who possesses that universal human curiosity regarding the "Odd secrets" of what lies beyond it. The line precisely demarcates the boundary between the realm of domestic errands and that of the eternal errand of redemption familiar to all New England Calvinists. Yet it also offers Dickinson a figure to mark the boundary between the world of workaday reality in which she locates Abiah and from which she can now depart and the realm of her own "golden dream," an aesthetic domain newly available to the incipient poet.

What we do learn from this letter, however, is consistent with the evidence of the later poems. First of all, the realm of Dickinson's golden dream is a place in which the wandering consciousness can challenge the justice of God's absolute sovereignty ("the same place that Satan hailed from") while simultaneously scrutinizing its own interior processes. It is also a place of isolation from the safety (and mundane toil) of a domestic life to which she halfheartedly returns "almost morning." Beyond this scant description Dickinson seems reluctant to disclose more to her reader ("but not to illustrate further I tell you I have been dreaming"), and we must ask ourselves why. The only logical answer again has to do with the developing poet's perceived perspective in regard to her audience. If Dickinson conceives of her reader as one still clinging to the ark of safety in this letter, then she presents herself, by contrast, as a kind of enfant terrible wandering freely in forbidden groves. Yet her restraint in divulging the details of her golden dream derives not so much from a personal fear of uttering minor heresies as from a reluctance to drive away, finally, a reader whose presence has already been notionally diminished to a "long lingering look" as it is. Further exposition in this instance would only hasten the inevitable, a total break with the actual reader, rather than her gradual displacement by an imagined absentee listener. This situation puts Dickinson into a rhetorical double bind, and thus she makes one final appeal to the estranged reader's abiding piety:

> Where are you now Abiah, where are your thoughts, and aspirings, where are your young affections, not with the *boots,* and *whiskers;* any with *me* ungrateful, *any* tho' drooping, dying? I presume you are loving your mother, and loving the stranger, and wanderer, visiting the poor, and afflicted, and reaping whole fields of blessings. Save me a *little* sheaf—only a very little one! Remember, and care for me sometimes, and scatter a fragrant flower in this wilderness life of mine by writing me, and by not forgetting, and by lingering longer in prayer, that the Father may bless one more!

Her implied farewell is once again unmistakable here ("Remember, and care for me sometimes"), and, to appreciate fully Dickinson's absolute renunciation of the life of Christian servitude used to portray Abiah in this passage, we need only recall a letter written five months earlier to Jane Humphrey. After facetiously remarking on the recommencement of the local philanthropic "Sewing Society," Dickinson boasts of her own refusal to participate: "I am already set down as one of those brands almost consumed—and my hardheartedness gets me many prayers."[17] Viewed together, the statement to Jane and her closing remarks to Abiah mark the extent of Dickinson's withdrawal from that community of professed believers *before* she reached her twenties. Thus, it is less with an air of sentimentality than with a sense of resolve regarding the choice she has made that Dickinson bids her absent (but scrupulously orthodox) reader well, and we should hear overtones of the "ubi sunt" motif in her concluding "Where are you now Abiah," rather than an earnest plea for the physical return of her departed friend. If the actual Abiah Root is absent in this scenario, it is because Emily Dickinson is leaving her far behind.

Still, throughout these letters Dickinson keeps calling herself back, as it were, to her fading reader's image and to a time when spiritual communion seemed possible between them. Beneath an undeniable nostalgia for the "sad times, sweet times" of childhood, however, lies an unsettling awareness of the growing separation between writer and reader that Dickinson repeatedly dramatizes in her writing while simultaneously striving to overcome it. This strategy receives full exposition in the letter Dickinson writes to her former classmate upon the death of their headmaster, Leonard Humphrey. In it she depicts herself as a "grandame . . . banding my silver hairs," while she portrays Abiah riding "rocking-horses in your present as in young sleeps—quite a pretty contrast indeed." Absent both in time and space, the reader once more becomes the object of the writer's quest, as inaccessible, perhaps, as the departed Humphrey himself:

> Where *are* you, my *antique* friend, or my very dear and young one . . . it *may* seem quite a presumption that I address you at all, knowing not if you habit here, or if my "bird has flown" in which world her wing is folded. When I think of the friends I love, and the little while we may dwell here, and then "we go away," I have a yearning feeling, a desire eager and anxious lest any be stolen away, so that I cannot behold them. I would have you here, all here, where I can *see* you, and *hear* you, and where I can say "Oh, no," if the "Son of Man" ever "cometh"![18]

Implicit in this letter is a progressive chain of analogies related to audience. In the first, between Humphrey's death and Abiah's absence, the loss of her former headmaster spurs Dickinson into a more profound contemplation of Abiah's remoteness. Both of her childhood friends have become unavailable in a mutually illustrative way, it seems. Indeed, Dickinson can no longer attest with certainty that her immediate correspondent even inhabits this world any longer. Pondering the inevitable loss of all the friends she loves, Dickinson next relates her awareness of absence to an anxious desire to have them all here—that is, to have all of her absent friends present in front of her. Since this sentiment expresses essentially the same "childish" hope Dickinson later voices to Mary Bowles, we can assume that even at this early stage the developing poet was aware of its futility. Simply put, people die and people go away over time. For Dickinson the response was to seek fulfillment by creating a new category of analogous presence that, rather than denying the death or absence of others, absolutely depended upon it:

> It is not enough, now, and then, at long and uncertain intervals to hear you're alive and well. I do not care for the body, I love the timid soul, the blushing, shrinking soul; it hides, for it is afraid . . . We are very small, Abiah—I think we grow still smaller—this tiny, insect life the portal to another; it seems strange—strange indeed.[19]

Only by imaginatively projecting herself and her reader beyond the portal of bodily life can Dickinson achieve the sought-after communion. She strives toward her end through a process of diminution, which effectively refines both writer and reader out of physical existence but into the spiritual essences that enable the rhetorical transactions of the later poems to remain plausible. Turning her back on such publicly agreed-upon categories as physical presence, the developing artist is forced to create and internalize an essential spiritual presence she can engage as audience. A comic articulation of this strategy occurs in Poem 288:

> I'm Nobody! Who are you!
> Are you—Nobody—Too?
> Then there's a pair of us!
> Don't tell! they'd advertise—you know!
>
> How dreary—to be—Somebody!
> How public—like a Frog—
> To tell one's name—the livelong June—
> To an admiring Bog!

On the face of it a Nobody addressing Nobody may sound like "the quality of silly playfulness" that Yvor Winters found so regrettable in Dickinson's style.[20] In the context of Dickinson's letters to Abiah Root, however, this concept appears an inevitable conclusion to a sequence of conspicuously frustrating attempts to locate her actual reader. Their continual "growing away from each other" in one sense must have sorely underlined the aspiring poet's need for a suitable audience to provide the desired "bond of spirit" so many of her later poems sought. But Dickinson triumphed in one respect by growing away from Abiah and turning to her golden dream of a place in which the absent reader was a tangible asset,

renunciation a "piercing Virtue." The losses of Leonard Humphrey and
Abiah Root (followed later by those of Ben Newton and, in a significant
sense, Susan Gilbert Dickinson) were no doubt substantial personal set-
backs in Dickinson's life. Yet Dickinson's ability not only to cope with
loss but also to transform it into a prerequisite for artistic growth remains
a lasting testament to her resourcefulness and a significant aspect of her
achievement. The most elaborate articulation of this process occurs in a
letter to Susan Gilbert, dated 1854 by Johnson. It shows the poet's grow-
ing confidence in her own antinomian powers and, in a sense, indicates
where the relationship with Abiah was heading as well:

> Sue—you can go or stay—There is but one alternative—We differ
> often lately, and this must be the last.
>
> You need not fear to leave me lest I should be alone, for I often
> part with things I fancy I have loved,—sometimes to the grave, and
> sometimes to an oblivion rather bitterer than death—thus my heart
> bleeds so frequently that I shant mind the hemorrhage, and I only
> add an agony to several previous ones, and at the end of day
> remark—a bubble burst!
>
> Such incidents would grieve me when I was but a child, and
> perhaps I could have wept when little feet hard by mine, stood still
> in the coffin, but eyes grow dry sometimes, and hearts get crisp and
> tinder, and had as lief burn.
>
> Sue—I have lived by this. It is the lingering emblem of the Heaven I
> once dreamed, and though if this is taken, I shall remain alone, and
> though in that last day, the Jesus Christ you love, remark he does not
> know me—there is a darker spirit will not disown it's child.
>
> Few have been given me, and if I love them so, that for *idolatry*,
> they are removed from me—I simply murmur *gone*, and the billow
> dies away into the boundless blue, and no one knows but me, that
> one went down today.[21]

Her situation in this regard was not vastly different from that articu-
lated by Wallace Stevens in "The Snow Man," whose chilly listener
finally becomes less absorbed with the "Nothing that is not there," than
with "the nothing that *is*" (my emphasis). Dickinson's "unreconciled
spirit," launched on its own epistemological voyage, would continue to
articulate the discoveries of its experience, even though it seemed cut off
by the inevitability of death and absence from reaching a sympathetic

audience this side of the grave. She confronted the problem by attempt-
ing to free herself from a restraining dependence on the actual presence
(and approval) of her childhood friends and by communicating in the
aftermath of their separation with her "timid soul," which quite literally
for the developing artist amounted to addressing "No-body."

It does not necessarily follow, however, that, in renouncing her
bodily audience and embarking on what seems like a solipsistic quest,
Dickinson intended to remain impenetrable to her later readers. That she
departs from a world of commonplace assumptions and material reality
cannot be questioned, but, by leaving a written record of her journey in
the letters and, more deliberately, in the poems, Dickinson is leaving the
door ajar for the competent navigator, implicit in each of the texts, to
recreate and individualize an essential experience. Her oft-quoted injunc-
tion to Abiah suggests this potential: "The shore is safer, Abiah, but I
love to buffet the sea—I can count the bitter wrecks here in these pleasant
waters, and hear the murmuring winds, but oh, I love the danger!"[22] Of
course, the ultimate danger for a developing writer lies in the threat of
becoming incomprehensible and thus totally cut off from the solid
ground offered by Abiah, in this instance, or by whatever potential audi-
ence might accurately be depicted as hugging the shore of safe, common-
place assumptions and untested, conventional beliefs. Yet it is also impor-
tant to note that, while the apostrophe to Abiah in this passage consigns
her *to* the shore of safety, thereby serving as yet one more distancing
device between writer and audience, *implicit* in the fundamentally unflat-
tering portrayal of the reader is a challenge for her to relinquish her hold
on that shore and, following Dickinson's lead, to strike out on her own
imaginative quest. And, although we should not overestimate Dickin-
son's reliance on her actual friend Abiah Root accepting this challenge,
neither should we overlook the poet's presentation of her own love of
danger as exemplary for the addressed reader as well.

Dickinson's attitude toward audience in this passage might be in-
structively compared with Mark Harris's well-known dictum in his essay
"Easy Does It Not": "I write. Let the reader learn to read."[23] Harris goes
on to explain the modern novelist's studied ambivalence toward audience
not in terms that solipsistically deny the mundane reader's capacity for
understanding but, rather, in terms that demand the reader expand her or
his capacity in order to measure up to the imaginative experience the
writer sets forth: "I must be as skillful as I can. I am obliged to be the best
craftsman I can be. I must be free to choose my subject and my language,

and I am at liberty to experiment, to grow, to express, if need be, the complexity of my experience with whatever resources are at hand." What Harris demands, then, much like Dickinson in the preceding century, is a reader possessed of the same openness to experience as the writer, the same daring, and at least a comparable degree of imaginative resourcefulness if the text is to be met on the terms of its own creation. Harris concludes his essay by calling for "people with ears to listen, people who will bring to the evening talents to challenge our own, who will work as goddam hard to read as we work to write."

Such an adventurous, self-reliant reader was unavailable to Emily Dickinson during her formative period (as it was to Poe and Hawthorne the generation before her), and so she would end up working double time in a sense, not by doing her reader's work for her (a practice abjured by Harris) but, instead, by continuing to formulate poems that *implied* a reader "with talents to challenge [her] own" and then dramatizing epistemological experiences to test the limits of those talents. Renunciation of the "admiring Bog" of vulgar readers, such as the unreceptively orthodox Abiah, should be seen as a crucial step in this process. But we do well to remember that this renunciation is part of a larger rhetorical—and not strictly pathological—response to a supremely talented writer's crisis of isolation if we hope to recognize Dickinson for what she was striving to become at this time: a hardworking artist with enough daring to strike out from the shore of Calvinist orthodoxy on her own and with a linguistic genius that would provide a route of access, however challenging, for the competent reader to follow her on her journey.

Much violence has been done to Dickinson's literary reputation by those who have approached her writings with the tacit assumption that they never finally transcend the merely personal. As a result, letters like those we have been examining to Abiah Root (or, more significantly, later letters to Susan Gilbert Dickinson and Kate Anthon) and poems such as "I'm Nobody! Who are you!" fall prey to analysis as expositions of the poet's personality disorders. Weisbuch suggests, on the other hand, that there often occurs between selected letters and individual poems that follow a "transformation of personal experiences into archetypal autobiography."[24] This transformation is precisely what we observe when we read "I'm Nobody! Who are You!" through the lens provided by Dickinson's letter to Abiah Root upon the death of Leonard Humphrey. In a strictly symbolic sense the poem has little, if anything, to do with Humphrey's death—or even with Dickinson's response to that event. Yet

Dickinson's letters to Abiah Root, when read together, present an arche-typal pattern that we can recognize as the poet's eternal quest for an audience, and, further, the letter on Humphrey's death in this context depicts a stage in the pattern that becomes dramatized in Poem 288 as a rhetorical relationship in which Nobody speaks to nobody.

All of this suggests that we should give greater emphasis to those rhetorical, rather than strictly personal, aspects of the letters and treat the correspondence in general, but especially the early correspondence, as a kind of writer's workshop in which the developing artist would likely experiment with her persona, formulate a durable reader-writer relation-ship, and sample various images and image clusters that might then reemerge meaningfully in the poems.[25] To demonstrate that Dickinson saw her correspondence as just such a workshop, we need look no further than her final few letters to Abiah Root, which, while they relinquished her need for a personal reunion with her old friend, reasserted a compen-sating vision of faith in spiritual reunions occurring in the beyond that could potentially bridge the gap between the aspiring poet and her absent reader.

The fact that Dickinson wrote only three more letters to Abiah Root between August 1851 and May 1852 before sending her final farewell over two years later, in July 1854, is all the evidence we need to conclude the personal friendship was running its course. It is equally clear that Abiah's elusiveness was becoming aesthetically problematic for Dickin-son, a type of that profounder transience and denied access haunting so many of the later poems. In the first place this elusiveness was becoming habitual. "you have the funniest manner of popping into town, and the most *lamentable* manner of popping *out* again of any one I know."[26] More significantly, Dickinson perceives a connection between what she terms her correspondent's "evanescence" and her own search for an "*enduring treasure*" of presence, which she was sadly discovering could only be found by looking elsewhere:

> It would seem my dear Abiah that out of all the moments crowding this little world a *few* might be vouchsafed to spend with those we love—a *separated* hour—an hour more pure and true than *ordinary* hours, when we could *pause* a moment before we journey on . . . Dont you think sometimes these brief imperfect meetings have a tale to tell—perhaps but for the sorrow which accompanies *them* we

would not be reminded of brevity and change—and would build the dwelling *earthward* whose site is in the skies—perhaps the treasure *here* would be *too dear* a treasure.

The brevity and imperfection of a recent face-to-face meeting with Abiah (she had been in Amherst for the college commencement) now serves as a memento mori for the developing writer, who is learning to subdue her desire for a "treasure *here*" and to set her sights *beyond* for fulfillment. Once eagerly sought after, those few vouchsafed moments of extraordinarily intense intimacy now serve in an essentially negative capacity: they teach Dickinson what *not* to value too much. That she had been expecting too much from Abiah as a friend and spiritual confidante is clear even from her earliest letters. This passage reveals just how far Dickinson has progressed from an overreliance on their primarily "earthward" relationship to a patterned use of renunciation as a means of achieving the proper perspective on all relationships this side of the grave.

Yet none of this distancing should obscure for us the persistence with which Dickinson returned to the theme of spiritual reunions throughout her final letters to Abiah Root. It would simply be erroneous to imply that Dickinson used renunciation as a final response to the dilemma of unsatisfactory reception in her writing. Even at this early stage in the poet's development she was acquiring enough discipline as a writer to sublimate her personal disappointment over Abiah's vacillations into a higher quest for fulfillment beyond the harassing realities of time and physical separation. It is in the process of imaginatively pursuing that quest that the aspiring poet transforms her elusive personal friend into a type of absentee reader and spiritual charge simultaneously: "I hope no change or time shall *blight* these loves of ou[r]'s, I would bear them all in my arms to my home in the glorious heaven and say, 'here am I my Father, and those whom thou hast given me.' " For the remainder of this letter Dickinson focuses her attention on the reader's "*eternal* feelings" ("how things *beyond* are to you"), closing with an imaginative excursion into Paradise, which, she later acknowledges, in Poem 370, "is so far of the Mind" but which also, when experienced jointly and intimately through the transient medium of language, could dissolve the barrier of absence and approximate immortality:

Shall it always be so Abiah—is there no *longer* day given for our communion with the spirits of our love?—writing is brief and fleeting—conversation will come again, yet if it *will,* it hastes and must be on it's way—earth is short Abiah, but Paradise is *long* there must be many moments in an eternal day—then *sometime we* shall tarry, while time and tide *roll on,* and till then Vale!

Within the short compass of this astonishing paragraph Dickinson transforms the frustrating imperfections of earthly love into an assurance of "that diviner thing," as she terms heavenly love in Poem 673, while bidding farewell to a personal friend who has disappointed her all the while. Consequently, the passage offers, in capsule summary, the progress of Dickinson's relationship as a writer with the only known audience available to her for the entire extent of those crucial formative years before she began gathering the poems into packets.

Dickinson adds what seem to be the finishing touches to her mature conception of audience in the next letter to Abiah Root by articulating a remarkable pattern of images that would recur in two poems on audience composed at least thirteen and twenty-seven years later, respectively. Departing for a six-month visit to Philadelphia, Abiah has failed to pay her friend a good-bye visit. Dickinson begins the letter by reasserting "the links which bind us to each other, and make the very thought of you, and time when I last saw you, a sacred thing to me."[27] After imaginatively embracing her departed reader with "a vine of fancies, towards which dear Abiah sustains the part of oak," Dickinson hints at the poetics of "faith" that was to become the crowning achievement of her artistic maturity: "as up each sturdy branch there climbs a little tendril so full of faith and confidence and the most holy trust, so let the hearts do also, of the dear 'estray'; then the farther we may be from home and from each other, the nearer by that faith which 'overcometh all things' and bringeth us to itself." As her slightly muddled allusion to the First Epistle of John suggests, by faith alone can Dickinson's alienated spirit hope to achieve victory over time, space, and the potential horrors of its own isolation. And yet this is not an easy victory for the writer still encumbered with an actual correspondent who in fact remains indifferent:

Amherst and Philadelphia, separate indeed, and yet how near, bridged by a thousand trusts and a "thousand times ten thousand" the travellers who cross, whom you and I may not see, nor hear the trip of their feet, yet faith tells us they are there, ever crossing and recrossing. Very likely, Abiah, you fancy me at home in my little

chamber, writing you a letter, but you are greatly mistaken. I am on
the blue Susquehanna paddling down to you; I am not much of a
sailor, so I get along rather slowly, and I am not much of a mermaid,
though I verily think I shall be, if the tide overtakes me at my present
jog. Hard-hearted girl! I don't believe you care, if you did you
would come quickly and help me out of this sea; but if I drown,
Abiah, and go down to dwell in the seaweed forever and forever, I
will not forget your name, nor all the wrong you did me!

Two things strike us about this passage in relation to Dickinson's
mature artistic vision. In the first place, as has already been noted, its
tone, imagery, and essential theme are nearly identical to "Faith—is the
Pierless Bridge" and "How brittle are the Piers," presenting faith as a
transcendent virtue, capable at once of overcoming the infinite distance
and the compelling loneliness separating the questing spirit from its de-
sired object. It is a virtue Dickinson applies to both imaginative and
spiritual ends, however, not only bridging the gap between the hearts
and minds of the distant correspondents but also sweeping them up into
an overwhelming pilgrimage of countless other invisible questers as they
silently cross that profounder gap between this world and the next. Here,
then, is the confluence of heart, mind, and spirit that best defines fulfill-
ment for the mature Emily Dickinson.

   Yet it is but a momentary fulfillment, and the second thing to strike
us about this passage is the stunning abruptness with which Dickinson
shifts from her rhapsodic vision of faith to anxiety about her reader's
callous reception. Renunciation, division, and bitterness mark her tone as
she accuses Abiah of a fatal indifference to her needs as a friend and, at
least implicitly, to her goals as a writer. We can see Dickinson, the aspir-
ing writer, doing all the groundwork in this fascinating passage—
building bridges, paddling down rivers, laboriously struggling to close
the gap between herself and her reader—only to realize that Abiah will
not hold up her side of the bargain:

Why did you go away and not come to see me? I felt so sure you
would come, because you promised me, that I watched and waited
for you, and bestowed a tear or two upon my absentee . . . perhaps,
my dear Abiah, it is well that I go without it; it might have added
anguish to our long separation, or made the miles still longer which
keep a friend away. I always try to think in any disappointment that

had I been gratified, it had been sadder still, and I weave from such suppositions, *at times,* considerable consolation; consolation upside down as I am pleased to call it.

This passage represents the culmination of Dickinson's uneasy adjustment to the vacillations of Abiah's friendship and presence. Denied a final face-to-face interview, Dickinson comforts herself with the paradoxical assumption that Abiah's physical presence somehow would have proven an outright hindrance to her imaginative communion with the absentee reader she would later seek to recall. For Dickinson the poet "consolation upside down" was to become much more than a method of equivocating over disappointing personal relationships. It would become part of the larger set of aesthetic assumptions involving faith in a world unseen, a compelling desire to render that world accessible through language, and a subsequent need to share that access intimately with a reader who had been left behind. This was a world of essence, however, and, as Sewall has told us, essence for Emily Dickinson required absence. By relinquishing her hold on the actual flesh-and-blood Abiah Root, the incipient poet could ensure a conjectured presence in the aftermath, which she would address as "my absentee." Thus, we have the spiritual, aesthetic, and rhetorical rationale for Dickinson's use of renunciation in her life and in her life's work.

Although she writes Abiah Root one more letter in May 1852 before her final "Vale" over two years later, the tone is decidedly restrained: "You and I have grown older since school-days, and our years have made us soberer."[28] Gone is the urgency giving the earlier letters to Abiah all of their vitality. Nonetheless, what Dickinson carries from this personally frustrating early relationship into the years of her artistic maturity is an image, the "long lingering look" of an absentee reader, and a rhetorical relationship she struggled to sustain with that reader, one that would reemerge in many of her later poems.

It has been persuasively argued that Emily Dickinson's poetic style does not evince a discernable pattern of development, and this is true inasmuch as we find it difficult to discuss her career in the convenient terminology of an early, a middle, or a late period.[29] This difficulty should not preclude us from examining whatever remains of her written record *prior* to the years when she began collecting her poetry into packets, however, if for no other reason than to consider the kinds of relational difficulties that would characteristically absorb the developing writer's interest. Although, as Dickinson's editors and biographers are quick to remind us, that record remains woefully incomplete, there are areas, such as her correspondence with Abiah Root, that are surprisingly abundant. There we discover a writer who, from her mid-teens, demonstrated a passionate interest in the capacities of language and the imagination to evoke a sense of presence in the wake of personal loss and absence. As a developing poet, Dickinson strove to exploit the restorative capacity of language to its fullest and to achieve a communion of feelings both frank and intimate in the process. Abiah's personal betrayal of that intimacy, rather than stifling the incipient poet in her quest, diverted her genius into a complex linguistic experiment whereby she would distance herself by renouncing her childhood friend (there are an extraordinary number of farewells in their correspondence) while developing a compensating vision of faith in reunions beyond. In this sense we could say Dickinson disembodied her actual reader in the process of attempting to create a more stable spiritual essence, which she began to address in these revealing early letters; it is often some more refined version of this essence that serves as a silent auditor in many of the nearly eighteen hundred poems to follow.

Once achieved, this stable absentee reader would actually liberate Emily Dickinson to depart *inward* to her own epistemological wilderness on a quest of enormous daring and complexity, but the process of reformulating a viable presence out of the gap left by her actual friend's departure was fraught with conflicting emotions for her. Dickinson apparently learned quite early that courting the spiritual freedom she so enjoyed (and required) also meant courting alienation. Her final letters to Abiah Root reveal an awareness of this dilemma, both in the uneasiness with which they treat the subject of her reader's "evanescence" and in the ambivalence of her term for the necessary process of renunciation—consolation upside down. Still, as troubling as the anguish of alienation was for Emily Dickinson, she obviously found the potential for a compensating spiritual communion inspiring enough to produce one of this nation's two major bodies of poems.

NOTES

1. Weisbuch, *Emily Dickinson's Poetry* (Chicago: University of Chicago Press, 1975), 59. For another discussion of Dickinson's biographical "doubleness,"

see Sewall, *The Life of Emily Dickinson*: "It should come as no surprise by now that there are at least two Emily Dickinsons. There may in fact be as many as there are biographers, but for expository purposes at this juncture, two will do" (532).

2. See *The Letters of Emily Dickinson*, ed. Thomas H. Johnson and Theodora Ward, 3 vols. (Cambridge: Harvard University Press, 1958; hereafter: *Letters*) 1: 32–33. Johnson notes, "The circle of five girls to whom she refers include, beside herself, Abiah Root, Abby Wood, Harriet Merrill, and Sarah Tracy." No letters are extant between Dickinson and any of the others among "the five."

3. *Letters*, 1:18.

4. *Letters*, 2:358.

5. *Letters*, 1:19.

6. *Letters*, 1:21.

7. Sewall, *Life of Emily Dickinson*, 380.

8. *Letters*, 1:60.

9. *Letters*, 1:66.

10. Kenneth Burke, *Counter-Statement* (Berkeley: University of California Press, 1968), 142–43.

11. *Letters*, 1:71.

12. Sewall, *Life of Emily Dickinson*, 617–18.

13. Sewall, *Life of Emily Dickinson*, 382–85. Actually, Sewall allows that the letters following October 1848 represent some of Dickinson's "most daring experiments in style," but he seems to be dating them from "the Mount Holyoke period" (September 1847–August 1848).

14. *Letters*, 1:86–89.

15. Porter, *Dickinson: The Modern Idiom* (Cambridge: Harvard University Press, 1981), 9.

16. *Letters*, 1:99.

17. *Letters*, 1:84.

18. *Letters*, 1:103.

19. *Letters*, 1:103–4.

20. Yvor Winters, "Emily Dickinson and the Limits of Judgment," in *Emily Dickinson: A Collection of Critical Essays*, ed. Richard Sewall (Englewood Cliffs, N.J.: Prentice-Hall, 1963), 29. This phrase appears quite early in the essay, as part of his savage attack on poem 585, "I like to see it lap the Miles—": "The poem is abominable; and the quality of silly playfulness which renders it abominable is diffused more or less perceptibly throughout most of her work, and this diffusion is facilitated by the limited range of her metrical schemes."

21. *Letters*, 1:305–6.

22. *Letters*, 1:104.

23. Mark Harris, "Preface: Easy Does It Not," *A Ticket for a Seamstitch* (Lincoln: University of Nebraska Press, 1984), xix.

24. Weisbuch, *Emily Dickinson's Poetry*, 43. Weisbuch's example for "archetypal

autobiography" is his perceived connection between a letter to Austin (letter 42), describing her father's wrath at her arriving home at 9 P.M., and Poem 207, "Tho' I get home how late—how late—," written several years later.

25. A still useful study that establishes the importance of Dickinson's "formative years" is David Porter's first book, *The Art of Emily Dickinson's Early Poetry* (Cambridge: Harvard University Press, 1964). Porter's aim is to plot "the boundary of the developmental period in her career and [discover] the early stylistic habits that equipped her for the enormous flood of poetry in the year 1862 and after" (ix). He concludes the opening chapter asserting that, by the time Dickinson corresponded with Higginson in 1862, "in her own mind certainly, the formative period had . . . reached an end" (15).

26. *Letters*, 1:129–31.

27. *Letters*, 1:166–67.

28. *Letters*, 1:206–7.

29. The two chief proponents of this view are Charles Anderson (*Emily Dickinson's Poetry: Stairway of Surprise* [Garden City, N.Y.: Doubleday, 1966], x–xi) and, surprisingly, Porter himself (*Dickinson*, 5, 184, and passim). For another study that attempts to chart different phases or stages in the poet's career, see Greg Johnson, *Emily Dickinson: Perception and the Poet's Quest* (Tuscaloosa: University of Alabama Press, 1985).

Homoeroticism and Audience:
Emily Dickinson's Female "Master"

Betsy Erkkila

I could not find a *chink* to put the worthy pastor; when he said "Our Heavenly Father," I said "My Darling Sue"; when he read the 100th Psalm, I kept saying your precious letter all over to myself, and Susie, when they sang—it would have made you laugh to hear one little voice, piping to the departed. I made up words and kept singing how I loved you, and you had gone, while all the choir were singing Hallelujahs. I presume nobody heard me, because I sang *so small,* but it was a kind of comfort to think I might put them out, singing of you.

—Emily Dickinson to Susan Gilbert (Dickinson), 1852

"What if the 'goods' refused to go to market?" asks Luce Irigaray in "Des marchandises entre elles" ("Female Commodities among Themselves"). Reflecting on the use of women as objects of mediation, exchange, and transference between men in a patriarchal and ultimately homosexual economy, Irigaray wonders: "What if they maintained among themselves 'another' kind of trade?" (1985, 196). Emily Dickinson's interaction with a select circle of female friends was her means of refusing to go to market. Getting the goods together in a separate community of female language and desire, Dickinson sought to maintain among women another kind of trade. Dickinson's community of women included her sister, Lavinia, and her sister-in-law, Susan Gilbert Dickinson; her childhood friends Abiah Root, Abby Wood, Emily Fowler Ford, and Jane Humphrey; and later her friend Elizabeth Holland and her cousins Louise and Frances Norcross.

At a time when women were subject to the authority of the father in the home, legally "covered" in marriage, and deprived of citizenship and political being under the Constitution of the United States, Dickinson's exchanges with women appear to have served the same function as gift giving in earlier societies, creating a noninstitutionalized form of social commerce that affirmed the social being and solidarity of women even as it became the site of competition, rivalry, and contest.[1] With her female friends Dickinson shared a culture of affection and dissidence, of writing and exchanging "papers," of gardening, secrets, and a joyous irreverence toward male law. "How many knights are slain and wounded, and how many now remain," she asks Jane Humphrey. "Keep a list of the conquests, Jennie, this is an *enemy's* Land!"[2] It is in her correspondence with women that we first hear the transgressive witch voice—the heh! heh! heh!—that would become the high tone of her poems. "I have lately come to the conclusion that I am Eve, alias Mrs. Adam," she wrote to Abiah Root in 1846. "You know there is no account of her death in the Bible, and why am not I Eve?" (*L* 1:24).

Among Dickinson's "bright circle" of female friends it was Sue Gilbert more than any other who was the presiding presence in the birth chambers of her poetic art. Having said this, one is immediately struck by the extent to which speculations about the male "Master" and narratives of heterosexual love still dominate critical interpretations of Dickinson's life and work. Critics endlessly debate which of a number of male figures—Charles Wadsworth, Samuel Bowles, Otis Lord, or God himself—played the commanding role in Dickinson's life. To get this Master plot, Dickinson's central and troubled love relationship with her sister-in-law, Susan Gilbert Dickinson, has been by turns erased, mutilated, demonized, and sentimentalized in the history of Dickinson scholarship. Dickinson's brother, Austin, quite literally erased and scissored out references to Sue in the correspondence he presented to his lover, Mabel Loomis Todd, who along with Thomas Higginson undertook to "edit" Dickinson's poetry and correspondence after her death.[3] According to Todd's daughter, Millicent Todd Bingham: "Mr. Dickinson stipulated that if Emily's letters to him were to be used, the name of one of her girlhood friends must be left out—that of Susan Gilbert—his wife. But omitting her name was not enough. Before turning over the letters he went through them, eliminating Susan Gilbert's name and in some instances making alterations to disguise a reference to her" (Bingham 1955, 54). Austin's attempt literally to cut Dickinson's intense and life-long love relationship with Susan Gilbert out of her life story might itself be read as part of the history of modern homosexuality, which began to emerge as a concept, a type, and a pathology among European sexologists in the late nineteenth century, at about the same that Dickinson's poetry and her correspondence were being edited and prepared for general circulation by friends and family.[4]

While Austin sought to cut out or cover over his sister's passionate references to his wife, after Susan's death in 1913 she was demonized by local Amherst society as a dark lady and a villain. Lavinia's friend Mary Lee Hall says she told her that "Sue had been cruel to Emily and herself, and they each had suffered keenly from her insincerities, her insane jealousies, as well as her intentional deceit" (qtd. in Sewall 1974, 256). According to Mabel Loomis Todd, Susan was "quite generally disliked and thoroughly distrusted" (278). Elaborating upon her mother's version of Sue as a lower-class woman who married above her station, Bingham calls her "a relentless alien," "a low being, the daughter of a stable keeper whom the Squire had married by mistake" (260, 300).[5] Referring to her as "Satan, or Sue," Mary Lee Hall wrote: "You cannot imagine such a fiend, for Sue could appear like 'an angel of light,' when it served her purpose to do so" (261). To Sarah Tuckerman, whose husband taught at Amherst College, Susan and her daughter Martha Dickinson [Bianchi] were "the two black devils" (256).

In *The Life and Letters of Emily Dickinson* (1924) Bianchi seeks to counter these negative versions of her mother with a story of her own, a carefully "edited" and sentimentalized version of the relationship between Dickinson and Sue as an idyllic friendship between sisters. In the last decade feminist critics, following Rebecca Patterson's lead and Adrienne Rich's call for a revisionary look at "intense woman-to woman-relationships" as "a central element in Dickinson's life and art" (1978, 157), have begun to break the historical and literary silence surrounding Dickinson's relationship with Sue Gilbert. But, in their attempt to enact and enforce a feminist and at times utopian model of loving sisterhood, these critics have also tended to romanticize the relationship between Dickinson and Gilbert, covering over the difference, the pain, and the "bladed" words that were also part of their love.[6]

Although the stories about Sue's cruelty and duplicity may not be true, they do suggest something of the role she played not only for the townspeople but also for Dickinson herself, as the "torrid Spirit," "Siren," and "Stranger" through whom and against whom she defined herself. It is Sue's story, finally, that never gets told. What we do know is that the "War Between the Houses" was a war between women, a war that had as its site and center the volcanic and transgressive love relationship between Dickinson and Sue.

Susan Gilbert arrived back in Amherst in 1848, after completing her formal schooling, and there is evidence that at some time in their late teens or early twenties she and Dickinson began writing poetry together. We "please ourselves with the fancy that we are the only poets, and everyone else is *prose*," Dickinson wrote to Sue in October 1851 (*L* 1:144). Sometime around March 1853 she sent Sue one of her first poems—"On this wondrous sea"—preceded with the injunction "*Write! Comrade, write!*" (1:206). The same month, in a letter to her brother, Austin, she made her first overt announcement of her own literary ambitions. Teasing her "Brother Pegasus" about the poem he enclosed in a letter to her, she says: "I'll tell you what it is—I've been in the habit *myself* of writing some few things, and it rather appears to me that you're getting away my patent, so you'd better be somewhat careful, or I'll call the police!" (1:235).

By the early 1850s Dickinson came to equate what she called "*real life*" with the world of the fathers. "We do not have much poetry," Dickinson wrote to Austin in 1851, "father having made up his mind that its pretty much all *real life*. Fathers real life and *mine* sometimes come into collision, but as yet, escape unhurt!" (*L* 1:161). Dickinson was aided in the process of resisting her father's "*real*" and discovering the sources of her own creative power by her passionate and erotically intense love relationship with Sue Gilbert. "Susie, will you indeed come home next Saturday, and be my own again, and kiss me as you used to?" she wrote in June 1852, when Sue was teaching in Baltimore. "I hope for you so much, and feel so eager for you, feel that I *cannot* wait, feel that *now* I must have you—that the expectation once more to see your face again, makes me feel hot and feverish, and my heart beats so fast—" (1:215).

When Dickinson speaks her desire in her correspondence with Sue, language breaks down. She speaks silence—not in words but, instead, with her body.

> Susie, forgive me Darling, for every word I say—my heart is full of you, none other than you in my thoughts, yet when I seek to say to you something not for the world, words fail me. If you were here— and Oh that you were, my Susie, we need not talk at all, our eyes would whisper for use, and your hand fast in mine, we would not ask for language. (*L* 1:211–12)

In her attempt to express what had been unnamed and unrepresented by her culture Dickinson's letters to Sue, like her letters to her other female friends, begin to speak the elliptical, hyperbolic, densely figural language of her verse. In fact, as their relationship grew, Dickinson's letters to Sue became shorter and shorter, until finally, in the last few decades of her life, the letters, and indeed the poems to Sue, have all the quality of cryptic code messages delivered across enemy lines.

Whether or not Dickinson's relationship with Sue was lesbian in the modern sense of the term is open to question.[7] Catharine Stimpson has argued that "lesbianism partakes of the body, partakes of the flesh. That carnality distinguishes it from gestures of political sympathy with homosexuals and from affectionate friendships in which women enjoy each other, support each other, and commingle a sense of identity and well-being. Lesbianism represents a commitment of skin, blood, breast, and bone" (1981, 364). In its early phases, at least, Dickinson's relationship with Sue had a physical dimension, but by the mid-1860s their relationship was carried on largely through writing and most often through poems. What is apparent is that the lifelong bond between them exists within what Adrienne Rich calls the "lesbian continuum" of woman-identified existence. Dickinson's relationship with Sue Gilbert is part of the history of women who "as witches, *femmes seules,* marriage resisters, spinsters, autonomous widows, and/or lesbians—have managed on varying levels *not* to collaborate" (Rich 1980, 635). Dickinson's love for Sue was a form of saying no to the masculine and heterosexual orders of church and state in order to say yes to herself and to her own poetic creation.

After Sue joined the church in August 1850, along with Dickinson's father, Dickinson sought in erotically charged images to seduce her back into her own personal religion of female love: "The bells are ringing, Susie, north, and east, and south, and *your own* village bell, and the people who love God, are expecting to go to meeting; don't *you* go Susie, not to *their* meeting, but come with me this morning to the church within our hearts, where the bells are always ringing, and the preacher whose name is Love—shall intercede there for us!" Having refused to go to "the usual meetinghouse, to hear the usual sermon," Dickinson has "the old *king feeling*" as, in the "sweet Sabbath" of their communion, she seeks to "poeticize" the world for Sue (*L* 1:181). As Sue's "Idolater" Dickinson makes her the "Shrine" of a female-centered religion that eclipses the religion of the New England patriarchs and releases her into song.

In an 1852 letter to Sue, quoted in the epigraph, Dickinson makes her own profession of faith. Over and over in her letters and poems

Dickinson rewrites scriptural passages to express her idolatry at what she calls the "Shrine of Sue" (2:458). She counters the Calvinistic religion of the fathers with a religion of female love, and, empowered by her love for Sue, she imagines *her small* voice growing so strong that she will "put out" the voice of Calvinist patriarchy in song.

But Sue Gilbert was not only a source of love. Cultured, worldly, mercurial, and magnetically attractive, she was also a source of knowledge and power. As Richard Sewall observes, hyperbole is the ruling figure in Dickinson's correspondence with Sue: "Images of uniqueness, size, power, totality abound" (1974, 202). Under Sue's influence Dickinson discovered an elastic power that enabled her to dance "like a bomb abroad" and to dream terrorist dreams of annihilating the Puritan fathers, New England culture, and, ultimately, the entire edifice of America itself. Writing to Sue of how her " 'life' was made a 'victim' at Church meeting," Dickinson longs for the assistance of her female friends in destroying the "Phantom" that pursues her. "How I did wish for you—how, for my own dear Vinnie—how for Goliah, or Samson—to pull the whole church down" (*L* 1:284).

When her father was sent as a delegate to the Whig convention in Baltimore in 1852, she wondered why she could not be a delegate. The knowledge of her exclusion from the constituted orders of masculine political power leads her into a fantasy of destruction. "I don't like this country at all, and I shant stay here any longer! 'Delenda est' America, Massachusetts and all!" (*L* 1:212). While Sue probably did not share Dickinson's terrorist dreams of violence against state and nation, it was Dickinson's explosive and transgressive desire for Sue that called forth and validated the volcanic persona who would emerge in the poems as a "Loaded Gun" and "Vesuvius at Home."

In her multiple incarnations as "absent Lover" and a "real beautiful hero," "Imagination" and an "Avalanche of Sun," an "emblem of Heaven" and the "garden *unseen*," Susan Gilbert served finally as a bewitching muse-like presence who poeticized Dickinson's world and called forth her own art of song. "You sketch my pictures for me," Dickinson wrote Sue in 1853, "and 'tis at their sweet colorings, rather than this dim real that I am used, so you see when you go away, the world looks staringly, and I find I need more vail" (*L* 1:229). At times Sue seemed the essence at once of creation and ecstasy. "Dear Susie, when you come, how many boundless blossoms among those silent beds!" (1:208), Dickinson wrote in words that seem to bear a hidden but nonetheless self-consciously sexual nuance.

Sue's presence brings the "warm and green, and birds" of spring. When she is absent it is waste and stone (1:304).

In the poem "Dying,! Dying in the night!" it is Sue as Dollie, and not Jesus Christ, who brings salvation and light:

> And "Jesus"! Where is *Jesus* gone?
> They said that Jesus—always came—
> Perhaps he does'nt know the House—
> This way, Jesus, Let him pass!
>
> Somebody run to the great gate
> And see if Dollie's coming! Wait!
> I hear her feet upon the stair!
> Death won't hurt—now Dollie's here![8]

Experiencing herself as hungry and insufficiently nurtured by either God the Father or her biological mother, in the early stages of their relationship Dickinson turned to Sue as a compensatory source of mother religion and mother love: "Oh Susie, I would nestle close to your warm heart, and never hear the wind blow, or the storm beat again," she wrote her in the winter of 1852. "Is there any room for me there, or shall I wander away all homeless and alone?" (*L* 1:177).

From the first, however, it was Sue's role as sister rather than maternal protectress that shaped the relationship between them. This sisterly relation might, as some feminist critics have argued, appear to foreground the familial and horizontal nature of their bond, in contrast to the more hierarchical relationship of dominance and submission that characterized Dickinson's relationship with the male figures in her life and poems.[9] But, as "precious Sister," Sue was also and always not the same. If their sisterhood was marked by passionate love, it was also a scene of struggle for possession, power, and dominion.

In "One Sister have I in our house" Dickinson represents Sue as a bird whose "different tune" becomes a source of sustenance in the journey from childhood to adulthood:

> She did not sing as we did—
> It was a different tune—
> Herself to her a music
> A Bumble bee of June.

Today is far from Childhood—
But up and down the hills
I held her hand the tighter—
Which shortened all the miles—

(*P* 14)

Even in this sisterly poem of praise, however, there are ambiguous references to a "hum" that "Deceives" and eyes that "lie," references that suggest that Sue's "different tune" was also a source of tension between them.

Sue's difference was, I would argue, at least in part a difference of class and privilege. As the orphaned daughter of a tavern owner, Sue was from a lower social class than Dickinson, and thus she could not, like Dickinson, exercise the privilege of choosing not to circulate. Smart and ambitious for status and power, Sue had designs in and on the social world that placed her at odds with Dickinson's dream of an exclusive female bond. "Sue always made a point of associating principally with daughters of the better class," wrote Mabel Loomis Todd. "She was a bright girl, who knew how to put herself on confidential terms with daughters of the upper class in Amherst, and for some years she and Lavinia and Emily were trusting friends" (Sewall 1974, 282).

Having made her own profession of faith and aspiring to rise socially, Sue may have been uneasy with the urgency, intensity, and seeming irreverence of Dickinson's love. It was probably what Dickinson called her "*idolatry*" that provoked a disagreement between them sometime in the mid-1850s: "Sue—you can go or stay—," Dickinson wrote abruptly. "We differ often lately, and this must be the last." She associates the causes of their disagreement with her own private worship at the shrine of Sue: "Sue—I have lived by this. It is the lingering emblem of the Heaven I once dreamed, and though if this is taken I shall remain alone, and though in that last day, the Jesus Christ you love, remark he does not know me—there is a darker spirit will not disown it's child" (*L* 1:306).

If Dickinson was angered by the loss of Sue to Jesus Christ, there is also evidence that Sue's marriage to Austin Dickinson in 1856 may be responsible for the mysterious silence—the total absence of letters—between 1856 and 1858. During the courtship of Sue and Austin, Dickinson expressed her own ambivalence about the potentially repressive rituals of heterosexual love and marriage: "You and I have been strangely silent upon this subject, Susie," she wrote in June 1852.

How dull our lives must seem to the bride, and the plighted maiden, whose days are fed with gold, and who gathers pearls every evening; but to the *wife*, Susie, sometimes the *wife forgotten*, our lives perhaps seem dearer than all others in the world; you have seen flowers at morning, *satisfied* with the dew, and those same sweet flowers at noon with their heads bowed in anguish before the mighty sun. . . . [T]hey know that the man of noon, is *mightier* than the morning and their life is henceforth to him. Oh, Susie, it is dangerous. . . . It does so rend me, Susie, the thought of it when it comes, that I tremble lest at sometime I, too, am yielded up. (*L* 1:210)

The imagery of female flowers being dried up by the "man of noon" suggests the threat that marriage represented to Dickinson during the period of her creative growth. But the letter is more than a confession of her own fear of being "yielded up" to male power. Dickinson's sexually and hyperbolically charged language may be an attempt to seduce Sue away from the "rending" heterosexual order of the phallus and back into the "boundless blossoms" of their own female love.

In "Ourselves were wed on summer—dear—," Dickinson represents the tale of her loss of Sue to the masculine orders of religion and marriage:

Ourselves were wed one summer—dear—
Your Vision—was in June—
And when Your little Lifetime failed,
I wearied—too—of mine.

(*P* 631)

The syntactical oddness of *Ourselves* suggests the "difference" of their female marriage—the autoerotic awakening to an enriched consciousness of self that a woman can experience in loving someone who is like rather than different from herself. Dickinson's syntactical construction might be paraphrased to read: we married our selves when we married each other.

Sue's "Vision" in June appears to telescope two events: her profession of faith in August 1850 and her marriage to Austin in July 1856. Associating their relationship with the creative bloom of summer, Dickinson experiences her loss of Sue to both religion and marriage as a kind of death in which Sue's life is "yielded up" to the masculine and heterosexual orders of man and God. She overcomes her own experience of death

and waste by yielding herself not to man or God but, rather, to the
"light" and call of her poetic muse:

> And overtaken in the Dark—
> Where You had put me down—
> By Some one carrying a Light—
> I—too—received the Sign.

(P 631)

Having received the "Sign" of her poetic vocation as another kind of
religious and marital vow, Dickinson inscribes the difference of her own
life in lines that suggest both the heroism of her quest and her experience
of loss:

> 'Tis true—Our Futures different lay—
> Your Cottage—faced the sun—
> While Oceans—and the North must be—
> On every side of mine
>
> 'Tis true, Your Garden led the Bloom,
> For mine—in Frosts—was sown—
> And yet, one Summer, we were Queens—
> But You—were crowned in June—

(P 631)

Whereas Sue's life is contained within the daily social round of cottage and
sun, Dickinson lives sterile and witchlike on the margins, facing the open
space of "Oceans" and "the North." Once again Sue is associated with the
creativity and bloom of a garden, but it is a garden circumscribed by the
round of the male order signified by sun/son. The line "Your Garden led
the Bloom" may in fact refer to the birth of Sue's son, Edward, on 19 June
1861. Dickinson sows her own garden—her poems—in "Frosts" that
suggest the cold and waste of her separation from Sue, her existence on the
margins of the social world, and a barrenness that gives birth to poems
rather than children. In their separation from each other, Dickinson sug-
gests, both have lost some of the potency of their primal bond together
when they were "Queens" under another law. And, thus, the "crown" of
power that Sue receives as the Bride of Christ and man is also a crown of
limits, blows, and thorns.

This loss of the female to the law of the fathers is a central and almost obsessively recurrent motif in Dickinson's letters and later in her poems. In her very first letter to Abiah Root, written when she was fourteen, Dickinson presents herself as part of a female universe of blooming gardens and singing birds, continually embattled by a tyrannical and all-powerful masculine force: "I have heard some sweet little birds sing, but I fear we shall have more cold weather and their little bills will be frozen up before their songs are finished. My plants look beautifully. Old King Frost has not had the pleasure of snatching any of them in his cold embrace as yet, and I hope will not" (L 1:9).

Dickinson's myth of paradise was not the biblical story of Adam and Eve in Genesis but, rather, the anterior matriarchal myth of female community inscribed by the myth of Demeter and Kore. Over and over in her poems Dickinson returns to the story of a primal female bond ruptured by the intrusion of a Plutonian figure in the shape of man, God, or death itself. The essence of this myth of origins is contained in the following poem:

We talked as Girls do—
Fond, and late—
We speculated fair, on every subject, but the Grave—
Of our's, none affair—

We handled Destinies, as cool—
As we—Disposers—be
And God, a Quiet Party
To our Authority—

But fondest, dwelt upon Ourself
As we eventual—be—
When Girls to Women, softly raised
We—occupy—Degree—

We parted with a contract
To cherish, and to write
But Heaven made both, impossible
Before another night.

(P 586)

The poem represents a fantasy of female power in which, as in Dickinson's "Oh Darling Sue" letter, "Girl" talk silences the "Authority" of the male voice. This female contract of two as one—figured in the grammatical fracture of *Ourself*—is at once affectional and creative: "To cherish, and to write." But this primal bond is interrupted by the masculine "Authority" of "Heaven," perhaps in the form of religion, marriage, adulthood, or death.

From a psychoanalytic point of view the poem might be read as an inscription of the daughter's desire to return to what French feminists have called the body and the language of the mother. But this underlying psychic drama of Dickinson's poems also had a particular historic formation, enacting dimensions of her early relationships with her sacred band of girlfriends. As a female poet seeking to "occupy" a subject position and "Degree" in a cultural economy in which the only socially valorized route from girlhood to womanhood was through the masculine orders of religion, marriage, and motherhood, Dickinson imagines the loss of paradise not as a fall away from man or God but, instead, the loss of a specifically female bond that enabled her to achieve a sense of agency, "Authority," and voice. The female contract "To cherish, and to write" calls up even as it breaks the woman's traditional marital vow "to love, cherish, and obey" her husband and her God.

When Sue Gilbert married Austin in 1856 Dickinson lost the possibility of an exclusive female relation under another law. Insofar as the social order is, as Lévi-Strauss argues, grounded in the incest taboo and the exchange of women among men, Dickinson's own refusal to marry and her attempt to create an alternative exchange among women might be read as a gesture of political resistance, an attempt to block the cultural and social order at its very foundations. In fact, if Sue's marriage to Austin separated her from Dickinson, Sue's new status as sister-in-law also served paradoxically to reinforce Dickinson's refusal to circulate by transforming their erotic bond into an actual kinship "in law" and thus a form of incest. By ultimately strengthening the kinship between Dickinson and Sue, Sue's marriage became a rather inventive means for Dickinson to love her and to make a family with her within the conventional domestic arrangements of nineteenth-century genteel New England society. Within this familial arrangement Dickinson undertook her own form of production, articulating one possible answer to what Luce Irigaray calls "the question of what the social status of women might be—in particular through its differentiation from a simple reproductive-maternal function" (1985, 128).

After Sue's legal incorporation into the family and sometime during the mysterious break in correspondence between 1856 and 1858, Dickinson began arranging and sewing her poems into groupings that Mabel Loomis Todd called "fascicles."[10] Among Dickinson's manuscripts there are thirty-nine groupings that have been threaded and bound together and twenty-five other groupings that have not been sewn. Although Dickinson may have been preparing her poems for eventual publication, she also may have been engaged in a private form of publication. Folding, sewing, and binding four to five sheets of paper together in groupings of eighteen to twenty poems, Dickinson, in effect, converted traditional female thread-and-needle work into a different kind of housework and her own form of productive industry.

"*My* Business is to *sing*," she wrote to Elizabeth Holland during the period of her most intense poetic creation, at a time when she was seeking to articulate a valuable and productive kind of women's work that did not merely subtend the interests and orders of men. In the same letter she wrote: "Perhaps you laugh at me! Perhaps the whole United States are laughing at me too! *I* can't stop for that ! *My* business is to love" (*L* 2:413). Like such female reformers as Emma Willard and Julia Ward Howe, who sought to ground their arguments for women's education and women's suffrage in domestic ideology and traditional notions of a "woman's sphere," Dickinson seeks to justify her poetic "business" by linking it with the traditionally feminine business of affection and love.[11] But, in her attempt to legitimize her creative work and to resist the traditionally commercial business of men with her own affectional economy, Dickinson paradoxically risks reinstating the very dichotomy of male and female work that underwrites the essential illegitimacy of her business as a writing woman. This dichotomy is a point of stress in Dickinson's poems, as her speaker swings between the more conventional notion of women's art as loving and healing inscribed in the lines "If I can stop one Heart from breaking / I shall not live in vain" and a more transgressive notion of women's art as the power to wound and to kill expressed in the poem "My Life had stood—a Loaded Gun" (*P* 919, 754).

Although Susan is often criticized for failing to cooperate in Mabel Loomis Todd's project to publish Dickinson's poems, the bowdlerized version in which her *Poems* first appeared in 1890 and 1891—with Dickinson's poems neatly titled and thematicized and her fracture of meter and rhyme, grammar and syntax, carefully corrected and regularized— suggests that Sue may have had a better understanding of the kind of poetic business in which Dickinson was engaged. Although Dickinson appears to have flirted with the notion of publishing, with the exception of a few poems, she in fact never did. This refusal to publish might be read as a further gesture in her refusal to go to market. She appears to have been engaged in a kind of cottage industry, a precapitalist mode of manuscript production and circulation that avoided the commodity and use values of the commercial marketplace.

Along with the manuscripts that Dickinson produced, threaded, and bound herself, she also engaged in a further form of self-production and self-publication by enclosing and circulating her poems in letters to her friends.[12] Within this private system of publication it was Sue Dickinson who received more poems than anyone else. As the recipient of at least 276 of Dickinson's poems, Sue served over many years as the primary audience for Dickinson's work. She was the subject of several poems and the inspiration for many more, perhaps even some of the marriage and Master poems that appear to be addressed to men.

Their exchange over "Safe in their Alabaster Chambers—" around 1861 indicates that she also served, perhaps frequently, as a knowledge-able critic of Dickinson's work. Commenting on the first stanza, Sue wrote: "You never made the peer for that verse, and I *guess* you[r] king-dom does'nt hold one. I always go to the fire and get warm after thinking of it, but I never *can* again." Sue's praise fed Dickinson's own ambitions as a poet. "Your praise is good—to me—because I *know* it *knows*—and *suppose*—it *means*. Could I make you and Austin proud—sometime—a great way off—'twould give me taller feet' " (*L* 2:380). When Thomas Higginson later asked her to define poetry, she borrowed Sue's "fire and ice" response to "Safe in their Alabaster Chambers—." "If I read a book [and] it makes my whole body so cold no fire ever can warm me, I know *that* is poetry" (2:474).

As a subscriber to the *Atlantic,* Sue may have urged Dickinson to respond to Thomas Higginson's "Letter to a Young Contributor" in the spring of 1862, and it may have been Sue who prevailed upon her friend and editor of the *Springfield Republic,* Samuel Bowles, to publish five of Dickinson's poems in that journal. After "Safe in their Alabaster Chambers—" appeared in the *Springfield Republican* on 1 March 1862, Sue sent Dickinson an enthusiastic note: "*Has girl read Republican?* It takes as long to start our Fleet as the Burnside" (Leyda 1960, 2:48). The note suggests that Dickinson's poetry writing was part of a collaborative enter-prise between them and that Sue was, at least momentarily, urging Dick-inson to "launch" her work and their "Fleet" in the world.

Although critics and biographers have suggested that the relationship between Sue and Dickinson broke off or changed radically in the mid-1850s, the letters and poems that Dickinson sent her over many years suggest that their relationship never really cooled—that Sue continued as sister-spirit, witch-goddess, erotic center, and muse at the very sources of Dickinson's poetic creation. But the relationship between them was not easy, and it was never free from ambivalence, tension, and pain. This ambivalence is evident even in their exchange over "Safe in their Alabaster Chambers—." Sue's words, "You never made the peer for that verse," might also suggest that Dickinson had written only one good poem. And Dickinson's response, "Your praise is good—to me—because I *know* it *knows*—and *suppose*—it *means*—," might also suggest that she is not really sure what and if Sue's advice *means;* it might only be *mean*. When the poem was published in the *Springfield Republican* it was in fact published in Dickinson's original version, the one Sue appears to have objected to.

This double nature of their relationship is suggested by a note that Dickinson wrote to Sue in 1864. "Sweet Sue—," she wrote from Cambridge, where she was being treated for eye trouble, "There is no first, or last, in Forever—It is Centre, there, all the time. . . . [F]or the Woman whom I prefer, Here is Festival—Where my Hands are cut, Her fingers will be found inside—" (*L* 2:430). As loved one, power, and muse, Sue was the "Sister of Ophir" and the "Festival" that enabled Dickinson to overcome her sense of amputation and lack under the regime of the fathers in order to give birth to herself and her poems. But, if Dickinson's "hands-cut-fingers" image suggests Sue's agency and power, the image also suggests the intensely erotic nature of the bond between them and the potentially painful nature of that bond as a wound that never heals, a love that is never finally consummated. Sue's "fingers" inside Dickinson's "cut" hands may be a source of Festival and power, but they also keep the wound always open.

The poems that Dickinson sent to Sue or that were inspired by her—and there were probably many more of these than we think—were not only poems of love, sisterhood, power, and *jouissance*. They were also and often poems that registered a sense of separation, loss, rejection, and inexpressible pain. "You love me—you are sure—," Dickinson wrote in one of her more anxious poetic addresses to Sue as "Dollie":

Be sure you're sure—you know—
I'll bear it better now—

If you'll just tell me so—
Than when—a little dull Balm grown—
Over this pain of mine—
You sting—again!

(P 156)

If Sue offered "Sunrise" and "Balm," she also had her "sting": she could
be cool, aloof, and—if we are to believe local Amherst gossip—
cunning, cruel, arrogant, and self-serving. "She dealt her pretty words
like Blades—," Dickinson wrote, perhaps with Sue in mind (*P* 479).
But Dickinson could also be a difficult, imperious, and demanding
friend, sister, and lover, and the art of bladed words was one to which
she was herself no stranger. In fact, "She dealt her pretty words like
Blades—" could also refer to her own wounding and killing power as
poet and sister.

In her desire to secure an alternative affectional relation among
women, Dickinson was not only in some sense possessed by Sue. She
also wanted to possess her. "To own a Susan of my own," she wrote:

Is of itself a Bliss—
Whatever Realm I forfeit, Lord,
Continue me in this!

(P 1401)

Having in effect forfeited God for Sue, Dickinson never fully accepted
the fact that she did not get Sue in exchange. "But Susan is a Stranger
yet—," she said in a rewrite of the poem "What mystery pervades a
well!" which she sent to her about 1877:

To pity those who know her not
Is helped by the regret
That those who know her know her less
The nearer her they get—

(L 2:598)

For all Dickinson's dream of female oneness and possession under an-
other law, Sue remained, finally, other—"A Different Peru," as Dickin-
son said in "Your Riches—taught me Poverty," an earlier poem she
addressed to her.

But, while it is important that we recognize Sue's difference from Dickinson, and the very real differences that marked the relationship between them, it is also important to recognize the centrality of this relationship in the text of Dickinson's life and work. Despite the efforts of the Dickinson family and later critics to erase and write over the erotic traces of this relationship,[13] it was Dickinson's intense, passionate, and sometimes troubled love relationship with Sue and not her love relationship with the Master—or any of the various men who have been proposed to play that role—that was the central and enduring relationship of her life. "With the exception of Shakespeare, you have told me of more knowledge than any one living—To say that sincerely is strange praise," Dickinson wrote to Sue in 1882 (L 3:733). If she could never really "own" a Susan of her "own," she could never finally separate herself from her either. "The tie between us is very fine, but a Hair never dissolves," she wrote to Sue shortly before her death in 1886 (L 3:893). Sue was at once both "Stranger" and "Sister," a woman like herself who called forth, mirrored, and affirmed the power, the knowledge, the creation, and the transgressive desire that became finally their Fleet and part of what Dickinson called "my letter to the World / That never wrote to Me—" (P 441).

NOTES

1. For a study of the ritual of gift giving in early societies, see Mauss 1954.
2. Dickinson 1960, 2:321 (hereafter cited in the text as "L").
3. For a discussion of Austin's "work" and the attempt to erase the specifically lesbian dimensions of this relationship, see Smith 1987.
4. See, for example, Richard von Krafft-Ebing, *Psychopathia Sexualis with Especial Reference to the Antipathic Sexual Instinct,* which was originally published in Stuttgart in 1886; and Havelock Ellis, "Sexual Inversion in Women" (1895) and *Sexual Inversion* (1901). In *The History of Sexuality: An Introduction* Michel Foucault observes: "The nineteenth-century homosexual became a personage, a past, a case history, and a childhood, in addition to being a type of life, a life form, and a morphology, with an indiscreet anatomy and possibly a mysterious physiology. . . . The sodomite had been a temporary aberration; the homosexual was now a species" (43).
5. In actuality, Sue's father was the owner of a tavern and livery stable in Amherst.
6. See, for example, Faderman 1978b; Mudge 1977; and Oberhaus 1983. In "To Fill a Gap" Martha Nell Smith argues that "their relationship knew anger as well as joy, ambivalence as well as clarity in feeling," but even she suggests

that theirs was a higher because a more egalitarian kind of love. Dickinson's poems to Sue, she says, "do not reflect the hierarchy and difference of heterosexual relations, but the sameness and equality of lesbian relations" (18). Adelaide Morris makes a similar argument in " 'The Love of Thee—a Prism Be.' "

7. In her now classic article "The Female World of Love and Ritual" Carroll Smith-Rosenberg argues that in the nineteenth century American girls routinely slept together, kissed, and hugged in relationships that were emotionally and sometimes erotically intense. In *The Riddle of Emily Dickinson* Rebecca Patterson argues that repressed homosexuality is the key to Dickinson's life. For a discussion of the homoerotic dimension of Dickinson's relationship with Susan Gilbert, see Faderman 1978a and b; and Smith 1993. In *Dickinson: The Anxiety of Gender* Vivian Pollak stresses the more negative, guilt-ridden homosexual dimension of Dickinson's love relationships with women, especially Sue Gilbert (1984, 133–56).

8. Dickinson 1955, 158 (hereafter cited in the text as "*P*").

9. For a comparison of the rhetoric of Dickinson's "Master" letters and her letters and poems to Sue Gilbert, see Morris 1983.

10. In *The Poetry of Emily Dickinson* Ruth Miller argues that these groupings are bounded by imagery, theme, and mood into long link-poems that progress from "quest" to "suffering" to "resolution."

11. In fact, Dickinson appears to echo Josiah Holland's rather conventional notion of women's role: "Her mission is to love, and it argues depravity of soul when a woman pants to enter the race and contend with man in the labor of life" (cited in Peckham 1940, 55).

12. In "To Fill a Gap" Martha Nell Smith argues: "If, in fact, she devised her own method of publication, which was to send her poems out in letters, then the manuscripts themselves, not their printed versions, should be the locus of study" (3).

13. For a recent instance of this kind of homoerotic erasure, see the 1994 edition of the *Norton Anthology of American Literature,* volume 1, which includes several of Dickinson's letters to Thomas Wentworth Higginson but excludes virtually all the poems and letters that Dickinson explicitly addressed to Susan Gilbert.

WORKS CITED

Bianchi, Martha Dickinson. 1924. *The Life and Letters of Emily Dickinson.* New York: Houghton Mifflin.

Bingham, Millicent Todd. 1955. *Emily Dickinson's Home: Letters of Edward Dickinson and His Family.* New York: Harper and Brothers.

Dickinson, Emily. 1955. *The Poems of Emily Dickinson.* Ed. Thomas H. Johnson. 3 vols. Cambridge: Belknap Press of Harvard University Press.

————. 1960. *The Letters of Emily Dickinson.* Ed. Thomas H. Johnson. 3 vols. Cambridge: Belknap Press of Harvard University Press.

Ellis, Havelock. 1901. *Sexual Inversion.* Philadelphia: F. A. Davis.

————. 1895. "Sexual Inversion in Women." *Alienist and Neurologist* 16.

Faderman, Lillian. 1978a. "Emily Dickinson's Homoerotic Poetry." *Higginson Journal* 18:19–27.

Faderman, Lillian. 1978b. "Emily Dickinson's Letters to Sue Gilbert." *Massachusetts Review* 18:197–225.

Foucault, Michel. 1978 (1977). *The History of Sexuality: An Introduction.* Trans. Robert Hurley. New York: Random House.

Higginson, Thomas. 1862. "Letter to a Young Contributor." *Atlantic Monthly* 9:401–11.

Irigaray, Luce. 1985 (1977). *This Sex Which Is Not One.* Trans. Catherine Porter. Ithaca: Cornell University Press.

Krafft-Ebing, Richard von. 1908 (1886). *Psychopathia Sexualis with Especial Reference to the Antipathic Sexual Instinct.* Trans. F. J. Rebman. Brooklyn: Physicians and Surgeons Book Company.

Lévi-Strauss, Claude. 1969. *The Elementary Structures of Kinship.* Ed. Rodney Needham. Trans. James Harle Bell, John Richard von Sturmer, and Rodney Needham. Boston: Beacon Press.

Leyda, Jay. 1960. *The Years and Hours of Emily Dickinson,* 2 vols. New Haven: Yale University Press.

Mauss, Marcel. 1954. *The Gift: Forms and Functions of Exchange in Archaic Societies.* Trans. Ian Cunnison. Glencoe, Ill.: Free Press.

Miller, Ruth. 1968. *The Poetry of Emily Dickinson.* Middleton, Conn.: Wesleyan University Press.

Morris, Adelaide. 1983. " 'The Love of Thee—a Prism Be': Men and Women in the Love Poetry of Emily Dickinson." In *Feminist Critics Read Emily Dickinson.* Ed. Suzanne Johasz, 98–113. Bloomington: Indiana University Press.

Mudge, Jean McClure. 1977. "Emily Dickinson and 'Sister Sue.' " *Prairie Schooner* 52:90–108.

Oberhaus, Dorothy Huff. 1983. "In Defense of Sue." *Dickinson Studies* 48:1–25.

Patterson, Rebecca. 1951. *The Riddle of Emily Dickinson.* Boston: Houghton Mifflin.

Peckham, Harry H. 1940. *Josiah Holland in Relation to His Time.* Philadelphia: University of Pennsylvania Press.

Pollak, Vivian. 1984. *Dickinson: The Anxiety of Gender.* Ithaca: Cornell University Press.

Rich, Adrienne. 1980. "Compulsory Heterosexuality and Lesbian Existence." *Signs* 5:631–60.

————. 1978. *On Lies, Secrets, and Silence: Selected Prose, 1966–1978.* New York: Norton.

Sewall, Richard. 1974. *The Life of Emily Dickinson.* New York: Farrar, Straus and Giroux.

Smith, Martha Nell. 1987. " 'To Fill a Gap.' " *San Jose Studies* 13:3–25.

———. 1993. *Rowing in Eden*. Austin: University of Texas Press.
Smith-Rosenberg, Carroll. 1975. "The Female World of Love and Ritual: Relations between Women in Nineteenth-Century America." *Signs* 1:1–29.
Stimpson, Catharine R. 1981. "Zero Degree Deviancy: The Lesbian Novel in English." *Critical Inquiry* 8:363–80.

"*My* Business is to *Sing*": Emily Dickinson's Letters to Elizabeth Holland

Stephanie A. Tingley

During the course of their thirty-three-year epistolary friendship the lively and outspoken Elizabeth Holland became one of Emily Dickinson's closest friends, perhaps the most precious of a small group of contemporary readers who possessed that "Rare Ear, not too dull."[1] The large number of letters Elizabeth Holland received from Emily Dickinson, together with their superior originality and quality, suggests that the poet considered this correspondence to be among her most important. Dickinson sent more letters and poems between 1854 and 1886 to Elizabeth than to any other single reader outside the immediate family circle, with the exception of T. W. Higginson. According to Holland's granddaughter Theodora Van Wagenen Ward, their friendship was warm and reciprocal, a mutually satisfying bond that would be sustained without interruption for over three decades.[2]

For Emily Dickinson such close friendships were precious and rare, relationships she equated on several occasions with "riches," or, as she describes them in Letter 150, "like gems—infrequent." Dickinson testifies to the strength and endurance of this particular relationship in a quatrain that ends one 1875 letter to her friend:

Nature assigns the Sun—
That—is Astronomy—
Nature cannot enact a Friend—
That—is Astrology.[3]

In the introduction to her collection of Dickinson's letters to her grandparents Ward suggests that a combination of strength of character and unflagging good humor was what attracted Emily Dickinson to her grandmother in the first place and what kept their friendship strong over the years.[4] Ward emphasizes Elizabeth Holland's individuality, "the quickness of her mind, . . . the wit of her conversation and the independence of her judgments." She concludes:

> She had the gift of meeting people on their own ground, yet retaining her own individuality in complete naturalness. She could be crisply outspoken, but never bitter, and her quick humor saved many an awkward situation.[5]

Dickinson's letters to Elizabeth Holland demonstrate that she overcame much of her natural reticence and took unusual risks with this correspondent. Daring to think aloud, she confides her joys, worries, doubts, and disappointments more freely in this epistolary friendship than she does with most other correspondents. In addition, as Theodora Ward reports, Elizabeth Holland's letters were always welcome in the Dickinson household for their "light touch, sense of humor, her connections with the larger world" (26).[6]

It is through this exchange of letters, then, that Elizabeth Holland became, for Emily Dickinson, the ideal friend Ralph Waldo Emerson defined and described in his essay "Friendship": "A friend is a person with whom I may be sincere. Before him [or her, in this case] I may think aloud."[7] Most often Dickinson's richest relationships were sustained primarily, and often exclusively, through an exchange of personal correspondence. Letters mediated between the extreme self-reliance that her self-imposed physical isolation necessitated and her need for emotional intimacy. Indeed, Emily Dickinson's epistolary relationship with Elizabeth Holland would thrive on the tension between physical distance and emotional proximity.

Significantly, Elizabeth was one of only a handful of correspondents who seemed never to disappoint the poet. Dickinson had a habit of disdainfully casting off those of her correspondents who failed to satisfy her rigorous standards for epistolary friendships. As she explains to Samuel Bowles: "My friends are very few. I can count them on my fingers— and besides, have fingers to spare" (L 223). One letter dated September 1873, however, reprimands Elizabeth for not writing back soon enough and suggests how angry Dickinson could become if she believed she was being neglected. The poet playfully reminds Elizabeth that she has failed to send a reply quickly enough and adds a mildly ironic reproof: "I have lost a Sister. Her name was not Austin and it was not Vinnie. She was scant of stature though expansive spirited and last seen in November." A few lines later she asks: "Possibly she perished? Extinction is eligible" (L 395). Apparently, Elizabeth managed to return to the poet's good graces, for they would continue to correspond regularly for another twelve years.

Most of Dickinson's biographers and critics have dismissed her friendship with Elizabeth Holland as a superficial exchange of domestic news between female friends and have chosen to focus, instead, on how Elizabeth's husband, Josiah Holland, might have hindered or helped Dickinson's attempts to publish her poetry or assumed that the poet wrote to them primarily as a couple.[8] Actually, Dickinson sent very few "union letters" to the Hollands, a fact she highlights in a letter to Elizabeth dated late November 1866 that offers a stringent reproof to those who send joint letters. "A mutual plum is not a plum," she complains (L 321). After 1865 she most often chose to address Elizabeth alone, although she usually asked her friend to pass along cordial greetings to her husband and children.[9]

Dickinson's correspondence with Elizabeth Holland contains much more than idle chatter or sharing of domestic details, for these letters serve two important, and intimately connected, purposes. First, this relationship helped satisfy the poet's need for a network of close, sympathetic female friends she could sustain and comfort with her words. In addition, she shares many of her poetic aspirations and inspirations with Elizabeth Holland. Those of us who read over Elizabeth's shoulder watch Emily Dickinson, always a highly self-conscious writer, in the process of exploring her vocation, refining her relationship with her audience, and developing her mature, original style.

As a result, Elizabeth received a large share of Dickinson's most challenging, innovative letters and some of her most sophisticated prose and poetry. Although, as with all of Emily Dickinson's readers, there were limits to Elizabeth Holland's understanding, Theodora Ward reports in *Emily Dickinson's Letters* that her grandmother "became expert at deciphering the strongly individual handwriting" (25). More important, over the years she also became increasingly adept at deciphering Dickinson's dense and difficult poetry and prose and was one of the few readers who apparently never ceased to appreciate the originality of her friend's compositions, even when she found them frustratingly elusive.

Complex, intellectually and stylistically challenging, and always en-
ergetic, most of Dickinson's letters to Elizabeth Holland are composed in
a cryptic, lyrical style reserved for only the most trusted, and most
astute, of the poet's highly select group of contemporary readers. Al-
though her earliest letters to Elizabeth Holland are somewhat pedestrian,
gradually their prose tightens, becoming increasingly encoded, aphoris-
tic, and lyrical. Such stylistic sophistication is significant, as Sharon Cam-
eron notes in *Lyric Time,* because "in Dickinson's letters we can observe
that the more vested the relationship with the letter recipient, the more
aphoristic, epigrammatic, and explicitly literary the letters become."[10]
Since Elizabeth Holland shared the poet's lively interest in literature and
learning, for example, Dickinson felt free to pack her letters to her friend
with aphorisms, comments on current events, and allusions to both popu-
lar literature and the classics, for, apparently, she could count on Eliza-
beth's lively and informed response.[11]

Even though many of Dickinson's letters to Elizabeth Holland are
just as complex linguistically as any composed for T. W. Higginson,
Samuel Bowles, or even the unnamed "Master," comparing the rhetori-
cal strategies of letters to these most privileged of her male correspon-
dents with those to Elizabeth Holland reveals crucial differences in ap-
proach and in the kind of relationship the poet establishes in each case
between writer and reader. To Higginson, for example, she tends to
present herself as a novice, an insignificant student in need of guidance
and reassurance. Even though we know that she had already composed
hundreds of her lyrics by the time she sent Higginson her initial letter in
1862, she asks him for editing advice, for "surgery" to help with her
organization and style. To Bowles and Master she most often takes on the
role of ardent lover and supplicant.[12]

In sharp contrast to the halting, overly deferential, self-denigrating
poses of little girl and unskilled amateur she adopts with these male
correspondents, the poet seems much more comfortable with declaring
her purpose and celebrating her talent in the privacy and relative security
of her exchange of personal letters with Elizabeth Holland, her support-
ive, ever-nurturing female friend. In this correspondence Dickinson cre-
ates a self-confident, authoritative persona, a poet who, although seem-
ingly reconciled to relative obscurity during her lifetime, feels free to
articulate her fervent hopes for immortality and posthumous fame. In
these letters Dickinson sounds much surer of her vocation and her pur-
pose as poet. Ignoring the "nuts and bolts" issues she discusses with

Higginson and abandoning the pleading tone of her epistolary relationships with Bowles and Master, she instead concentrates on describing her artistic vision and aesthetic aims.

Always adept at using and reshaping the social vocabulary of her culture, in her letters to Elizabeth Holland Emily Dickinson appropriates some of the conventional, highly sentimental language and imagery common to Victorian correspondence between female friends to conduct her most sustained evaluation and critique of her dual, and often conflicting, roles as mid-Victorian woman and lyric poet. Such readily recognizable, culturally sanctioned images and language, packed with code words familiar to both reader and writer, become a kind of shorthand—a quick way to refer to complex ideas about her writerly roles as sympathetic sister, fellow sufferer, and singer. As the years pass and as their friendship grows and deepens, these conventional images and associations gradually take on heightened significance until complex ideas can be alluded to with only a single word or, at most, a brief phrase.

Dickinson draws freely on the effusive, highly stylized sentimental rhetoric of sisterhood common to letters exchanged between female friends during the nineteenth century in her letters to Elizabeth Holland.[13] Letters from Emily Dickinson's half of the correspondence make clear, Richard Sewall notes, that the poet casts Elizabeth in the role of "spiritual sister," what feminist historian Carol Lasser describes as "fictive kin" in her study of nineteenth-century female friendships.[14] Although Dickinson complained bitterly in one early letter to J. G. and Elizabeth Holland that God had been stingy with her by allotting her only one sister—writing "sisters are brittle things. . . . God was penurious with me, which makes me shrewd with Him" (L 207)—she affectionately addresses her closest female friend in letter salutations as "Sister," "Little Sister," "Loved Little Sister," or "Elder Sister." These affectionate salutations highlight Elizabeth's special status in her extended family circle. Dickinson also granted her girlhood friend and future sister-in-law, Susan Gilbert, special status as sister, as Adelaide Morris has argued convincingly in her essay "The Love of Thee."[15] Once established the kinship bond between Elizabeth Holland and Emily Dickinson, like that between Susan and Emily, remained strong and unbroken until Dickinson's death in 1886.

As the work of Lasser and other cultural historians demonstrates,[16] friendships among nineteenth-century women who were unrelated by blood or marriage were crucial bonds that committed both parties to

lifelong "demonstrative affection, emotional mutuality, and the fulfill-
ment of obligations to support and nurture" one another (169). As Lasser
explains, "Sisters expected from each other mutual care and intense love.
They turned to each other in times of distress as well as success, looking
for solace as well as celebration" (165). The relationship between Eliza-
beth Holland and Emily Dickinson, sustained primarily through the ex-
change of personal letters, clearly fulfilled these rigorous requirements,
for these women wrote to encourage and sustain one another. Even more
significant, the emotional bond between them remained strong despite
physical distance and striking differences in life circumstances.

Dickinson's epistolary kinship with Elizabeth Holland exemplifies
how the poet envisioned using letters to connect reader and writer in an
intricate web of confidences and kinship. By adopting and then adapting
the language and imagery conventionally associated with what Carroll
Smith-Rosenberg has labeled "the female world of love and ritual," a
world familiar to both writer and reader, Dickinson suggests that for her
the ideal relationship between writer and reader necessitates both inti-
macy and reciprocity. Correspondence between those designated spiri-
tual sisters, then, took the form of an ongoing, intimate conversation
conducted through the mail.

In addition to shaping her correspondence with Elizabeth Holland
into a model epistolary friendship, Dickinson also finds ways to use the
stereotypical notion that a Victorian woman's correspondence was the
spontaneous outpouring of a sensitive, suffering soul to say something
important about her reasons for writing both letters and lyrics. Dickin-
son employs the conventional Victorian language of consolation in these
letters to comfort her friend at times of pain, disappointment, or bereave-
ment. The painful experiences that the two women share help strengthen
the bond between them. In most of these verses and letters the poet
depicts herself as a sensitive fellow sufferer whose words are intended to
comfort and inspire the one who reads them. In addition, just as the
conventional language of sisterhood offers Dickinson a convenient and
efficient way to describe the key features of an ideal relationship between
writer and audience, using the Victorian language of consolation in letters
and poems to Elizabeth provides the poet with ample opportunity to
investigate the impetus for her art and explore her ideas about a female
poet's role and responsibilities.

Both women suffered a devastating series of deaths of loved ones
over the years. Dickinson's losses included, among others, both of her

parents, her young nephew Gilbert, Samuel Bowles, and Judge Otis Lord. In December 1882, shortly after the death of her mother, Dickinson begins a letter with a description of the numbing effect the cumulative losses have had on her. "To speak seemed taken from me—," she tells Elizabeth. "Blow has followed blow, till the wondering terror of the Mind clutches what it is left, helpless of an accent—" (L 792). Elizabeth Holland grieved over several miscarriages during her early married life and lost a brother and a sister within a year of each other in the 1880s. Her worst blow, however, would come with Josiah's sudden death from a heart attack on 12 October 1881. After hearing the news, Emily Dickinson sent her friend a series of elegiac messages that offered comfort and counseled her friend to "cling tight to the hearts that will not let you fall" (L 731). This sequence of consolatory letters culminates in one of Dickinson's most lyrical and linguistically complex letter-poems:

> Dear Sister.
> The Things that never can come back, are several
> —Childhood—some forms of Hope—the Dead—
> Though Joys—like Men—may sometimes make a Journey—
> And still abide—
> We do not mourn for Traveler, or Sailor,
> Their Routes are fair—
> But think enlarged of all that they will tell us
> Returning here—
> "Here!" There are typic "Heres"—
> Foretold Locations—
> The Spirit does not stand—
> Himself—at whatsoever Fathom
> His Native Land—
>
> Emily, in love—
>
> (Poem 733)

In other consolatory poems and letters sent to Elizabeth, Dickinson describes those who are left behind to mourn the deaths of loved ones as "the Birds—that stay," the "[s]hiverers round Farmers' doors—" (Poem 334), who are able to survive the cold of winter, or the depths of despair, on just a few meager crumbs of bread or consolation.

In addition to mourning the loss of a large number of loved ones, both women suffered from health problems. Both endured chronic ill health in their later years. Elizabeth Holland's activities were severely restricted by arthritis; Emily Dickinson suffered from what she described in one letter to her friend as "nervous prostration" (L 873). Most important, lifelong eye trouble plagued them both; both feared blindness.

Not surprisingly, Dickinson's letters to Elizabeth Holland are filled with references to vision and sight. Dickinson makes their common fear of losing their vision most explicit in a wry comment in one late November 1871 letter: "Beg the Oculist to commute your Sentence," she writes, "that you may also commute mine. Doubtless he has no friend and to curtail Communion is all that remains to him." In the next paragraph she goes on to assure her friend that both of them will eventually triumph over their vision problems: "This transitive malice will doubtless retire— offering you anew to us and ourselves to you" (L 369).

Ever solicitous of Holland's vision problems, Dickinson frequently warns Elizabeth not to strain her eyes with too much letter writing or reading, assuring her that "the vitality of [her] syllables compensates for their infrequency" (L 492) and, later, "Were it not for the eyes," Dickinson complains, "we would know of your oftener. Have they no remorse for their selfishness?" (L 551). On another occasion she reluctantly recommends Robinson's life of Emily Brontë to her friend, writing, "I wish the dear Eyes would so far relent as to let you read 'Emily Brontë'— more electric far than anything since 'Jane Eyre' " (L 822). Dickinson made several extended trips to Boston for eye treatments during the 1860s, including one 1864 trip lasting seven months. Elizabeth Holland's eye problems were even more severe, causing her a great deal of pain and resulting in permanently impaired vision. The severity of her condition prompted her husband to plan an 1868 trip abroad for the whole family designed not only to educate the children but also to offer his wife the chance to consult Dr. Albrecht von Grafe of Berlin, a doctor who, as Holland biographer Henry H. Peckham explains, "was at that time probably the foremost oculist in Europe."[17]

The need to respond to their shared eye troubles provides Dickinson with the impetus she needs to explore her poetics of deprivation, her theory that suffering inspires poetic expression. Far from rendering her inarticulate or even mute, Dickinson tells Elizabeth over and over during their thirty-three-year correspondence that her own fear, pain, and loss actually motivate her to write and enhance her creativity. As she confesses in one letter, she often writes verses to "relieve . . . a palsy" (L 265), and in another, to Higginson, "I sing as the Boy does by the Burying Ground—because I am afraid—" (L 261).

Thus, a number of letters concentrate on showing her friend how to transform unfortunate experiences into occasions to celebrate through the power of language. When Holland eventually had one eye surgically removed, for example, an operation that Emily Dickinson read about in the *Springfield Daily Republican*,[18] the poet was quick both to praise Elizabeth's valor and to offer solace in a letter dated August 1872: "To have lost an Enemy is an Event with all of us—almost more memorable perhaps than to find a friend. This severe success befalls our little Sister— and though the Tears insist at first, as in all good fortune, Gratitude grieves best" (L 377). By describing Holland's surgery as "good fortune" and a "severe success," Dickinson demonstrates how she uses the power of lyrical language to transform her friend's tragedy into a triumph.

Over the years loss of sight gradually becomes a metaphor in Dickinson's letters to Elizabeth Holland for the more general vulnerability of all women in mid-Victorian culture—a shorthand way for Dickinson to critique the limitations her culture put upon female poet and female reader alike.[19] In this context the Dickinson lyric that begins

> Before I got my eye put out
> I liked as well to see—
> As other Creatures, that have Eyes
> And know no other way—
>
> (Poem 327)

as well as the large number of poems in which Dickinson uses references to eyes or vision as metaphors for perceiving or knowing, take on additional significance. Here and elsewhere she suggests that the physical disability both she and Elizabeth Holland endure is symptomatic of a far-reaching cultural and spiritual malaise.

In addition, her friend's frustration with her impaired vision and her fear of blindness give Dickinson an opportunity to experiment with ways to capture the essence of an object or an experience in words—to articulate and test her ideas about language. For example, she composes many poems and passages of lyrical letter prose, which she explicitly labels "word pictures" or "word portraits," designed to tell her friend what she sees. In an 1877 letter, for example, Dickinson introduces a lighthearted poetic word picture of a bumblebee by writing, "I must just show you a

Bee, that is eating a Lilac at the Window. There—there—he is gone!
How glad his family will be to see him!" A poem describing the bee's
appearance and behavior follows:

> Bees are Black, with gilt Surcingles—
> Buccaneers of Buzz.
> Ride abroad in ostentation
> And subsist on Fuzz.
>
> Fuzz ordained—not Fuzz contingent—
> Marrows of the Hill.
> Jugs—a Universe's fracture
> Could not jar or spill.
>
> (L 502)

One late letter even contains a pen portrait of Elizabeth Holland herself,
which Dickinson introduces by asking, "May I present your portrait to
your Sons in Law?" The poem that follows pays tribute to the warmth
and depth of their friendship:

> To see her is a Picture—
> To hear her is a Tune—
> To know her an Intemperance
> As innocent as June—
> To know her not—Affliction—
> To own her as a Friend
> A warmth as near as if the Sun
> Were shining in your Hand.
>
> (L 802)

Always concerned with capturing the immediacy of these experi-
ences, as well as the emotions associated with an occasion or an observa-
tion, such word pictures depend on metaphor and are packed with words
that appeal to all of the senses. As Elizabeth Phillips astutely notes in her
discussion of the style of Dickinson's letters to the Hollands in *Emily
Dickinson: Personae and Performance,* "[W]hen she 'paints,' it is as an ex-
pressionist. Changes of season or differences of opinions are emotional
events."[20] In a single sentence that depends upon synesthesia for its im-
pact, for instance, the poet captures the essence of early spring: "The

lawn is full of south and the odors tangle, and I hear today for the first the river in the tree" (L 318).

By announcing her intention to craft pictures with words, then, Dickinson suggests something important about how she defines her vocation as poet. Her job is to articulate what every person knows instinctively—to translate her observations, feelings, and insights into language for sensitive readers such as Elizabeth Holland. For Dickinson as female poet, as for Emerson, the poet functions primarily as a seer and a namer. Like Emerson, too, she is often forced to acknowledge her frustration at the limits of language, to admit that, despite her considerable talent and skill, both spoken and written expression must forever remain woefully and inescapably inadequate. As she reminds Elizabeth in a letter dated October 1881: "One who only said 'I am sorry' helped me the most when father ceased—it was too soon for language" (L 730). Despite the inevitable imperfections of written expression, however, as Phillips notes, Dickinson's letters to Elizabeth Holland "are at least a partial record of the anxieties they shared and their reliance on language to sustain one another" (143). Dickinson seemed to find considerable comfort in making the attempt to articulate what she saw and what she felt, for the effort linked poet and world, writer and reader.

Dickinson also reshapes the conventional language of birds, bees, and flowers flavoring Victorian prose and poetry, particularly that written by women, in her correspondence with Elizabeth Holland. One passage in an early letter, for example, is packed with these clichés. She writes:

I'm so glad you are not a blossom, for those in my garden fade, and then a 'reaper whose name is Death' has come to get a few to help him make a bouquet for himself, so I'm glad you are not a rose—and I'm glad you are not a bee, for where they go when summer's done, only the thyme knows, and even were you a robin, when the west winds came, you would cooly wink at me, and away, some morning! (L 185)

With such highly stylized phrases and images the young poet contrasts the transience of these natural objects, which will fade away or leave her when the winter winds blow, with the constancy of Elizabeth Holland's friendship.

More particularly, Dickinson transforms the stereotypical image of the Victorian poetess as a songbird, an image popularized by, among others, her celebrated contemporary Lydia Sigourney, "the Sweet Singer of Hartford."[21] The stock images and clichés allow her to comment on her poetic vocation and define, both for herself and for Elizabeth, one of the most trusted of her readers, the relationship between her life and her art—her reasons for singing.

In letter after letter she describes herself and her friend as avian creatures and assigns both of them birdlike traits as a quick, efficient way to comment on similarities in the two women's personalities and habits. Both women are compared to small, plain, rather common birds. In one letter Dickinson reflects on a recent visit Elizabeth had made with her by asking, "Your little Trip still lingers, for is not all petite you do—you are such a Linnet?" (L 547), while late in 1884 the poet tells her friend, "You always were a Wren, you know, the tenant of a Twig" (L 990). Theodora Ward suggests in her collection of Dickinson's letters to Elizabeth Holland that what the poet thought of as birdlike in her grandmother's behavior was "the quickness of her mind" and the "nimbleness of her small body," her ability to "dart into the heart of a human problem as a hummingbird darts into the heart of a flower" (18). Dickinson describes herself, too, as a small, nimble-witted and -footed, rather plain bird, most often a wren, bluebird, or, most significant, American robin. In the poem that begins "The Robin's My Criterion for Tune—" (Poem 285) Dickinson develops the parallels between herself as female poet and songbird. The female robin is small, and her feathers are drab brown, but she possesses a magnificent singing voice. In addition, Dickinson firmly identifies herself with *American* subject matter by explaining that both she and the robin dwell in an American landscape. The speaker adds: "I see— New Englandly—."

Victorian conventions dictated that women belong at home, just as mother birds belong in their nests. Home and nest both serve as safe havens from the exigencies of the male-dominated, public world of commerce and work. Once Dickinson develops her metaphor in this way she can easily contrast her life choices and circumstances with Elizabeth's. With only a word or a short phrase, for example, she could delineate the differences between her own life choices and the more traditional roles that Elizabeth Holland undertook. In contrast to Elizabeth, the family-oriented mother bird, the poet describes herself as a single-minded career woman, as a solitary songbird rather than a nesting bird comfortably surrounded by her nestlings. Elizabeth's selfless attention to her duties as wife and mother of three thus are compared to the actions of a mother bird who builds a secure nest for her chicks. By extension, then, the poet may find shelter and comfort in her friend's nest, or loving heart and home. In an early quatrain Dickinson describes Elizabeth's love for her as a safe haven, a nest for her sparrow self:

Her heart is fit for *home*—
I—a Sparrow—build there
Sweet of twigs and twine
My perennial nest.

(Poem 84)

The songbird in flight, then, in contrast to the nesting bird, becomes one of Emily Dickinson's most significant metaphors for her poetic identity,[22] for what distinguishes her from Elizabeth, the poet notes on a number of occasions, is her ability to fly free and her exquisite singing voice. In a series of letters that develop this image Dickinson reveals much to Elizabeth Holland about her complex attitude toward her poetic vocation—her chosen role as solitary singer.

Dickinson often employs bird imagery in the Holland correspondence, for example, when she wishes to describe her relationship with her audience. The very first time she mentions her chosen vocation as poet to the Hollands she writes: "Swift little ornithology! Dancer, and floor, and cadence quite gathered away, and I, a phantom, to you a phantom, rehearse the story! An orator of feather unto an audience of fuzz,—and pantomimic plaudits" (L 195). This ornithological wordplay soon becomes an ongoing pattern in Dickinson's letters to Elizabeth Holland. Several years later, in perhaps her most explicit and most poignant comment on the relationship between poet and audience, art and immortality, she admits to fears that her audience will misunderstand her or find her comical: "Perhaps you laugh at me! Perhaps the whole United States are laughing at me too!" She adds, "*I* can't stop for that! *My* business is to love." Her anxiety on this occasion is only momentary, however, for she ends this letter with a brief fable that suggests she intends to continue to write, to sing, no matter what the response:

I found a bird, this morning, down—down—on a little bush at the foot of the garden, and wherefore sing, I said, since nobody *hears?*

One sob in the throat, one flutter of bosom—'*My* business is to *sing*'—and away she rose! How do I know but cherubim, once, themselves, as patient, listened, and applauded her unnoticed hymn? (L 269)

By explicitly assigning the bird a female identity and by stressing the fact that this is a songbird, Dickinson's story comments on her attitude toward her own vocation as poet and her ambivalence about poetry, fame, and immortality.

Dickinson also uses bird imagery in her letters to Elizabeth Holland to comment on the impetus for her art. In earlier letters the songbird sings out of pure joy. Letter 391, written in 1873, for example, ends with a lyric that focuses on the songbird's high spirits as the sole inspiration for its art:

The most triumphant Bird I ever knew or met
Embarked upon a twig today
And till Dominion set
I famish to behold so eminent a sight
And sang for nothing scrutable
But intimate Delight.
Retired, and resumed his transitive Estate—
To what delicious Accident
Does finest Glory fit!

(L 391)

Before too many years have passed, however, the songbirds that appear in her letters to Elizabeth begin, instead, to sing out of frustrated longing, pain, or fear. By 1881 the solitary songbird is homeless and desolate, as in Letter 685, which ends: "I knew a Bird that would sing as firm in the centre of Dissolution as in it's [*sic*] Father's nest" (L 685, III, 687). The death of Judge Otis Lord in 1884 is the impetus for the bleakest image of all. Dickinson writes:

Quite empty, quite at rest,
The Robin locks her Nest, and tries her Wings.
She does not know a Route
But puts her Craft about
For *rumored* Springs—

She does not ask for Noon—
She does not ask for Boon—
Crumbless and homeless, of but one request—
The Birds she lost—.

(L 890)

Here images of loss, desertion, disorientation, and cold coalesce to com-
ment on Dickinson's despair at being left "crumbless and homeless" at
the end of her life. She confides to Elizabeth her doubts that spring and
hope will ever return to her. Significantly, even at this lowest point, she
continues to sing, although the impetus for her creativity is pain and loss
rather than joy.

In the Holland-Dickinson correspondence, then, Emily Dickinson
engages in her most extended exploration of her vocation as poet and her
position as Victorian woman. By gradually transforming Victorian con-
ventions, which assigned a female writer the roles of sympathetic sister,
fellow sufferer, and singer, and making these roles her own, she tests the
limits of gender and genre. In letters and lyrics sent to her trusted friend
Elizabeth Holland she writes most powerfully, and often most poi-
gnantly, about the interconnections between singing and solitude, lan-
guage and loss. Most important, she articulates the aesthetic aims of a
poet whose "business is to sing."

NOTES

1. Poem 842, in *The Complete Poems of Emily Dickinson*, ed. Thomas H. Johnson
   (Boston: Little Brown, 1960) (hereafter cited in the text by poem number).
2. An inexplicable gap does occur in the extant correspondence between 1860
   and 1865. This is curious, as, according to many, these were the years of
   Dickinson's greatest poetic productivity. Holland's granddaughter is sure,
   though, that "the contact . . . was never broken" (*Emily Dickinson's Letters to
   Dr. and Mrs. Josiah Gilbert Holland.* Edited by Theodora Van Wagenen Ward.
   Cambridge: Harvard University Press, 1951), 24).
3. Letter 439, in *The Letters of Emily Dickinson,* ed. Thomas H. Johnson, 3 vols.
   (Cambridge: Belknap Press of Harvard University Press, 1955) (hereafter
   cited in the text by letter number).
4. Very little biographical information about Elizabeth Chapin Holland exists.
   Most of the scanty details must be culled from brief and infrequent mentions
   in biographies of her husband, Josiah Gilbert Holland. Most accounts empha-
   size her physical appearance and her roles as supportive spouse and nurturer

of the couple's three children, Annie, Kate, and Theodore and, later, their numerous grandchildren. Typical is a brief pen portrait found in Harriette Merrick Plunkett's laudatory 1895 biography *Josiah Gilbert Holland* (New York: Scribners, 1895). Plunkett describes Elizabeth's appearance at the time of her marriage:

> A miniature of Mrs. Holland, made at this time, shows her with a fair complexion, a rosy bloom, a pair of remarkably frank and fearless bluish-gray eyes, and a wealth of soft brown hair. She was of medium height, but looked fairly petite beside the tall and stalwart figure of her husband. (25–26)

5. Theodora Van Wagenen Ward, ed. *Emily Dickinson's Letters to Dr. and Mrs. Josiah Gilbert Holland* (Cambridge: Harvard University Press, 1951), 19. One would hardly expect Elizabeth Holland's granddaughter to paint anything other than a positive and sympathetic portrait of her grandmother. Still, Dickinson's own positive response to the Hollands corroborates Ward's impressions. Dickinson records the beginning of her friendship with Elizabeth Holland, who was seven years her senior, in a letter written to her brother Austin dated 10 July 1853: "Dr. Holland and his wife spent last Friday with us—came unexpectedly—we had a charming time, and have promised to visit them after Commencement" (L 132). Dickinson's thank-you letter, written in the autumn of 1853, shortly after she and Lavinia had returned home from their eagerly anticipated visit, also communicates her enthusiasm for her new friends and suggests something of the warmth and depth of the friendship that would soon develop and grow between Emily and Elizabeth.

6. Even after Emily Dickinson decided, in the early 1860s, to never leave "her Father's house and grounds," Elizabeth Holland continued to pay occasional visits to her friend in Amherst. The reclusive poet always welcomed her warmly, even in the later years, when she seldom granted a face-to-face interview to anyone.

7. Ralph Waldo Emerson, "Friendship," *Essays and Lectures* (New York: Library of America, 1983), 341.

8. Certainly, Emily Dickinson did know Josiah Gilbert Holland first, for in August of 1851, almost two years before her first visit to the Holland home in Springfield, she met the prominent newspaper editor and author at a reception held in her father's parlor to celebrate Holland's receipt of an honorary master's degree from Amherst College. In addition, Edward Dickinson and his daughters had long enjoyed Holland's lively essays in the *Springfield Republican,* and Emily knew of Holland's attempts to discover, encourage, and publish new writers and, more particularly, admired his commitment to promoting the work of female writers. According to Dickinson's biographer Cynthia Griffin Woolf, however, she was uncomfortable with J. G. Holland's conservative ideas about appropriate subject matter and style for poetry, particularly for the work of "lady poets" (*Emily Dickinson*

[New York: Knopf, 1986], 244–45). The ambivalence seemed to be mutual, for Holland's granddaughter Theodora Ward reports that "Dr. Holland is quoted as having said that Emily's verse was too ethereal for publication" (*Letters*, 25). In any case, despite his considerable literary connections, at some point Emily Dickinson apparently decided that he could not, or would not, help her with her attempt to publish her poetry. Even though the majority of the letters Thomas H. Johnson lists as having been written to "the Hollands," in appendix 3 of his 1958 variorum edition of Dickinson's letters, were actually addressed solely to Elizabeth, there is no separate entry for her in his appendix, "Biographical Sketches of Recipients of Letters and Persons Mentioned in Them." Instead, the scanty bits of information included are subsumed into her husband's entry, which describes some of the highlights of his life and career, including among them his marriage to Elizabeth Luna Chapin in 1845. Johnson does acknowledge in passing the especially close relationship between Elizabeth and Emily but insists on treating the Hollands as a unit and describing their relationship with Emily Dickinson as a joint and equal partnership: "Both were vivacious, candid, and perceptive" (*Letters*, 945).

The Hollands' granddaughter Theodora Van Wagenen Ward, in the introduction to her collection *Emily Dickinson's Letters to Dr. and Mrs. Josiah Gilbert Holland,* is one of the few critics who attempts to redress this neglect of her grandmother's centrality to Dickinson's mid-Victorian audience. In addition, Richard Sewall's chapter in his book *Life of Emily Dickinson,* although titled "Dr. and Mrs. Josiah Gilbert Holland," is packed with astute observations about the subject matter and style of Dickinson's letters to the Hollands, and he begins to suggest how important this particular friendship with Elizabeth was to the mature Emily Dickinson.

9. In Thomas H. Johnson's 1955 variorum edition of the letters only fourteen of the ninety-four pieces extant are addressed to both Josiah and Elizabeth Holland, the remaining eighty letters are addressed solely to Elizabeth

10. Sharon Cameron, *Lyric Time: Dickinson and the Limits of Genre* (Baltimore: Johns Hopkins University Press, 1979), 12.

11. Unfortunately, as far as I can determine, none of Elizabeth Holland's letters to Emily Dickinson remain, as Emily Dickinson instructed her sister Lavinia to burn the letters she had received from others at her death. In addition, what remains of Dickinson's half of their correspondence is probably not complete.

12. I tend to agree with Richard Sewall and Judith Farr, among others, who argue that Samuel Bowles is the best candidate for "Master."

13. Carroll Smith-Rosenberg's essay "The Female World Of Love and Ritual," reprinted in her collection *Disorderly Conduct: Visions of Gender in Victorian America* (New York: Knopf, 1985), examines the rhetorical strategies and vocabulary typical of American Victorian women's letters and diaries. In addition, the first chapter of Karen Lystra's *Searching the Heart: Women, Men, and Romantic Love in Nineteenth-Century America* (1989) examines the rhetoric

of the Victorian love letter and the language of affection, both between
friends of the same sex and between lovers.

14. Carol Lasser, " 'Let Us Be Sisters Forever': The Sororal Model of Nineteenth-
Century Female Friendship," *Signs* 14 (Autumn 1988): 158–81; and Richard
Sewall, *The Life of Emily Dickinson* (New York: Farrar, Straus, and Giroux,
1974), 633.

15. Adalaide Morris, " 'The Love of Thee—a Prism Be': Men and Women in the
Love Poetry of Emily Dickinson," in *Feminist Critics Read Emily Dickinson*,
ed. Suzanne Juhasz, 98–113 (Bloomington: Indiana University Press, 1983).

16. See also chapter 5, "Sisterhood," in Nancy Cott, *The Bonds of Womanhood:
"Woman's Sphere" in New England, 1780–1835* (New Haven: Yale University
Press, 1977), esp. 183–96.

17. Harry H. Peckham, *Josiah Gilbert Holland in Relation to His Times* (Philadel-
phia: University of Pennsylvania Press, 1940), 166.

18. Jay Leyda includes an excerpt from the *Republican*'s 29 August 1872 report of
the surgery, in *The Years and Hours of Emily Dickinson*, 2 vols. (New Haven:
Yale University Press, 1960), which reads, in part:

> Many of the friends of Dr. Holland and his wife will be saddened to
> learn that Mrs. Holland has been obliged to have one of her eyes re-
> moved on account of its diseased condition. The operation has been
> successfully performed, and she is otherwise in improved health.
> (2:189)

19. Sandra Gilbert and Susan Gubar, in their book *The Madwoman in the Attic:
The Woman Writer and the Nineteenth-Century Literary Imagination* (New
Haven: Yale University Press, 1979), argue that this connection between
seeing and identity and, conversely, eye disease and "I-dis-ease" becomes a
central motif in the work of nineteenth-century female writers on both sides
of the Atlantic. "Whether she is a passive angel or an active monster," they
write, "the woman writer feels herself to be literally or figuratively crippled
by the debilitating alternatives her culture offers her" (57).

20. Elizabeth Phillips, *Emily Dickinson: Personae and Performance* (University
Park: Penn State University Press, 1988), 140.

21. See Cheryl Walker, *The Nightingale's Burden: Women Poets and American Culture
before 1900* (Bloomington: Indiana University Press, 1982); and Joanne Dob-
son, *Dickinson and the Strategies of Reticence: The Woman Writer in Nineteenth-
Century America* (Bloomington: Indiana University Press, 1989), for extended
discussions of conventions describing the female poet as a songbird.

22. Dickinson's use of bird imagery has been explored in a number of contexts,
including James R. Guthrie's essay "The Modest Poet's Tactics of Conceal-
ment and Surprise: Bird Symbolism in Dickinson's Poetry," *ESQ* 27 (1981):
230–37; and Cynthia Griffin Wolff's biography *Emily Dickinson* (New York:
Knopf, 1986).

Ruth Miller, in *The Poetry of Emily Dickinson* (Middletown, Conn.: Wesleyan University Press, 1968), is the first to note that Dickinson does not use such imagery consistently, for "[a] bird may in one case be simply a bird, another time it may be a symbol of the song of the poet, singing of Heaven or Eternity; it may be a sign of regeneration of nature, or redemption of man; a bird may render as well the inaccessibility of the Divine" (195). Despite this variety, the use of imagery in the Dickinson–Holland correspondence, I would argue, consistently explores and refines the poet-songbird analogy.

Emily Dickinson's Perfect Audience: Helen Hunt Jackson

Richard B. Sewall

Almost every phase of Emily Dickinson's life leaves us with questions and few more so than the story of the publication of her poems during her lifetime. Why so few poems (barely a dozen) and all anonymous? Was it her own doing? An uneasiness about her work ("I could not weigh myself—Myself—" [L 261])? An ambivalence toward publicity and fame? Was it the failure of her intimates and advisors to understand her (and her work) and to give her the support she needed? Or were her verses too eccentric for public consumption—and for the editors who decided on such matters? And, in all of this, to what extent was she writing for, and seeking, an audience?

There is no doubt that, early on, she had glowing ambitions. We have the evidence in her own words. At nineteen she challenged an Amherst student, in a rollicking prose valentine (L 34), to join her in a literary project to wake up the world. When she was twenty-seven she and her cousin Louise Norcross "decided to be distinguished. It's a great thing to be 'great,' Loo . . ." (L 149). A year later she wrote her sister-in-law, "Could I make you and Austin . . . proud . . . sometime . . . a great way off . . . 'twould give me taller feet . . ." (L 238). By then, 1861, she had been sending poems to Samuel Bowles of the *Springfield Daily Republican* for several years.

When she was barely into her thirties, however, there came a change. She made a curious about-face in her first exchange of letters with Thomas Wentworth Higginson, in April 1862. She had asked him for an opinion of her poems (she had enclosed four of her best). When he advised her to "delay to publish," she "smiled." Publication, she wrote him, "is foreign to my thought as Firmament to Fin. . . . My Barefoot-Rank is better." She added that only recently, "this winter," she had refused "Two Editors of Journals" who had "asked me for my Mind" (L 265). Then, about a year later, came the poem in which she dismissed publication as the "auction of the Mind," a paltry business transaction. Although she kept on writing steadily—a rough estimate of 363 poems in 1862 and the usual outpouring of letters—she settled (gradually, her brother Austin insisted) into a reclusiveness that ended, apparently, whatever efforts she might have made toward fulfilling the ambition she had talked about with her cousin.

Then, in the mid-1870s, the friend of her childhood, Helen (Fiske) Hunt Jackson, reentered her life with an urgent plea that she "sing aloud" (L 444a). The episode, all by correspondence—Emily in Amherst, Helen in Colorado Springs—is full of meaning, I think, for both of them, above and beyond the matter of getting Emily to go public.

Helen was in full career as a national figure. Emily was well on her way to becoming a "myth" even to her fellow citizens in Amherst. Except for one poem that Helen succeeded in getting published (she had aimed at Emily's portfolio), her mission failed. But after all those years the meeting of minds was in itself a fulfillment. Emily found, at last, what I have chosen to call "a perfect audience," and Helen had the stimulating, and perhaps chastening, experience of direct contact with a literary power far beyond her own. I am tempted to call the experience, for both of them, redemptive. To justify this high claim, let me rehearse the background, the temperament, and, above all, the sense of vocation that each of them brought to this mid-1870s reconvergence.

To go back, way back: Emily and Helen were born in Amherst about two months apart in the fall of 1830 and delivered by the same doctor—which, it could be said without too much stretching, was about all of significance they had in common for the next forty years. As a child, Helen was tomboyish, outgoing, something of a handful. Her mother described her as a "born rebel . . . quite inclined to question the authority of everything, the Bible she says does not *feel* as if it were true" (YH 1:36).[1] Her parents, Professor and Mrs. Nathan Welby Fiske, took her out of Amherst Academy when she was eleven and sent her away to school. This was the beginning of an unsettled and knockabout youth. Her mother died when Helen was thirteen and her father three years later. From then on, until she married Lieutenant Edward Hunt, when she was twenty-one, she made her home with aunts, uncles, and guardians. (Contrast this with Emily's settled life in the Homestead, her family intact and protective.) Helen's attempt to establish a home of her own was interrupted and finally brought to an end by sadness after sadness. Her first child died in infancy. Her husband was killed in a wartime accident in 1863. Her beloved son Renny died two years later.

From then on she had to live pretty much by her wits. She began to write. Poetry came first as, presumably, a way to deal with her grief. She developed a knack for journalism and with it a good business sense. (Emily, by this time, had been writing for years, in private.) Things turned very much her way when, early in 1866, she took up residence in Mrs. Hannah Dane's "literary boarding house" in Newport, Rhode Island, and became a fellow boarder with the Higginsons. Higginson took an immediate interest in her writing and became not only her literary "mentor" (YH 2:213) but also her chief advocate in the world of publishing. In due course they compared notes about Amherst and Emily Dickinson. When Higginson produced the poems Emily had been sending him, Helen had her first experience of her friend's work (YH 2:111). Her own book *Verses* was published in 1870. It met with resounding praise—from Bowles and (among others) Emerson. Higginson called Helen "one of the most gifted poetesses in America" (YH 2:131). Emily joined in the praise, from afar (L 368).

Then came Helen's western sojourns, first for her health then, in 1875, to settle permanently in Colorado Springs with her new husband, William S. Jackson. She became interested in the cause of the American Indian and turned to her true vocation: the fight for truth and justice. Her study *Century of Dishonor* (1881) and her novel *Ramona* (1884) were of major importance in calling the plight of the Indians to national attention.

Emily's response to *Ramona* shows how far apart the two women were. "Pity me," she wrote to Helen, "I have finished Ramona. Would that like Shakespeare, it were just published!" (L 976). Not a word about the Indians and Helen's valiant stand. It is safe to say that the very mention of Shakespeare must have baffled Helen. She had written a novel, in prose and for a cause. *Ramona*, she hoped, would do for the Indian what *Uncle Tom's Cabin* had done for the American Negro. She was a crusader.

Emily, clearly, was not. Much has been made, for instance, of her alleged indifference to the Civil War and the issues it was fought for. But its tragedy did not elude her; it simply intensified those questions—the eternal ones—that she wrestled with all her creative life: the "Flood subject," immortality (L 319); those "odd secrets of the line," of which she imagined herself as the "pale Reporter" (Poem 160); what happens at "the Being's Centre" (Poem 553), in the dark "Cellars of the Soul" (Poem 1225). These were her "causes" and her vocation, very different from Helen's. What is notable about this late (epistolary) meeting of the two women is that, for all their differences, the prevailing note was delight in each other—and joy.

To understand the joy in it for Emily, and what I have presumed to call its redemptive quality, it is well to be reminded of a theme that runs through her life, in her home, in the town of Amherst, and in her relations with the literary world beyond Amherst. (The redemptive aspect for Helen began, I suggest, with those boardinghouse sessions over Emily's poems with Higginson.) Emily learned early the price an original mind usually pays in every generation: the failure to be understood by one's contemporaries, even one's intimates; the sense that, no matter how intense or urgent your communications may be, they are falling on deaf ears. We would call it alienation. Emily's sense of alienation was never, as far as we know, violently expressed. No foot stampings are recorded, no diatribes, no "Howl," no "No, in Thunder." (I find the word *rage* misapplied to her.) She kept those thoughts, if she had them, to herself or, in whimsical letters or in poems whose metaphors (I think she hoped) provided sufficient disguise, followed her own advice to "Tell all the truth but tell it slant" (Poem 1229). When she was twenty-two she wrote to a friend (in her preferred spelling), "I find I need more vail" (L 107).

Even her family, she soon found, were not understanding her. There are the often quoted remarks about her mother: "I never had a mother. I suppose a mother is one to whom you hurry when you are troubled" (L 342b). "I always ran Home to Awe when I was a child, if anything befell me. He was an awful Mother, but I liked him better than none" (L 405). The problem was not "mother rejection" or even, as I see it, "mother inadequacy." Mrs. Dickinson was in many ways quite adequate; she was essential to the home that Emily dearly loved, and, as Emily said much later, "When she became our Child, the Affection came" (L 792). Emily summed up the problem in a sentence: "My Mother does not care for thought" (L 261).

Nor did she find the understanding and sustenance she sought for in her father. He was "too busy with his Briefs . . . to notice what we do" (L 261). "My father seems to me often the oldest and oddest sort of a foreigner. Sometimes I say something and he stares in a curious sort of bewilderment though I speak a thought quite as old as his daughter" (*Life* 66). She could joke about him when he was alive, but after his death the thought of his "lonely Life and lonelier Death" haunted her (L 457). Again, a summing up that explains a great deal about the relationship between father and daughter: "His Heart was pure and terrible and I think no other like it exists" (L 418).

Sister Vinnie, younger than she by two and a half years, was her constant companion in the household. But mentally and temperamentally the two were poles apart. Emily described her difficulty in a letter to Joseph Lyman, who had once been enamored of Vinnie:

> And Vinnie, Joseph, it is so weird and so vastly mysterious, she sleeps by my side, her care is in some sort motherly . . . yet if we had come up for the first time from two wells where we had hitherto been bred her astonishment would not be greater at some things I say. (*Life* 145)

So, again, bewilderment. Shortly after Emily's death Vinnie was asked if she had ever studied her sister's poems extensively. "Certainly not," she replied, "I never looked at Emily's poems except those she herself showed me. Had she wished me to do so, she would have made her wishes known" (*Life* 155). Once, summing up the family, Vinnie made a clear distinction: "Emily had to think—she was the only one of us who had that to do. . . . I had the family to keep track of" (*Life* 128).

Her brother, Austin, understood her better, I think, than anyone else in the family, and, certainly, during their youth together he was her greatest source of fun and cheer in the household. But there is nothing on record to indicate that he was sympathetic with, or helpful in, her developing literary interests. When she was twenty she wrote him a saucy letter:

> You say you dont comprehend me, you want a simpler style. *Gratitude* indeed for all my fine philosophy! . . . [So, from now on] as *simple* as you please, the *simplest* sort of simple. (L 45)

So, even the lordly Austin, three years older and a graduate of Amherst College, was mystified. No "audience" here. That he ever developed an ear for her poetry is doubtful.

The only one in the family circle who took the interest in her work she sought (and who had the ear for it) was her sister-in-law, Susan, living just next door. Their exchange of letters in the summer of 1861 on the poem "Safe in their Alabaster Chambers" shows Sue as a perceptive critic and Emily as quick to take criticism and grateful for it (L 238; and Poem 216). But there is not further record of such collaboration.

Samuel G. Ward, an early Transcendentalist and a writer for the *Dial,* wrote Higginson on the occasion of the publication in 1890 of the first selection of Emily's poems. He stressed the New England innerness of the poems: "We conversed with our own souls till we lost the art of communicating with other people"—an observation that led him to speculate on the nature of the family that nourished our poet: "The typical family grew up strangers to each other, as in this case. It was *awfully* high, but awfully lonesome" (*Life* 26). Strangers, perhaps, but, as Emily said again and again, *loving* strangers. So, if for Emily life even in her family meant a degree of alienation, it was a special Dickinson kind, and she seems to have been content with it. In her later years she wrote to a friend, "We have no statutes here, but each does as it will, which is the sweetest jurisprudence" (L 545).

Now to take Emily out of her home and into Amherst and "the world." The pattern is much the same. She had a sociable youth— parties, promenades, sleigh rides, sugarings off, a reading club, valentines, and all the rest that made her exclaim, at age nineteen, "Amherst is alive with fun this winter" (L 29). But, as her girlhood friends married or left town or died or, like Abiah Root, would not follow her independent path, she began to withdraw. (Austin says the process began in her early twenties [*Life* 222].) By her thirties she had given up going to church. She avoided sewing circles, revivals, and "august assemblies," as she called commencements. Increasingly, she found that their language was not hers, as hers was certainly not theirs. She anticipated bewilderment on both sides and withdrew to her writing desk—like Thoreau, "to transact some private business with the fewest obstacles." Indeed, about this time she used the "business" metaphor in her famous letter to the Hollands in Springfield (Dr. Holland was Bowles's partner on the *Republican*), attempting to explain to them what it was that so absorbed her:

Perhaps you laugh at me! Perhaps the whole United States are laughing at me too! *I* can't stop for that! My business is to love. I found a bird, this morning, down—down—on a little bush at the foot of the garden, and wherefore sing, I said, since nobody *hears?*

One sob in the throat, one flutter of bosom—*My* business is to *sing*—and away she rose! How do I know but cherubim, once

themselves, as patient, listened, and applauded her unnoticed hymn.
(L 269)

These urgent lines (the underscoring is hers) were written, as far as can be ascertained, in the summer of 1862. This was perhaps the most productive year of her life, a time when the desire to be "heard" must have been great. Why, then, did she brush aside, in the letter to Higginson, the mere thought of publication, when, to the Hollands, she is the bird singing though nobody hears—a poet without an audience? I think she was more honest with the Hollands.

To be sure, she had known some success. The *Republican* had printed "I taste a liquor never brewed" (Poem 214) in May 1861—anonymously, clumsily altered, and under a title that was not hers, "May-Wine"—and "Safe in their Alabaster Chambers" (Poem 216), again anonymously and with the title "The Sleepers" added. But she had reason to expect better from Bowles. He was a close friend, and she had been sending him poems for nearly four years. Once again she experienced the frustration of an original mind in an uncomprehending time. Bowles's (and Holland's) taste in poetry was thoroughly conventional. The Fannie Ferns and Minnie Myrtles dominated the *Republican*'s poetry section.

Then, in August 1862, Higginson joined the company of the "bewildered." He had in hand a dozen of her finest, but he seemed still unmoved, and, though it was unusual for her, she confronted him: "You say 'Beyond your knowledge.' You would not jest with me, because I believe you—but Preceptor—you cannot mean it? All men say 'What' to me, but I thought it a fashion" (L 271). Although Higginson was delighted (and no doubt surprised) by the extraordinary success of the posthumous *Poems,* which he helped edit in 1890 ("How could we ever have doubted about them?" he wrote to Mabel Todd [*Life* 528]), he insisted to the end that Helen Hunt Jackson was the finest female poet America had produced. Emily's irregularities, her "spasmodic gait" (L 265), the "Fiery mist" (L 330a) with which (he complained) she surrounded herself, were too much for him. Yet Emily continued her correspondence with him throughout her life. Jay Leyda's comment is relevant to our theme: "She needed one sensitive literary stranger's reaction to her work, and she aimed to keep him interested in both her work and herself" (YH 1:iv).

Within six months or so of this August letter to Higginson, Samuel Bowles sent an unfortunate message to Emily in a letter to his close friend

Austin. If it was sensitivity she was looking for, one wonders at her
response to this:

> . . . to the Queen Recluse my especial sympathy—that she has
> "overcome the world."—Is it really true that they ring [sing?] "Old
> Hundred" & "Aleluia" perpetually in heaven—ask her; and are dan-
> delions, asphodels, & Maiden's [*vows?*] the standard flowers of the
> ethereal? (YH 2:76)

In her late twenties the 1857 edition of Thomas à Kempis's work *Of the
Imitation of Christ* had made its way into the Dickinson enclave. Its stir-
ring exhortation to "fly the tumultuousness of the world . . . take refuge
within the closet of thine heart . . . diligently search into and set in order
both the outward and the inward man" may have given authority to, and
hastened, her tendency toward withdrawal. Bowles seems gratuitously
to be mocking the injunctions of the saint. One wonders if he ever took
her, and her poetry, seriously. Of this passage in the letter to Austin, Jay
Leyda writes: "His joshing deflection of ED's emotion, especially as
reflected in her poetry, may have altered her life" (YH 1:xxxii).

There was one more failure to see her work for what it was and to
give it the hearing it needed. In some ways it was the unkindest cut of all.
It happened in the early 1870s in New York City. Her old and dear friend
Dr. Holland, now editor of the new magazine *Scribner's,* had a chance
meeting with Emily's childhood friend Emily Fowler, now Mrs. Gordon
Lester Ford of Brooklyn. Here is how Mrs. Ford described the meeting
to Mable Loomis Todd, then busy collecting Emily's letters in the 1890s:

> Once I met Dr. Holland, the editor of *Scribner's Magazine,* who said,
> "You know Emily Dickinson. I have some poems of hers under
> consideration for publication—but they really are not suitable—they
> are too ethereal." But I said, "They are beautiful, so concentrated,
> but they remind me of orchids, air-plants that have no roots in
> earth." He said, "That is true,—a perfect description. I dare not use
> them"; and I think these lyric ejaculations, these breathed out projec-
> tiles sharp as lances, would at that time have fallen into idle ears.
> (*Life* 377)

Mrs. Ford had a volume of verses to her credit (whose roots went no
deeper than the sub-Tennysonian mode of the day), and she was no doubt

exercising her sensitivities to the limit. Dr. Holland had been sharing Emily's letters and the poems that frequently went with them for years with his wife (much loved by Emily). He could scarcely have missed the symbolism, for instance, of the bird whose "business" was to sing. Perhaps the two New Yorkers were right about the current taste in poetry. But, in view of the extraordinary success the poems had less than twenty years later, perhaps all they needed in the mid-1870s was the backing of a few influential literary people. Neither the editor nor the poet, in this instance, had the perception and the courage of Helen Hunt Jackson.

For all the distance, geographic and temperamental, between Helen and Emily since their childhood separation, Helen had been loyal to her Amherst origins. She visited frequently and, at least twice, called on Emily. She came in August 1860 to introduce her new husband, Lieutenant Hunt, who, as Emily told Higginson ten years later, "interested her more than any man she ever saw" (L 342b). But there seems to have been no literary talk. Helen had not yet taken up the pen, and Emily, apparently, said nothing about her poetry. Although the poetry Helen wrote after her husband's death led, under Higginson's tutelage, to the *Verses* of 1870, she had to be concerned with more lucrative work—children's stories, travel, feuilletons of various sorts. She had a facile style and a fine sense of the market, and by the mid-1870s she had some four hundred items to her credit.

Her experience of Emily's poetry, which Higginson had brought to her attention, must have had a sobering effect. For all the praise showered on *Verses* (even Emily joined in: "Mrs. Hunt's poems are stronger than any written by women since Mrs. Browning, with the exception of Mrs. Lewes" [L 368]), she could hardly have helped seeing the difference between her work and Emily's. In her journalistic writing she had made fun of female poetasters. A passage on the final page of Ruth Odell's *Life of Helen* (1939) suggests a radical change of heart:

> [She] says that her own work was not much better than that of Fanny Ferns and the Minnie Myrtles she had derided. Her success had been too easy, too early, too rapid. She had sold her birthright.

Whatever Emily's part might have been in this change, Helen's later writing, as Joseph Gordon has pointed out,[2] has more concern for truth than for the marketplace and a heightened sense of style. Many readers saw Emily's hand in the *Sax Holm* stories (1872) and thought of the work as a collaboration of the two women. The heroine of Helen's novel *Mercy Phillbrick's Choice* (1876) is patently modeled, in part, on Emily Dickinson:

> Truth, truth, truth was still the war-cry of her soul, and there was an intensity in every word of her written or spoken pleadings on this subject which might well have revealed to a careful analyzer of them that they had sprung out of the profoundest experiences. Her influence as a writer was very great. As she grew older, she wrote less and less for the delight of the ear, and more and more for the stirring of the heart. (3)

And it is notable that Helen signed her full name to the most important works, *A Century of Dishonor* and *Ramona*.

In estimating all that the fruitful convergence of the two women in the mid-1870s did for Emily, it is well to keep in mind her long experience of failed communication, from her family, who did everything but understand her, to Bowles and Higginson, whose failure she generalized into what sounds like a confession of despair: "All men say 'What' to me." (Of Dr. Holland's timidity we hope she was unaware.) Vinnie, it will be recalled, said that Emily was always on the lookout for the "rewarding person," someone with whom she could talk on even terms, someone who would not turn away from her or from her poetry in mystification—someone, in short, who could write to her like this: "You are a great poet, and it is wrong to the day you live in that you will not sing aloud. When you are what men call dead you will be sorry you were stingy" (L 444a).

Although there are two envelopes addressed but never sent to "Mrs. Helen Hunt," one dated 1868 and the other undated but addressed in Emily's handwriting of about 1872, the first letter we have between the two women is Emily's letter congratulating her on her marriage to Mr. Jackson in October 1875. It is a very short note—only six words—but it includes a poem (or, to be precise, one-half of a poem):

> Have I a word but joy?
>   E. Dickinson
>   Who fleeing from the Spring
>   The Spring avenging fling
>   To Dooms of Balm—
>
>   (Poem 1337; L 444)

The rest of the story is familiar. Helen sent the note back, asking Emily to explain the verse, especially those "dooms," and insisting that she return the note, which Helen prized. But the note was not returned. A few months later Helen complained: "But you did not send it back, though you wrote that you would. Was this an accident, or a late withdrawal of your consent? Remember that it is mine—not yours—and be honest." And then two sentences—one an apology, the other a renewed plea for help with those dooms (Helen was not inclined to give up): "Thank you for not being angry with my impudent request for interpretations. I do wish I knew just what 'dooms' you meant, though!" (L 444a).

And who can blame her? Although the word *doom* may be read as neutral, signifying "destiny," it has a frosty sound. *Balm* suggests anything that soothes or heals or palliates—but why did Emily link it with that ambiguous word *Dooms?* Those of us who have the complete canon before us (Helen had only a handful of poems) can see further reason for her bewilderment. *Balm,* too, was a highly charged word for Emily Dickinson. From the "little dull Balm" of Poem 156 to the note she added to Poem 1510 ("Heaven the Balm of a surly Technicality") the word is a flag of warning, the most notable example being Poem 252: "Give Balm—to Giants— / And they'll wilt, like Men—." The six-word note to Helen is about Joy, and Emily may be warning her never to forget her "Spring," the joy of the present, the "moment" that may be frittered away in the "balm" of her new (and secure, comfortable) life in Colorado. In Poem 492 *balm* is equated with narcotics. And then there is the epigram that Emily lived (and wrote) by: "Forever— is composed of Nows—" (Poem 624).

Whether Helen ever saw such meaning in those three lines we do not know. The important thing is that she recognized a mystery worth solving. A year after her marriage she visited Emily in Amherst, perhaps to discuss such matters, and shortly thereafter wrote her a letter that contained a significant confession. In view of the long failure of even Emily's closest associates to understand her, to express anything much beyond delighted bewilderment at her poems, it is not difficult to imagine what might have been her lift of spirit on reading the following (I have underscored the key sentence): "This morning I have read over again the last verses you sent me. I find them more clear than I thought they were. *Part of the dimness must have been in me.*" Here at last was someone, and someone of literary stature, who believed in her, recognized her greatness, and was willing to work not only for but also on her poems.

Helen's death in August 1885 (preceding Emily's by only nine months) came as a shock. The friendship had grown since the mid-1870s. It was in 1878 that, through Helen's efforts, Emily's "Success is counted sweetest" appeared in the *No Name Series* (a collection of poems by well-known authors, printed anonymously).[3] There followed a promising exchange between Emily and the editor of the series, Thomas Niles of Roberts Brothers, but it came to nothing and with it Helen's hope that Emily would "sing aloud" to her own day. The warmth of their friendship is wonderfully expressed in a rough draft (which is all we have) of Emily's letter of condolence to Mr. Jackson:

> Helen of Troy will die, but Helen of Colorado, never. Dear friend, can you walk, were the last words that I wrote her. Dear friend, I can fly—her immortal (soaring) reply. I never saw Mrs. Jackson but twice, but those twice are indelible, and one Day more I am deified, was the only impression she ever left on any Heart (House) she entered—.

It's not too much to say, I think, that this final friendship—open, uncomplicated, unanguished, based on interests and ambitions held in common—is one of the reasons for the mood of serenity and poise, a kind of Olympian summing up that I take to be the prevailing vision of Emily's last few years. There are sadnesses and grievous losses (her nephew Gilbert and Judge Lord) and her own lingering illness. But her tensions, the swings of mood, have largely disappeared. The tone is sometimes prophetic, as Emily wrote Mrs. Holland late in 1884: "All grows strangely emphatic, and I think if I should see you again, I sh'd begin every sentence with 'I say unto you—' " (L 950). A little poem of the early 1880s, seemingly so unpretentious, may be seen, if read analogically, as a summing up of her career. The first ten lines went to Mr. Niles (and perhaps to Helen) and may have been a gentle way of calling them both off. The last four were written later and the whole sent to Higginson, who had been ill, in a letter of late 1882:

> How happy is the little Stone
> That rambles in the Road alone,
> And doesn't care about Careers
> And exigencies never fears—
> Whose Coat of elemental Brown
> A passing Universe put on,

And independent as the Sun
Associates or glows alone,
Fulfilling absolute Decree
In casual simplicity—

(Poem 1510)

Obtaining but or own Extent
In whatsoever Realm—
'Twas Christ's own personal Expanse
That bore him from the Tomb—

(L 767; Poem 1543)

The Christology of the last two lines may have been a kind of blessing on
Higginson in his illness—but who's to say that she did not have in mind
her own literary immortality? (She often identified her sufferings with
Christ's.) She had written to Austin and Sue, twenty years before, that
she hoped to make them proud "a great way off." Here it's "In whatso-
ever Realm—." I like to think that Helen helped her toward such confi-
dence, so much can come from a "perfect audience," even of one.

NOTES

This essay is what survives of two talks, the first in Colorado Springs (1988),
as one of the series to honor Helen Hunt Jackson; the second in Amherst (27
October 1989), as part of a conference on the theme "Emily Dickinson and
Audience." I have added and subtracted, of course. The key to the references
that follow is. L = *The Letters of Emily Dickinson*, ed. Thomas H. Johnson and
Theodora Ward, 3 vols. (Cambridge: Harvard University Press, 1958); Poem
= *The Poems of Emily Dickinson*, ed. Thomas H. Johnson (Cambridge: Har-
vard University Press, 1955); YH = Jay Leyda, *The Years and Hours of Emily
Dickinson*, 2 vols. (New Haven: Yale University Press, 1960); *Life* = R. B.
Sewall, *The Life of Emily Dickinson*, 2 vols. (New Haven: Yale University
Press, 1974).

1. Sometime after Emily's death her brother, Austin, comparing Emily and
   Helen as children, wrote of Emily's brilliance and Helen's "wild romping
   rebellious Spirit and ways" (see *Life*, 222).
2. In " 'So Threads Cross': Helen Hunt Jackson and Emily Dickinson, A Literary
   Friendship," the first of a series of talks to honor Helen Jackson, Colorado
   Springs, 9 November 1988.
3. For readers the game was to identify the authors. Emily must have been
   pleased to learn that her poem "Success" was attributed to Emerson.

Part 3:
"A Fairer House than Prose": Dickinson the Nineteenth-Century American Poet

I dwell in Possibility—
A fairer House than Prose—
More numerous of Windows—
Superior—for Doors—

—Poem 657

Dickinson's Elected Audience

Robert Regan

Emily Dickinson probably had no knowledge of the tome of Saint Leo the Great, but if she had known it she would have liked its reasoned argument against the heretic Eutyches, who had questioned the reality of Christ's human nature: "The Lord of the universe assumed the aspect of servitude with a shadow veiling His majesty. . . . He who is true God is also true man; there is no falsity in this union, wherein the lowliness of man and the greatness of divinity are mutually united."[1] She attacks the same heresy, and she is the better rhetorician:

> What Soft—Cherubic Creatures—
> These Gentlewomen are—
> One would as soon assault a Plush—
> Or violate a Star—
>
> Such Dimity Convictions—
> A Horror so refined
> Of freckled Human Nature—
> Of Deity—ashamed—
>
> It's such a common—Glory—
> A Fisherman's—Degree—
> Redemption—Brittle Lady—
> Be so—ashamed of Thee—

(Poem 401)

She does not, like Leo, support her argument with scriptural quotation, but she has a text in mind: "Whosoever therefore shall be ashamed of me and of my words in this adulterous and sinful generation; of him also shall the Son of man be ashamed, when he cometh in the glory of his

217

Father with the holy angels" (Mark 8.38). We cannot fail to detect in the last two lines of the poem the echo of Christ's powerful denunciation of those who were ashamed of his humanity—his "freckled Human Nature." It is not, however, merely the isolated verse that Dickinson's words recall; it is the whole passage (8.27–38) setting forth the disciples' first questioning of the dual nature of Christ.

The prophecy Jesus delivers to the twelve in verse 31, "that the Son of man must suffer many things, and be rejected of the elders, and of the chief priests, and scribes, and be killed, and after three days rise again," elicits a "rebuke" from Peter, who seems to speak for all the disciples. But Jesus at once rebukes Peter: "Get thee behind me, Satan: for thou savourest not the things that be of God, but the things that be of men" (8.33). Saint Luke, who was not disposed to deal with the disciples as Dickinson deals with her "Gentlewomen," transfers the words Mark has Jesus speak here, "Get thee behind me, Satan," to the temptation in the wilderness and has them addressed to Satan himself (Luke 4.8), but their doctrinal significance is the same: Jesus had been tempted to escape the rejections and sufferings that were the inescapable inheritance of "freckled Human Nature." Did the meditative poet Emily Dickinson project herself into the scene Saint Mark sketched? Did she see herself tempted by "gentlewomanly" editors to please and publish and win a worldly crown of fame? Perhaps further attention to her sacred texts will clarify those questions.

What Saint Mark's Jesus rebuked in Peter, what Leo rebuked in Eutyches, what Dickinson rebuked in her Gentlewomen, is the Monophysite heresy, the denial of the human side of the double nature of Christ. The disciples and their spokesman, Peter, welcomed the idea of a triumphant Messiah, a miracle worker, a king, a bestower of gifts, but at the idea of divine suffering, divine defenselessness, they were aghast. Like them, Dickinson's Gentlewomen are horrified, "ashamed," of "freckled Human Nature—of Deity—." But the word *Deity* should remind us that Dickinson does not subscribe to the opposite heresy, Arianism (or Unitarianism), and the resounding metonymy of *Redemption* for *Jesus* attests to the orthodox Christology of this unorthodox Christian poet.

The distinction I have suggested between the attitude of the earliest of the four Evangelists, Mark, toward the disciples and that of Luke (and Matthew and John as well) is advanced by the New Testament scholar Theodore J. Weeden, Sr., in his influential study *Mark: Traditions in Con-*

flict.[2] Drawing his methods from "the new literary criticism," Weeden asks "how the first reader might have looked at the Gospel" and, contextualizing the work in the dominant genres of the age, concludes that that reader "would have instinctively turned to the Markan characters, their portrayal, and the events which engulfed them as the starting point for understanding the composition." It is through the portrayal of his characters that Mark makes his point. Weeden's Mark "is assiduously involved in a vendetta against the disciples." The issue is Christology. Mark depicts disciples who see Jesus as a "divine man," one who has established his authority through "signs and wonders." By signs and wonders they intend to establish their own authority. Christians who accept that Christology and model themselves upon the disciples—"evangelists" we might call them today, or perhaps "televangelists"—have, according to Weeden's scenario, arrived in the young Christian community in which Mark presides as elder and authority. "These pneumatic exhibitionists have experienced such oneness with the exalted Lord that the demarcation between Jesus and themselves is lost in their own consciousness." Against them Mark argues, and makes his Jesus argue, "for a suffering-servant Christology," and for a suffering-servant model of discipleship.[3] Weeden acknowledges his debt to literary criticism—to reader-response theory, I assume he means. Emily Dickinson's critics are well positioned to demand repayment of principal and interest. On two issues of considerable interest Weeden will prove his worth: Why did Dickinson "keep the Sabbath . . . staying at Home" (Poem 324)? And why did she deem "Publication" to be "the Auction Of the Mind" (Poem 709)? If we will follow Weeden's example by asking what audience our latter-day Markan saint inscribes in her gospel and what opponents she tasks for their apostasy, we may conclude that the two questions are intertwined.

Dickinson's knowledge of the Gospels was intimate. She quotes from them more often than from any other source; she alludes to them more often than to any other texts. She makes reference to Mark, the earliest, shortest, and least ornamented of the Synoptic Gospels, less frequently than to Luke and Matthew (in most cases, of course, more than one of the Synoptics may supply her biblical source), but one allusion in which Mark is her only possible source suggests her spiritual kinship with that Evangelist. In "I like to see it lap the Miles—" (Poem 585) she makes her iron horse "neigh like Boanerges," an allusion to Mark 3.17, in which Jesus "surnamed" James and John "Boanerges, which is, The sons of thunder." There are linguistic and textual problems that may explain the disappearance of the name and its gloss from Matthew and Luke: no one knows why Mark thought *Boanerges* means "sons of thunder." Preoccupied with those issues, Mark's commentators have neglected the irony of the verse, but, if we concern ourselves exclusively with the English version, Dickinson's implied gloss is convincing: these preachers are a noisy pair—as noisy as a locomotive. The allusion does the steam engine no damage, but it does undermine the disciples and in the same manner that Mark's "Boanerges" had undermined them. A horse—even an iron horse—may neigh without attracting undue attention, but it is primarily Saint James and Saint John the poem represents as neighing—displaying *horsiness?* saying *nay?*

Another "pneumatic exhibitionist" suffers deflation in the familiar lines

> He preached upon "Breadth" till it argued him narrow—
> The Broad are too broad to define
> And of "Truth" until it proclaimed him a Liar—
> The Truth never flaunted a Sign—
>
> (Poem 1207)

If *Truth* here is, as I take it to be, another metonymy for *Jesus,* Dickinson may again intend us to recall verses from Mark: "Why doth this generation seek after a sign?" (8.12; or Matt. 16.4; or Luke 11.29); and "false Christs and false prophets shall rise, and shall show signs and wonders, to seduce, if it were possible, even the elect" (13.22; or Matt. 24.24). The end of the poem lends some support to that reading:

> What confusion would cover the innocent Jesus
> To meet so enabled a Man!

A worksheet draft of the poem contains seven alternatives for *enabled: learned, Religious, accomplished, discerning, accoutred, established, conclusive.* Her underlining *Religious* suggests that it was the runner-up. The right word won, surely, but *Religious,* the most ironically loaded of the candidates, is key to them all. Pondering her alternative readings, Dickinson was distancing herself from all the attributes of the prophetic caste of her community—"false Christs, and false prophets." The poem she has left us challenges us to consider our affiliations with all prophetic castes, as

Mark (or Weeden's Mark) challenged his readers to consider their affilia-
tions. There was, however, one prophet in her community Dickinson
regarded with respect, Ralph Waldo Emerson. To him she would turn for
a delineation of the poet's role and for ghostly counsel on the troubling
issue of publication.

Dickinson read Emerson, read him text and subtext, read him, I am con-
vinced, more carefully than he read himself. The key document for her is
the essay "The Poet." Eventually, she read much more of him, but for the
period of her greatest productivity the *Essays* were her Emerson. Her
familiarity with "The Poet" she proclaims, archly, in "I taste a liquor never
brewed—" (Poem 214). Emerson had argued that "the Poet knows that he
speaks adequately . . . only when he speaks somewhat wildly . . . not
with intellect alone, but with the intellect inebriated by nectar." "Nectar,"
mind you, not "wine, mead, narcotics, coffee, tea, opium, the fumes of
sandal-wood and tobacco," for "the air should suffice for his inspiration,
and he should be tipsy with water."[4] I wish I could believe that Emerson
found this funny—but, if that had been the case, it wouldn't have fallen to
Emily Dickinson to find it funny.

> Inebriate of Air—am I
> And Debauchee of Dew—
> Reeling—thro endless summer days—
> From inns of Molten Blue—
>
> When "Landlords" turn the drunken Bee
> Out of the Foxglove's door—
> When Butterflies—renounce their "drams"—
> I shall but drink the more!
>
> Till Seraphs swing their snowy Hats—
> And Saints—to windows run—
> To see the little Tippler
> Leaning against the—Sun—

(214)

But if she is here having a bit of fun at her mentor's expense, he remains
her mentor. It was he who taught her that the gentlewomanly "Seraphs"
and "Saints" who occupy the walk-up apartments above the Foxglove
Tavern—Castalian Spring Water on tap—will "swing their snowy hats"

and wag their fingers at the "reeling" nectar abuser below, who gropes
for the steadying lamppost of the "Sun." The cast of characters gives us
the apparent Unregenerate and the soi-disant Elect, the poet and the
public. And that is the cast of characters we encounter throughout "The
Poet" and many of Emerson's other essays.

    "The birth of a poet is the principal event of chronology"—*kairos* to
the New Testament scholar Emerson was—and the poet is the third
person of Emerson's trinity, "theologically, the Father, the Spirit, and the
Son, but which we will call here the Knower, the Doer and the Sayer"—
or the Logos (3:7, 5). Cheering words for the poet, these should be. But
are they? The opening paragraph of the essay announces its subject: "the
consideration of the nature and functions of the Poet . . . the means and
materials he uses . . . the general aspect of his art in the present time"
(3:4). But, when Emerson opens his second paragraph with the confes-
sion that "the breadth of the problem is great, for the poet is representa-
tive," the reader might be excused for asking "What problem?" A prob-
lem there is, and Emerson is not slow to expose it. He interposes four
short, upbeat sentences, but then the truth slips out: the poet "is isolated
among his contemporaries by truth and by his art." *Isolated* was in Emer-
son's day a word with a brief history, but *among* does not seem the
preposition naturally attached to it. Emerson is struggling against his
perception of the tragic predicament of the poet. He does offer the poet
"this consolation in his pursuits" (he knows that the poet needs a consola-
tion): "that they will draw all men sooner or later" (3:4). That verb
occurs again later in the essay: "He is the poet, and shall draw us with
love and terror, who sees through the flowing vest, the firm nature, and
can declare it" (3:21). "With love and terror," we note. In "Friendship"
Emerson had used the same verb:

> We walk alone in the world. Friends, such as we desire, are dreams
> and fables. But a sublime hope cheers ever the faithful heart, that
> elsewhere, in other regions of the universal power, souls are now
> acting, enduring and daring, which can love us and which we can
> love. . . . You demonstrate yourself, so as to put yourself out of the
> reach of false relations, and you draw to you the first-born of the
> world,—those rare pilgrims whereof only one or two wander in
> nature at once, and before whom the vulgar great show as spectres
> and shadows merely. (2:125)

"Acting, enduring, and daring": an arresting triplet, the middle term not really fitting in the set. For a graduate of a divinity school Emerson was little given to biblical echoes—I hesitate to say *allusions,* for I am not sure he was quite conscious of this one—but few in his audience can have missed it: "Now is the judgment of this world: now shall the prince of this world be cast out. And I, if I be lifted up from the earth, will draw all men unto me. This he said, signifying what death he should die" (John 12.31–33; see also 3.14, 8.28, 12.34). The Emersonian Poet is the Logos, the Messiah—but the crucified Messiah. Christology provides the governing metaphor of "The Poet"—suffering servant Christology. Emerson's essay is full of bad news.

At the center of the essay is a little parable. Nature makes a poet. To ensure against

> the risk of losing this wonder at a blow . . . she detaches from him a new self . . . [his] poems or songs, . . . a fearless, vivacious offspring, clad with wings. . . . The songs, thus flying immortal from their mortal parent, are pursued by clamorous flights of censures, which swarm in far greater numbers, and threaten to devour them; but these last are not winged. (3:14)

Why the "*flights* of censures" are not "*winged*" is not clear, but the poems somehow escape, leaving behind a swarm of dead critics—and a dead poet.

The essay ends with what Emerson intends as words to "cheer" the "faithful heart"; they are directed to the poet:

> Stand there, balked and dumb, stuttering and stammering, hissed and hooted, stand and strive. . . . The world is full of renunciations and apprenticeships, and this is thine; thou must pass for a fool and a churl for a long season. . . . [T]hou shalt be known only to thine own, and they shall console thee with tenderest love. (3:23–24)

It is a Pietà tableau that Emerson's words finally evoke.

I have ignored the most salient points of the argument of "The Poet." Dickinson did not ignore those points. "Bare lists of words . . . excited" her, and she must have felt a bond with Emerson's Lord Chatham (William Pitt), who was "accustomed to read in Bailey's Dictionary, when he

was preparing to speak in Parliament" (3:11). She would have agreed that
"it is not metres, but a metre-making argument that makes a poem" (3:6).
She saw "the gliding train of cars" (3:11) as an appropriate subject for a
poem. And, most to the point, she "dared to write [her] autobiography in
colossal cipher, or into universality" (3:21). But she also read the text I
have highlighted—Emerson's involuntarily inscribed subtext, we may
call it. She saw her world divided between "flights of censures" and "one
or two" "isolated" poets, "hissed and hooted" by a multitude. Yet she
must also have accepted Emerson's counsel that "very idle is all curiosity
concerning other people's estimate of us, and all fear of remaining un-
known is not less so." For "the world is full of judgment-days . . ."
(2:91), and "never was a sincere word utterly lost" (2:92). The world of
the future would reverse the hard judgments of the present: "We think our
civilization near its meridian, but we are yet only at the cock-crowing and
the morning star. In our barbarous society the influence of character is in
its infancy." But "every thought which genius and piety throw into the
world, alters the world" (3:126–27). Those final sentences are not from
"The Poet"—there is more assurance in them than the context of "The
Poet" could accommodate—but they are not inconsistent with the sum of
meaning that accumulates there.

Dickinson was not the only New England poet of her time to read
these Emersonian counsels and to take them to heart.

The late Yvor Winters was one of the most penetrating of the New
Critics—and one of the most perplexing. Here is the opening paragraph
of his foreword to N. Scott Momaday's edition of Tuckerman's poems:

> F. G. Tuckerman (1821–73) was one of the three most remarkable
> American poets of the nineteenth century. The others were Jones
> Very (1813–80) and Emily Dickinson (1830–86). Emerson had tal-
> ent, which was badly damaged by foolish thinking; Bryant might be
> described as a fine second-rate poet, better than most of the British
> poets of the century. Of Poe and Whitman, the less said the better.
> Very was Tuckerman's tutor at Harvard for a brief period, but their
> connections thereafter seem to have been slight. Tuckerman spent
> most of his mature life within eighteen miles of Amherst, but there
> is no evidence that he and Emily Dickinson even met or even knew
> of each other's existence. Miss Dickinson knew Tuckerman's son
> and probably knew his brother the Amherst botanist, a specialist in

mosses, and the distinguished member of the family (a ravine was named after him).[5]

Our first reaction to this provocative opening may be to judge it ungenerous to one or another of our favorite poets. I am convinced, however, that generosity is precisely what impels this witty and trenchant paragraph—generosity to two poets Winters saw as wronged by long critical neglect and deserving of another judgment day and generosity to Momaday, an important writer Winters was the first to hail for more significant talents than his editorial labors displayed.[6] Winters's generosity, however, is not what most arrests our attention here. Few will accept the judgment that more than one of Winters's three poets deserves quite so high a rank as he accords them all, and most will sense that he is suggesting something that, typically, he doesn't explicitly state: that the three constitute for him a set of some kind. Of what kind, then?

He provides one hint of what he has in mind: "All three of these poets were isolated personally (I suspect as a result of boredom)."[7] Of Tuckerman we know too little to be sure on the count of boredom, but Very, habituated to spiritual ecstasies, seems proof against that state, and Dickinson summarizes what many of her poems say in one sentence set down by Higginson: "I find ecstasy in living—the mere sense of living is joy enough" (Letter 342a). What Winters intended to suggest, I suspect, was not that his poets were bored but, rather, that the world from which they were radically isolated was orthodox, conformist, and, consequently, boring, dominated by such figures as "a specialist in mosses" who would give his name to "a ravine." Their society alienated them not by malevolence but by indifference. And perhaps what constitutes them a set is their awareness of that indifference—an indifference all of them could, indeed, figure as malevolence.

The three seem to have attained a common understanding of their world and the poet's place in it. They may not have required the assistance of Ralph Waldo Emerson to bring them to that understanding, but he was available to them all. All were readers of the texts from which I have attempted to extract Emerson's bad news about the fate of the poet. And the good news also: "that they will draw all men sooner or later." "Sooner," each was to discover, was not to be hoped for; "later," however, was quite another matter. On deferred judgment days they staked their reputations.

Tuckerman saw the English audience as more receptive than the

American. He had had a volume of his poems privately printed in the
United States in 1860 (Tuckerman was financially independent) and had
sent copies to Emerson, Hawthorne, and a number of other literary fig-
ures, but for regular publication he turned to a British publisher, for in the
United States, he fancied, his book "would be but coldly received." He
addresses his book "to those only who understand it,"[8] and he appears not
to have expected to find such readers in his own country. The sonnets of
the third, fourth, and fifth series, "The Cricket," which Winters, perhaps
a bit hyperbolically, called "the greatest poem in English of the century,"[9]
and a dozen later poems, these Tuckerman never sought to publish at all.
"The poet," Samuel L. Golden comments, "had marched a step ahead of
his age and had to wait for time to catch up with him."[10] He had to wait,
in point of fact, for posthumous recognition, and he seems to have been
content to wait. Very, at twenty-five, placed his manuscripts in Emer-
son's hands and left their preparation for the press entirely to him; later he
would send some of his verse to minor journals, but the greater part of his
mature work remained unpublished when he died forty years later. The
story of Dickinson's aspirations to publish and her decision to wait for a
more favorable day need hardly be detailed here. Their contemporaries
had no trouble seeing that the "Household" (or "Fireside") Poets consti-
tuted a set. They were "the gracious singers," as Mark Twain wickedly
put it, "to whom we and the world pay loving reverence and homage."[11]
They bore some resemblance to Weeden's "pneumatic exhibitionists."
Their contemporaries lacked the opportunity to recognize Tuckerman,
Very, and Dickinson as a set, for the three chose to remain invisible. It is
precisely that choice that makes them appear as a set to us.

To seek fame, to strive to be published, was, for Dickinson, for
Very, and probably for Tuckerman, unbecoming, shameful, sinful. Dick-
inson registers the point in an underrated poem:

> Publication—is the Auction
> Of the Mind of Man—
> Poverty—be justifying
> For so foul a thing
>
> Possibly—but We—would rather
> From Our Garret go
> White—Unto the White Creator—
> Than invest—Our Snow—

Thought belong to Him who gave it—
Then—to Him Who bear
It's Corporeal illustration—Sell
The Royal Air—

In the Parcel—Be the Merchant
Of the Heavenly Grace—
But reduce no Human Spirit
To Disgrace of Price—

(Poem 709)

The arresting enjambment of *Possibly*—not quite a real enjambment—
underscores the point of the poem: it is hardly possible for the poet to
contemplate "the Auction of the Mind," for the "Mind," "Thought," is
the property of God the Father; indeed, it is God, God the Son, the
"Corporeal illustration," the Incarnation, of Deity. The positioning of
"Sell / The Royal Air" also invites—demands—attention: when Dickin-
son places a word on the "wrong" line, she intends us to notice. Only a
Judas would sell the "Corporeal illustration" of God, his Air/Heir. The
pun reminds us of her text, the first chapter of the Gospel according to
Saint John. "In the beginning was the Word [Logos], and the Word was
with God, and the word was God" (1.1). Goethe's Faust had also medi-
tated on the translation of Logos: "*Im Anfang war das Wort!*" Better,
perhaps, "*Im Anfang war der Sinn*" (the Thought) or "*die Kraft*" (the
Power), or, finally, "*die Tat*" (the Deed).[12] Dickinson's Deed is her Word,
her Power, her Thought, and it belongs to the God "who gave it." The
Word was not her own, she could not sell it for fame. But in another
meditation on John 1.1 she asserts her faith—her Emersonian faith—in
its immortality:

A Word that breathes distinctly
Has not the power to die
Cohesive as the Spirit
It may expire if He—

(Poem 1651)

Tuckerman seems not to have theologized about poetry—certainly not
his own—but Very was of one mind with Dickinson: he saw himself as
"will-less," his poetry as inspired by the Divine will, and if it fell on deaf

ears in the present, it would one day be heard, and it would, as Emerson prophesied, alter the world. With such confidence Very asserts that

> The word goes forth! I see its conquering way,
> O'er seas and mountains sweeps it mighty on;
> The tribes of men are bowing 'neath its sway.[13]

Yet for all their faith Winters's three poets did not leave the fate of their poems to chance. The three chose remarkably similar strategies for ensuring that their work would reach the very special audience they had in mind. Tuckerman sent copies of his privately printed poems to Hawthorne, Emerson, Longfellow, Very, Bryant, Ellery Channing, and several other literary men of influence, and he crossed an ocean to visit, impress, and enthrall Tennyson.[14] Very delivered his early manuscripts to Emerson—delivered them with quietist theatricality. Dickinson turned to Thomas Wentworth Higginson. It is hardly necessary here to review the devices by which she rendered herself enigmatic and fascinating for the man who was to ensure her enduring reputation—indeed, her immortality (David Porter ably covers that topic in his essay in this collection). Suffice it to say that her extraordinary letters and the riveting performance she rendered when Higginson visited her in Amherst were her assurance that her "letter to the world" (Poem 441) would not be consigned to a dead letter office.

Weeden's Mark, advocate of a suffering servant Christology, warns his audience to reject the disciples—dense, thick-witted, selfish, noisy, faithless men—as role models and to reject those proclaimers of the faith who model themselves on the disciples, the serpent handlers, the miracle workers, the demon exorcisers, who were winning the admiration of the infant Christian community. It was a battle Mark was in large measure to lose. His Gospel was to be relegated to a place after Matthew's, and nine verses from another hand (16.12–20) were to be appended to its last chapter to soften its rejection of the doubting disciples (16.11) and to bring its interpretation of the resurrection into conformity with the later Gospels.

Emily Dickinson—indeed, Emily Dickinson, F. G. Tuckerman, and Jones Very—viewed success for the poet much as Mark viewed success for the miracle worker: it was a sure sign that something was wrong, for only a regenerate community can welcome its Redeemer, and, though regeneration might be hoped for, even expected, it had no more arrived in the three poets' community than in Mark's. The poet's role must, therefore, be that of the suffering servant who calls readers to suffering servanthood and who looks forward with them to a redemptive event in the future. Redemptive suffering figures conspicuously in the work of all three, but it is at the very center of the experience Dickinson conveys.

A poem remarkable for the density and allusive force of its imagery and for its inscribing a chapter—a future chapter—of the poet's autobiography in Emerson's "colossal cipher" begins

> Essential Oils—are wrung—
> The Attar from the Rose
> Be not expressed by Suns—alone—
> It is the gift of Screws—

The "Screws" and the press are instruments of the Inquisition, to which Dickinson makes several references (Poems 384, 414, 474, 536), but the words *Oils* and *expressed* point to another, prototypical agony, Christ's Agony in the Garden of Gethsemane, for the Hebrew etymology of *Gethsemene* is "oil press." George Herbert had exploited that etymology, for centuries a commonplace of homiletic and devotional literature, in his poem "The Agonie," and he too had exploited it without stating the word *Gethsemane*. His poem foregrounds the prototype, presenting Christ as "a man so wrung with pain" by the "presse and vice" of sin that "his skinne, his garments bloudie be," and he urges his readers to "taste" in the wine of the Eucharist the "liquor sweet" expressed by the Agony. Dickinson's poem foregrounds the ectype, the individual victim, inviting her readers to breathe the sweetness of the perfume "expressed" by a personal agony, the *essence,* the odor of sanctity: the "Attar" of the "Rose."

> The General Rose—decay—
> But this—in Lady's Drawer
> Make Summer—When the Lady lie
> In Ceaseless Rosemary—

> (Poem 675)

The poems, the remembrancers of their dead author, the relics of one of the "Martyr Poets" (Poem 544), shall live on when roses not subjected to "the gift of Screws" will have decayed. But what justifies this reading? Nowhere does the text speak of poems or of a poet. Yet the poem demands that we read it in dual contexts: in the context of suffering servant hagiography and in that of Emily Dickinson's autobiography. It is the former that writes the latter into "colossal cipher."

A very different poem, one almost devoid of imagery, functions similarly:

> The Province of the Saved
> Should be the Art—To save—
> Through Skill obtained in Themselves—
> The Science of the Grave
>
> No Man can understand
> But He that hath endured
> The Dissolution—in Himself—
> That Man—be qualified
>
> To qualify Despair
> To Those who failing new—
> Mistake Defeat for Death—Each time—
> Till acclimated—to—
>
> (Poem 539)

"No Man" and "That Man" stand at the center of the poem. They may denote Everyman, but both gender and number (capitalization, of course, will not help us) suggest that the prototype of Christ takes priority here over the ectype of the poet or her responsive reader.

"Failing new": behind this modern "failing" stands its type, the failing of the Crucifixion. *Failing* also recalls the familiar "I died for Beauty" (Poem 449). The "Two Kinsmen," Higginson's title for the poem, have in the judgment of the world failed, the one for "Beauty," the other for "Truth." Failure, rejection, is what validates Keats's proposition that "Beauty is truth, truth beauty" and makes the two "Brethren." To the Brotherhood, the fellowship, the community of failure Emily Dickinson, like Saint Mark, like Emerson, calls her readers, and with words that "qualify Despair": "the world," as Emerson has it, "is full of judgment days."

NOTES

1. Saint Leo the Great, *Letters,* trans. by Brother Edmund Hunt, C.S.C. (New York: Fathers of the Church, 1957), 97.
2. Theodore J. Weeden, Sr., *Mark: Traditions in Conflict* (Philadelphia: Fortress Press, 1971). Among the studies reacting to Weeden's are Mary Ann Beavis, *Mark's Audience: The Literary and Social Setting of Mark 4.11–12* (Sheffield: Sheffield Academic Press, 1989); and C. Clifton Black, *The Disciples according to Mark: Markan Redaction in Current Debate* (Sheffield: Sheffield Academic Press, 1989).
3. Weeden, *Mark,* viii, 16, 18, 50, 55, 75, 95.
4. *The Collected Works of Ralph Waldo Emerson,* ed. by Alfred R. Ferguson and Jean Ferguson Carr. Vol. 3: *Essays,* 2d ser. (Cambridge, Mass.: Harvard University Press, 1983) 16–17. Subsequent references to this edition and to Vol. 2 (*Essays, 1st ser.*) appear in parentheses. Jay Leyda, *The Years and Hours of Emily Dickinson* (New Haven: Yale University Press, 1960), 2:20–21, first invited attention to this source. See also Jack L. Capps, *Emily Dickinson's Reading* (Cambridge: Harvard University Press, 1966), 114–16, 173, 216 n.32.
5. *The Complete Poems of Frederick Goddard Tuckerman,* ed. N. Scott Momaday (New York: Oxford University Press, 1965), ix.
6. Winters, *Forms of Discovery* (Denver: Alan Swallow, 1967), 289–94.
7. Momaday, foreword, in *Complete Poems of Frederick Goddard Tuckerman,* ix.
8. Letter to Hawthorne, quoted in Julian Hawthorne, *Nathaniel Hawthorne and His Wife* (Boston: Houghton, Mifflin, 1893), 2:274–75.
9. Momaday, *Complete Poems of Frederick Goddard Tuckerman,* xvi.
10. Samuel L. Golden, *Frederick Goddard Tuckerman* (New York: Twayne, 1966), 133.
11. "The Whittier Birthday Speech" (1877), in *Mark Twain Speaking,* ed. Paul Fatout (Iowa City: University of Iowa Press, 1976), 114.
12. Goethe, Johann Wolfgang von, *Faust: A Tragedy* (Boston: Houghton-Mifflin, 1912), 1:1224–37.
13. *Poems and Essays by Jones Very* (Boston: Houghton Mifflin, 1886), 108. See William Irving Bartlett, *Jones Very: Emerson's "Brave Saint"* (Durham: Duke University Press, 1942), esp. 47–48, 54–55; and Edwin Gittleman, *Jones Very: The Effective Years, 1833–1840* (New York: Columbia University Press, 1967), esp. 188–89, 217, 294.
14. Golden, *Frederick Goddard Tuckerman,* 37–40, 128–33.

Emily Dickinson and the Reading Life

Willis J. Buckingham

The right function of poetry is to animate, to console, to rejoice—in one
word, to *strengthen*.

—Matthew Arnold (1875)

With every page I turn and return I grow more and more in love.
—Louise Chandler Moulton (reviewing
Emily Dickinson, 1890)

At first glance Dickinson's descriptions of reading appear to stress only
its excitement, interiority, and isolation. Her remark to Higginson that
she knows poetry physically ("If I [feel] so cold no fire ever can warm
me") gives the impression of Dickinson as an age-of-sensibility reader,
taking pleasure in the solitary consumption of joy, terror, and pathos.[1] In
"He fumbles at your soul" she portrays the writer as a "soul-scalping"
visionary who leaves the reader ecstatic but annihilated.[2] This privatized
construction of the reading act, combined on the one hand with the
marked inwardness of her poems and on the other with her reclusive life
and refusal to publish, have led to the widespread conclusion that reading
and writing for Dickinson were intensely self-centered. Rather than par-
ticipating in the literary ethos of her generation by writing for others, for
their moral or spiritual uplift, she is believed to have composed only for
her own benefit.[3]

Yet the subject of poems must not be confused with their cultural
negotiation of reader-writer relations. Being the most subjective and
confidential of poetic genres, the lyric nevertheless exists as much to
communicate with others as does verse narrative and drama. The speaker
of "The way I read a letter's this" (Poem 636) retires not to deny sociality
but, rather, to "Peruse how infinite" she is to her correspondent and to
reexperience how important that person, in his or her absence, is to her.[4]

In "The martyr poets did not tell" (Poem 544) she makes art and healing
synonymous. Sometimes her similitude for reading is presence at a pag-
eant, spectacle, or "opera," as in "I cannot dance upon my Toes" (Poem
326). Whether the writer is physician, performer, or antagonist who
"scalps your naked soul" (Poem 315), writing has affective power. Dickin-
son also characteristically insists that the reader does not remain passive:
"The tune is in thee" (Poem 526). With this "giving back," author and
reader establish a relation of exchange.

    How is poetry reading modeled as communication in the book
world Dickinson entered in the 1840s and 1850s? This essay looks at
period poetry reviews to reconstruct the platform of reader-writer rela-
tions in place at mid-century, considering them not as a direct influence
on her but, instead, as "a set of dispositions" learned (often unconsciously
absorbed) from the social field of her literary culture. These reviews
provide what Robert Daly calls (adopting a phrase from Pierre Bourdieu)
a "feel for the game" of reading, a collectively sanctioned "play" between
poet and reader.[5] What community of desire did Dickinson enter as a
reader and soon-to-be writer of poems? How did her circle of readers
construct and sanction poetry as a social practice? What expectations and
rules, what assignment of roles, governed the game played between
reader and lyric poet among educated Americans of the 1840s? From
study of the antebellum cultural imagination this essay then turns to
Dickinson's appropriation of culturally sanctioned scenes of reading.
What interactions between poet and reader do her poems enact? What
dramas of give-and-take do they narrate? These issues require us to inter-
pret a connection between literary texts and, in Robert Scholes's words,
"a larger cultural text, which is the matrix or master code that the literary
text both depends upon and modifies."[6]

The Reviewing Culture: Poetry Reading as Exchange

Dickinson came to her majority during a period of reaction against
one-way models of literary participation that imagined readers as self-
indulgent recipients of authorial invention and genius.[7] American literary
culture of the 1830s and 1840s guards against solipsism by demanding
that poetry work both centripetally, as individual illumination, *and* cen-
trifugally, as sympathetic connection with others. Antebellum reviewers
continue to imagine poetry reading as a passive reception of power but
seem newly determined to equalize the power exchange within the

reading situation. They uphold the paradigm of the giving genius and the gratefully receiving reader while insisting on a new set of pro-community relations in which readers are given a presumption of fraternity with writers.

Contributing to this development were dramatic improvements, during the poet's early adulthood, in the post office, in printing technology, and in the production of mass-produced books, magazines, and newspapers. Republican interest in an informed citizenry brought new levels of literacy to women as well as men. More and more Americans inherited leisure-class conditions, making them part of a widening community of readers—and writers, for it was a decade in which personal correspondence, not only printed documents, began to replace direct experience and face-to-face conversations, especially for women.[8] These changes, as they affected the reading tactics of Dickinson's generation, achieve their most direct expression in those periodicals and newspapers making it their business to appeal to "the literary classes." Their reviews and articles express what they believed their readers enjoyed, wanted to enjoy, and should enjoy when they opened a book of verse. Among them was the newly founded *Literary World,* a "high-culture" New York opinion journal that took as its model the leading London weeklies.[9] One of its first articles is a "times have changed" editorial entitled "Bad News for the Transcendental Poets." Noting that "transcendentalism . . . is beginning to be considered a bad card for a young author to play," the writer quotes both the *Boston Courier* and the *London Athenaeum* to the effect that the world has had its fill of "visionary bardlings" who affect misty imitations of Carlyle.[10]

Reviewing an 1846 edition of Emerson's poems a few weeks later, the *Literary World* indicates that his undoubted genius can be enjoyed only by the like-minded few and that what most readers want is less intellect and more humanity. Wordsworth comes a step closer and Byron still nearer. Emerson and Byron both wrote on the loss of a child, for example, but "in one we have the voice of lamentation lost in a vague speculation on fate—interesting only to the intellect: in the other, piercing to the very well-springs of the heart." Emerson may satisfy the rare and rarified reader, but "mankind at large" consists of a "more animated circle of readers" who rightfully care more for the poet able to render "the external world identified with human passion."[11]

Other editorials argue that the "traits" most needed in American poetry are "freshness, vivacity, and genuine force." American poets abound but few ease the reader's famine of soul: instead of "dramatic power," they offer only "descriptive talent," "elegance" rather than "energy," and "for passion, [only] sentimentality."[12] Readers need more than agreeable charm and sociability; they yearn profoundly for the voice of a master spirit "like Chaucer's scholar, 'Sounding in moral virtue, was his speech.' "[13] Because it is "spontaneous [and] individual," the "lyric spirit" best facilitates expression of this kind:

> It is in such poems the poet writes his life, gives his experience; proclaims his joy and praises, embalms a friend or an enemy; deepens a sentiment or renders his description most vivid. The regular forms of poetry seem strained and elaborate compared with this. They want, apparently, the impulse which gives truth to these, and which infuses its life in them. Other verse is more reflective or philosophical: [the lyric] gives the essence of the art; the true poetic afflatus.[14]

By invoking Chaucer's "scholar" as a model of the true poet, the *Literary World* pictures the ideal reader-writer relationship as that of preceptor and enamored pupil, between whom there are bonds of equality and friendship. A similar figure of the reader is sketched in pages of the *North American Review* during the late 1840s. The problem with a poet like Byron, according to the *Review*'s essay on him in 1845, is his unreliability as a friend. He has passion, originality, and all the outward marks of true poetic genius, but

> his readers were to be his vassals, and reflect the changes of his own feelings. He loved power for its own sake, and took delight in its mere exercise. An impulse or a whim he would obey, as other men obey a law or a principle. And then he seems, at times, a mere actor, with the world for his audience, striving to produce brilliant effects, and by no means careless of the applause of the pit.[15]

In his sarcasm and flippancy Byron reveals "sullen hatred" of humankind. As stage performer, he is brilliant but essentially unpoetical because so recklessly out of accord with the heart's native language and thus perversely untrue even to himself. Byron fails in genuineness and sincerity; in his outright manipulation, he is "haughty and self-aggrandizing." Though he may temporarily divert his readers, he will leave them undernourished, for he is not speaking to them in a situation in which heart may speak to heart, the listener's best self drawn to the moral attractiveness of the speaker.[16]

The *North American* finds the situation worse with the young William Wetmore Story, whose 1847 *Poems* are "delicate and tasteful" but personally withdrawn from his readers, who fail to receive from him "a single decisive blow." Story "is not much in earnest . . . he is exercising himself rather for his own amusement, than with a view of kindling or imparting delight to others." Story lacks power, deep truthfulness to the human heart, described kinetically here as a "decisive blow." And he wants the other essential, "earnestness." He remains an anonymous, autonomous stranger to his readers.[17]

The *North American*'s and *Literary World*'s two clusters of phrases for reader desire are repeated throughout mid-century reviewing. One set has to do with the need for authorial power and includes such designators as *force, vividness, passion, spontaneity, originality, imagination.* Other terms convey reader expectations for fellowship: *genuineness, honesty, earnestness,* and, above all, *sympathy.* Byron violates "sympathy" by not speaking earnestly; Story fails by not recognizing the human faces of his hearers and not showing his own. In Christian terms both exhibit love of self and prideful exclusion of others. In political terms they sin against equality.

These notices reveal the personal and egalitarian platform upon which poetry is to be transacted. The community of two enacted in silent reading is a microcosm of an ideal human community of best selves bonded in sympathy. Here there is no room for manipulation or for self-absorbed performance. It doesn't matter whether words come easily to the speaker or whether they are labored; poetic experience is "rapture," the reception of power in the context of love.

In its first (1850) issue *Harper's New Monthly Magazine,* another defender of the literary high ground, reprinted with evident approval an article from the London *Eclectic Review* entitled "Have Great Poets Become Impossible?"[18] In enthusiastic, even exalted, language the *Eclectic* argues that all ages have been poetic ages for they all have called forth the central human passions that in fine excess (as in the Crusades) bespeak "the roots of the human soul." Those who say the present century is unpoetical ignore "the volcano in the next mountain—while admiring or deploring those which have been extinct for centuries." The great poets "count the beatings of the human heart." "It is the essence of poetry to increase and multiply—to create an echo and shadow of its own power, even as the voice of the cataract summons the spirits of the wilderness to return it in thunder." The "genius" of poets today "should be less epic and didactic, than lyrical and popular."[19] Notice the careful joining of power and fellowship; the poet still commands epic force yet communicates within a distinctly egalitarian community of echoing and reciprocating souls.

The *Eclectic* does not ignore this contradiction. Poetry multiplies in loaves-and-fishes fashion by creating like responses in the hearts of listeners. Readers' sympathetic vibrations come back as echoes and shadows. But, as mere echo and shadow, the receiving reader would seem to suffer loss of self. The *Eclectic* meets the issue with a curious adjustment of its imagery: instead of annihilating, the "cataract" empowers the "spirits of the wilderness" to echo with their *own* thunder. For the *Eclectic* the poet's inspiriting powers remain intact, but reading as a transaction occurs between equals. The reader is raised to the poet's heights. Should the poet thunder, readers can thunder back.

Harper's expresses this two-directional pull a year later when taking up a new book of poems by Richard Henry Stoddard. The journal's reviewer pictures Stoddard as the ideal poet-reader and reader-poet. He is bold and deeply reflective, but, the reviewer quickly adds, "on themes of tender and pathetic interest, [Stoddard's] words murmur with a plaintive melody that reaches the hidden source of tears."[20] Stoddard "reaches" his audience, stirring them at a personal dimension of depth with communion that is at once emotional and intellectual. This implied nearness to his readers (Stoddard communicates at "hidden" levels) *Harper's* takes a remarkable step farther. A derivative style gives Stoddard more, not less, credibility as a poet. His voice "betrays the influence of frequent communings with his favorite poets," because Stoddard "is eminently susceptible and receptive":

> He does not wander in the spicy groves of poetical enchantment, without bearing away sweet odors. But this is no impeachment of his own individuality. He is not only drawn by the subtle affinities of genius to the study of the best models, but all the impressions which he receives take a new form from his own plastic nature.[21]

This is *Harper's* garden party setting of the wilderness responding to the cataract. Stoddard's powers as a reader are powers of reception, of affinity, of *sharing* authorial "genius." Superficially, Stoddard resembles Emerson's reclusive artist (described at the end of the latter's essay "The Poet"), who renounces the world to "know the muse only." But Emerson's originating genius stands alone before a holy ideal, while *Harper's* figure ambulates with friendly muses (other poets), giving and receiving and sharing "affinities." Emerson cautions the prospective poet that only "the ideal shall be real to thee, and the impressions of the actual world shall fall like summer rain, copious, but not troublesome, to thy invulnerable essence." Unarmored, malleable, even porous, Stoddard earns the sacred title of poet by walking Calliope's neighborhood. He is able to give to the extent he is able to receive. For *Harper's* fellowship, not isolation, enables human creativity.

These documents reveal pressure, during Dickinson's first years as an adult, to democratize and familialize the poet-reader relationship. The period's literary press demonstrates this development in a multitude of ways. A glance at the contents of periodicals of the time shows strong interest in the lives of authors, in their homes, their regions, their comings and goings. Accounts of visits with a writer or of pilgrimages to an author's home are enormously popular features, given their frequency, in a range of publications, from local papers to the *North American Review*.

Moreover, reviewing during the antebellum period becomes increasingly informal; critics present themselves as cultivated but neighborly, inviting the reader in for after-dinner conversation around the library table. Shortly after *Harper's Monthly* began publication it instituted popular departments entitled "The Editor's Drawer," "The Editor's Study," and "The Editor's Easy Chair." There arose a new sort of book commentator, the "literary correspondent," often a regular contributor to dailies and weeklies. Papers in Philadelphia, for example, or New Orleans would regularly print a column full of Boston or New York "intelligence." Writers of these literary letters adopt the tone of social conversation about literary gatherings or the book trade, addressing their readers as genial friends. Literary magazines also regularly reserved space for "bric-a-brac," scraps of unrelated information about authors and books. Mid-Victorian readers talked together as if they were a transatlantic family with common reading desires and experience. It was a huge community with distinct local, regional, and national constituencies. It was both select (appealing to "discerning" readers) and open to all. The unpretentious tone of "Our Literary Corner" columns made it easy for any reader

to feel at ease. This spirit of affiliation often took concrete form in the
century's many authors' clubs and readers' societies.

Reviewers further presuppose this personalist and devotionalist
readerly ethos by the ways they pay attention to binding and decoration,
praising them as "delicate," "pretty," and "handsome." In June and De-
cember, especially, they would share advice about gift giving, surveying
books designed for the wedding and holiday trade. During Dickinson's
early years the literary annuals were still in vogue, collections of short
pieces, often poems, commissioned for their appropriateness as gifts to
women. To take a single example, *The Hare-Bell; A Token of Friendship*
contained assorted short, heartfelt pieces, with such titles as "Oh, Soft
Sleep the Hills" and "Sonnet to a Friend." The volume treats poetry as a
public form of personal correspondence throughout; it ends with twin
poems, the first by Mrs. Sigourney with, on the facing page, a verse
reply from the friend (she had been his houseguest on Staten Island) her
poem addresses.[22]

Book chat columns of the period offer another vehicle for this spirited
literary sociality of fondness and veneration. They combine clubhouse and
church, a place for gossip, for information, and for talks about writers by
skilled, appreciative readers. Here member-readers also find pictures of
their favorite writers. Leading magazines competed with one another in
the quality of their engravings. *Harper's* first major article on Bryant be-
gins with an arresting half-page portrait and, inside, a view of the poet's
home.[23] This need for visualization runs parallel to "literalness about close
relations with the divine" that led devotionalists to humanize the Father in
the figure of Jesus: "For the first time [in the 1840s] in Protestant America,
there was a healthy market for engravings of Renaissance paintings for
Christ, the Madonna and Child, and the Annunciation."[24]

Indeed, spiritual attachment as the model for the poet-reader relation-
ship owes much to the religious movement of devotionalism that devel-
oped in the United States during Dickinson's childhood years. As de-
scribed by Richard Rabinowitz, for middle-class women "devotionalism
offered a flowing of one's internal spirituality that compensated for a
woman's declining role in social and economic spheres." Devotionalism
cultivated consciousness, expressing the need for intense subjective expe-
rience. Institutions, biblical narrative, and the public arena for moral
action yielded to the individual mind as the place where the battle for
truth was fought.[25] Deepened personal relationships became increasingly
important, not only between Christ and the individual but also among

human beings. Heightened sympathy for a special friend became a religious experience; sufficiently strengthened and intense, it became a foretaste of heaven. Also, as Rabinowitz notes, during the 1830s, 1840s, and 1850s "personal experience became increasingly vicarious; one lived through one's fantasies of other people's lives."[26] Within this devotionalist culture one might well read poems expecting profound communion with a spiritually attractive mentor and soulmate.

Antebellum fiction reviewers, Nina Baym has shown, reflect similar needs and fulfillments. They most admire those stories that would convey energy, occasioning a power transfer from writer to reader:

> The greater the power of the text, the greater the reader's interest, which at its height becomes enchantment, absorption, or fascination. Power is thus experienced as power *over* the reader; but power works by creating interest *in* the reader, so that the reader too becomes strong. Interest refers less to intellect than emotions. . . . Interest in the novel is a kind of excitement.[27]

From this perspective the benefit of verse reading (emotional attachment to, sympathy for, and interest in the poet-speaker) appears scarcely different from the human appeal readers expect to feel for likable characters in fiction.[28] Mid-century readers made a place alongside poet-prophets (like Byron) for poet-neighbors (like Longfellow). Both could mediate the moral sublime. "He is the poet," said *Harper's* of Longfellow as late as 1882, "of the household, of the fireside, of the universal home feeling. The infinite tenderness and patience, the pathos, and the beauty of daily life, of familiar emotion, and the common scene."[29] This willingness to appreciate both examples of the poet is visible in the titles given poetry anthologies. In the Dickinsons' library were Rufus Griswold's *Sacred Poets of England and America* (1849) and Charles Dana's *Household Book of Poetry* (6th ed., 1860).[30]

Republican ideals, literacy and leisure for women, changes in information diffusion and in spiritual experience, the century's need to defend against disheartening mechanization and skepticism, all shaped the conditions for poetry reading when Emily Dickinson came of age. In particular, as Jane Tompkins has pointed out, a great "faceless" middle class became the audience for poetry, rather than, as in the eighteenth century, a small, elite readership. "There was no longer any way," she continues, "for the poet to measure the impact of his work on an audience, since the author and the audience were no longer personally known to each other."[31] But far from fearing this development—or accepting depersonalization—the American literary establishment made egalitarianism the basis for insisting on poetry's social and socializing function. While it is true, as Tompkins says, that literature in general "became synonymous with emotionalism, individualism, and the contemplative life," the reading life in Victorian America was understood as more than self-regarding enrichment.[32] Of all the genres poetry could most directly express heartfelt communion; it was the preeminent literary medium for social exchange at its dimension of depth. In Dickinson's literary culture reading at its best energized the human capacity for personal attachment.[33] This congruence between personal relationships and those between reader and writer held for those who lived into the turn of the century: Howells would title one of his memoirs *Literary Friends and Acquaintance* (1900); Harriet Prescott Spofford called hers *A Little Book of Friends* (1916).[34]

Dickinson's Stories of Reading

To what extent did Emily Dickinson participate in this poetry reading culture? We know her to have been a passionate reader and to have enjoyed the ardors and intimacies of the Victorian woman's literary life, "one of the richest and deepest," as Allen Tate has famously remarked of Dickinson, "ever lived on this continent."[35] The devotionalist, friendship ethos cultivated reverie and the inner life, integrating poetry making with other satisfying work (like letter writing and gift giving) that would nourish and strengthen others. Dickinson describes making poems as such an activity in her lines beginning "I fit for them," the likely reference being to her private audience of friends and correspondents. "I fit for them," she continues, in the hope "that abstinence of mine produce / A purer food for them" (Poem 1109). From the side of receiving poetry she frequently equates consumption with nourishment, rapture, and the opening of one's secret heart: "Strong Draughts of Their Refreshing Minds / To drink—enables Mine" (Poem 711).[36]

The presumption of intimacy works at many levels in Dickinson's poetry. Her verse often begins with a striking self-reference, as in an urgent communication with a friend: "I can't tell you—but you feel it—" (Poem 65); "I had some things that I called mine—" (Poem 116); "I learned—at least—what Home could be—" (Poem 944). Accentuating that confidentiality, as if opening a private window into her interiority, the poems adopt a notable syntactic abbreviation, replicating the structures of inner speech, the condensed speech for oneself.[37] If her poems resemble letters, her letters, as many have remarked, often resemble poems.[38] She indicated the radical personalism of her verse making in refusing to publish, to "auction" her "mind" (Poem 709) by submitting it to the nonoccasional neutrality of print.[39] Her initial question to Higginson about her poems asked whether he thought they "breathed" (L 260).

Within this context of deeply personal (more intense for not being face-to-face) communication Dickinson nevertheless also gives distancing eminence to the poet vis-à-vis her reader. In the give-and-take of this sacralized one-sided dialogue her speakers frequently role-play the professional to the layperson. "The World—feels Dusty" (Poem 715), for example, figures this hierarchical difference in the power it gives the speaker to attend, and to fully meet, the eleventh-hour needs of the dying: "Mine be the Ministry / When thy Thirst comes—." Dickinson's poems are almost obsessively about the social transactions of giving and taking. They contain stories of "service," narratives of relation between self and others that correlate with the readership conditions indicated in poetry reviewing at mid-century. Two poems, in particular, illustrate this connection between literary text and readership culture. Both are about service, and, though neither poem speaks directly to poet-reader relations, each posits a power structure resting on professionalism. These poems, and others like them, demonstrate how Dickinson modifies Victorian literary friendship codes to include tensions and problems of intimacy in the reader-writer relationship. The first of these poems has been little noticed; to the second modern scholarship is granting preeminence. Both imagine their speakers as persons of compelling competence.

> I think the longest Hour of all
> Is when the Cars have come—
> And we are waiting for the Coach—
> It seems as though the Time
>
> Indignant—that the Joy was come—
> Did block the Gilded Hands—
> And would not let the Seconds by—
> But slowest instant—ends—

The Pendulum begins to count—
Like little Scholars—loud—
The steps grow thicker—in the Hall—
The Heart begins to crowd—

Then I—my timid service done—
Tho' service 'twas, of Love—
Take up my little Violin—
And further North—remove.

(Poem 635)

Here the speaker, a violinist, performs for friends and relatives brought from afar (in railcars, evidently) to witness their beloved's deathbed moment when "Joy was come." They experience an intersection of the timeless with time that seems to stop the clock. "Indignant"—Dickinson's variant is *affronted*—at this intrusion, chronometric time soon ends this haunted, extraquotidian interval (Dickinson elsewhere describes it as "a Wilderness of Size" [Poem 856]). The pendulum begins again, there is noise of steps in the hall, the bustle of life resumes, and the speaker, her "timid service" finished, retires with her "little" instrument "further North," North being the place, in Dickinson's geography, of solitude and "lovelessness."[40]

We have seen that reviewing in Dickinson's era brought an egalitarian personalization to the office of the poet, while simultaneously maintaining earlier figurations of the poet as uplifting visionary. Is the poet in this poem one of many or one out of many? Apparently both. On the one side, she is hardly self-assured, and the capacity of her instrument to affect others is "small."[41] At best she is only an accompanist to this extradiurnal experience. Her audience seems to be absorbed with her (rather than by her) in a strange "waiting"—out of space, out of time. She does not appear until the poem's last stanza, giving herself the status of an afterthought. Nevertheless, in that final verse the word *Tho'* offsets these many diminishments with two oppositional indicators of power: "service" and "love." An accompanist to immortality, a facilitator of awe, she is a professional. However little those benefiting are aware, hers is a skilled enablement motivated by and conveying human affection.

Distinguishing itself from softer versions of the Victorian (female) ministering angel is the note here of professionalism. *Service* in the poem carries a certain privacy and distance from the event and implies distinctly nonamateur capacities. Though timid, the speaker wields an authority validated by her masterly description of death's "slowest instant" as experienced by the living. She is an artist of unquotidian, nonhabitual consciousness. She is a performer who when finished picks up her instrument and leaves. For how well she accomplishes her task (the realization of awe) the poem itself exists as sufficient evidence.

The poem's scene suggests an initial separation of mourners from the speaker, indicating individuation with the opening words *I think*. The speaker is the only one with a violin, having thereby a special status of musician called to serve at a special event. During performance, while waiting for death's "Coach," however, distinction is eclipsed. Souls in a shared privacy vibrate collectively to the only sound, hers, that accompanies this mighty arrival. Her instrument's "discourse" is that of background music. When the service is over, however, first-person separation returns. Three events constitute this narrative: (1) being called, or at least acting instinctively on a presumed desire; (2) serving (to good effect and in a context of extreme intimacy and privacy); and (3) retiring. In terms of social transaction two potentials are realized, both intense community and intense loneliness, the speaker finally aware (perhaps in the commodification of skill) of a formidable barrier between herself and those she serves.

"I think the longest Hour of all" focuses on a haunted moment of enchantment rather than on the office of the poet; nevertheless, it contains a set of dispositions pertaining to the reader-writer relationship that accord well with ideas voiced in mid-century reviewing: the affiliation and mutuality of the writer and reader, yet, equally, the authority and distancing professionalism of the artist. "My Life had stood—a Loaded Gun—" provides another example of reader-writer give-and-take. Being, apparently, a meditation by the speaker about her relation to her beloved, the underlying situation of this alliance is, as in "I think the longest Hour of all," one of service. If we substitute writer or artist for the speaker, and reader or consumer of art for the beloved (the "owner" in this poem) a social narrative emerges markedly similar to that in "I think the longest Hour of all."

My Life had stood—a Loaded Gun—
In Corners—till a Day
The Owner passed—identified—
And carried Me away—

And now We roam in Sovreign Woods—
And now We hunt the Doe—
And every time I speak for Him—
The Mountains straight reply—

And do I smile, such cordial light
Upon the Valley glow—
It is as a Vesuvian face
Had let it's pleasure through—

And when at Night—Our good Day done—
I guard My Master's Head—
'Tis better than the Eider-Duck's
Deep Pillow—to have shared—

To foe of His—I'm deadly foe—
None stir the second time—
On whom I lay a Yellow Eye—
Or an emphatic Thumb—

Though I than He—may longer live
He longer must—than I—
For I have but the power to kill,
Without—the power to die—

                                                    (Poem 754)

The speaker begins her professional work when her abilities are recognized and claimed. Her service for the requester is to put under enchantment the various activities of daily life. (Authors do the same for readers once readers know them and "carry away" their books.) The reader experiences intimacy and empowerment from the artist-professional. The reader, having exchanged the writer's voice for his or her own, finds his or her position in the world so strengthened that all nature is put under obedience ("mountains straight reply"). Other daily activities, such as work ("hunting") and competition ("To foe of His—I'm deadly foe—") come to fruition when the day is done, by a "deep pillowed" night of refreshment infused with erotic satisfaction. Of its nature, however, this enchantment is transitory, conditioned by the mortality of the reader. He or she has the "power" of finitude, of stepping out of time into eternity ("Though I than He—may longer live / He longer must—than

I—"). The writer, in what she has written, may continue to be present in
this world as she enhances the lives of other reader-consumers ("the
power to kill, / Without the power to die—"). But this power of service
is a shadowy, ancillary power, dependent on being called into her role as
giver by those who request "ownership" or clientship of her.

With her paradigmatic stress on service in both these poems Dickin-
son understands the role difference between reader and writer as that
between purchaser and merchant. Like the reviewers' maintenance of
paradoxical modes of relation, the writer, as both friend and inspirer—
both one with and other to the reader—Dickinson articulates a relation of
layperson to professional, buyer to seller. The reader enjoys an infusion
of power (or, in the other poem, an immersion in the sublime) along with
a relation of intimacy with the writer; the writer, as a holder of the power
to enchant, retains presumptive superiority to the reader. Yet that advan-
tage is finally only pure capacity; it can be given again and again but only
on demand from the purchasing, "owning" client-reader. There can be
jubilation in serving and being served ("And now We roam in Sovereign
Woods") but, along with it, the chastening reminder that relations be-
tween reader and writer, in so far as they are professional, are between
quite distinct entities. The artist's power carries with it the sadness of
difference. As creator, she is embodied in her artifacts; she is in a sense
inferior to those she serves, for, in having a vitality that can die, they
enjoy a humanity she can join and enrich but then must leave—"And
further North—remove."

It is a commonplace that in Dickinson's poems scenes of death and
scenes of love are marked by an inexorable journeying of the speaker
away from the adored and longed-for other. These narratives are like
scenes of reading from the point of view of the reader, who must finally
close the book, and from the point of view of the writer, whose "services
of love" are no longer needed. Dickinson's literary culture dichotomized
its portraits of the artist as both companion and hero. She responded with
a central conception of reading as service that retains both writerly roles
(friend and professional) but, in its metaphor of service, introduces a
poignant note of writerly subordination and indenture that is absent in
antebellum reviewing.[42]

Dickinson's poems conflate the reading life and the writing life in
recurring dramas of being called ("identification"), of enchantment and
connection, and of inexorable separation. Served and server temporarily

achieve sympathetic republican communion but inevitably retreat to different spheres. "Because I could not stop for death" (712), for example, follows this progression, in which parties from different worlds join, a layperson gives herself up to a professional, they are closely in contact as they experience worldly/unworldly strangeness, then they separate, with the speaker feeling the aftermath of heightened awareness, a sense of the timeless within time. Implicit within this poem is a characteristic scene of the reading life from the point of view of the reader. Whether from the reader's side (as in this poem or "I think I was enchanted" [Poem 593], Dickinson's poem in tribute to Barrett Browning) or from the writer's perspective (as in "I think the longest Hour of all" and "My life had stood—a Loaded Gun—"), the experience is accompanied by feelings of joy followed by loss, of bonding followed by loneliness.[43]

This plot informs even such well-known "nature" poems as "A Bird came down the Walk—" (Poem 328), in which two unlike creatures, bird and speaker, almost join. In the bird's presence the speaker's world turns surrealistically and wonderfully strange—but only for a moment. The bird, as "author" of the experience, just as suddenly abandons the speaker, leaving her alone with the aftermath of its absence. A similar drama governs "A Route of Evanescence" (Poem 1463) with a powerful giver (the hummingbird) vanishing as the visited blossoms adjust their tumbled heads. Their everyday world is invested with other-worldly ("from Tunis") enchantment.

Perhaps Betsy Erkilla is right to insist that Dickinson often follows aristocratic impulses.[44] But Dickinson appears to imagine reader-writer relations even more democratically than reviewers of her time. For example, in another of her poems the writer, though strong, seems to vanish, while the (poetic) lamps she lights continue their life of service ("The Poets light but Lamps—" [Poem 883]). The destiny of genius is to become poignantly divorced from its originating vitality. Though superior in power, the artist waits until called, then her power seems put under a law of separation even from her. From the author's side more than from the reader's, the reading act is haunted by its end. The taker profits; the giver learns that around capacity hovers effacement.

Similarly, in "A Word made Flesh" Dickinson pictures reading as a Christian service of communion. The reader is, of course, both suppliant and beneficiary, but the figure of the servant-writer emphasizes the humility and self-emptying of Jesus rather than his powers of divinity. Jesus' situation is egalitarian, for, like writers and all professionals, his ability to

give depends upon being called. The poem's stress on intimacy further
implies a give-and-take between equals:

> A Word made Flesh is seldom
> And tremblingly partook
> Nor then perhaps reported
> But have I not mistook
> Each one of us has tasted
> With ecstasies of stealth
> The very food debated
> To our specific strength—
>
> A Word that breathes distinctly
> Has not the power to die
> Cohesive as the Spirit
> It may expire if He—
> "Made Flesh and dwelt among us"
> Could condescension be
> Like this consent of Language
> This loved Philology.
>
>   (Poem 1651)

This story of agency and benefit is told from the point of view of the
taker, but it shares a common plot with implied stories in other poems.
The opening lines of the second stanza, "A Word that breathes distinctly /
Has not the power to die," rehearse the situation of the speaker in "My
Life had stood   a Loaded Gun   ," who had extraordinary consensual
power to act but, lacking finitude, had no power to be acted on.[45] The
reading life precipitates a paradoxical exchange of power, enacting "con-
descension" that simultaneously exalts and annuls the giver. Here are
sacralized request and compliance ("consent"), professional capacity
("Philology"), affective (ad)ministration ("loved"), rhapsodic privacy
("ecstasies of stealth"), intimacy, nourishment, and self-emptying ("con-
descension"). What we might call the "shadow drama" in this poem is a
three-part enactment of consent occasioning nearness/performance fol-
lowed by separation/effacement. At the individual level one might call
this ur-story an intimacy replacement fantasy. While on the one hand it
speaks to and springs out of Dickinson's enjoyment of reading as an act of
privacy, on the other it enacts an experience of "self-in-relation."[46] As the

reviewers of her generations insisted, literary affiliation is not one emo-
tion cultivated among others in an interiorized culture of the feelings.
Rather, it signifies an ethical standard of literary relations by which writ-
ers who fail to make human connection, as persons, are severely judged.

Dickinson, too, believes that books matter most on a personal level.
In her letters she refers to authors as if she, they, and her correspondents
are all members of the same intimate circle. At its fullest, or most "po-
etic," literature profoundly resembles correspondence: it is "home feel-
ing," privacy and community combined. Within this cultural field of
poet-reader relations Dickinson constructs haunted narratives of access
and effacement.

NOTES

1. *The Letters of Emily Dickinson,* ed. Thomas H. Johnson, 3 vols. (Cambridge:
   Harvard University Press, 1958), 2:473–74 (as numbered in this edition,
   Letter 342a). Letter numbers cited parenthetically in the text (with the prefix
   "L") follow this edition.
2. *The Poems of Emily Dickinson,* ed. Thomas H. Johnson, 3 vols. (Cambridge:
   Harvard University Press, 1955), 1:238–39 (as numbered in this edition, Poem
   315). Poem numbers cited parenthetically in the text follow this edition.
3. Joanne Dobson, for example, notes that Dickinson is "reticent" about social
   issues and that she wrote "for the relief of her own mind not for the moral
   betterment of the reader" (*Dickinson and the Strategies of Reticence* [Blooming-
   ton: Indiana University Press, 1989], 91–95). Yet, as Dobson justly notes,
   Dickinson was living at a time when "writing was perceived as a hierarchi-
   cally constituted moral act in which the lines of responsibility ran like a
   telegraph line directly from heaven through the writer to the world" (95).
4. See Christopher E. G. Benfey (*Emily Dickinson and the Problem of Others*
   [Amherst: University of Massachusetts Press, 1984]) on poet-reader relations
   implied in this poem. He believes its last two lines indicate Dickinson's
   characteristic "shift from salvation through God to salvation through other
   people" (48–50). I am indebted to Benfey's volume in many ways, especially
   his careful discussion of intimacy in Dickinson and his application to her of
   the term *effacement.*
5. Robert Daly, "Cooper's Allegories of Reading and 'The Wreck of the Past,' "
   in *Readers in History: Nineteenth-Century American Literature and the Contexts of
   Response,* ed. James L. Machor (Baltimore: Johns Hopkins University Press,
   1993), 117.
6. Robert Scholes, *Textual Power: Literary Theory and the Teaching of English*
   (New Haven: Yale University Press, 1985), 33.

7. It is clearer in the twentieth century that benevolence, teaching, and empathy were present in both age-of-sensibility and Romantic traditions; see, for example, Janet Todd, *Sensibility: An Introduction* (London: Methuen, 1986).

8. Richard Brown, *Knowledge Is Power: The Diffusion of Information in Early America, 1700–1865* (New York: Oxford University Press, 1989), 162–65.

9. Richard Broadhead discusses the mid-century emergence of elite literary journals in *Cultures of Letters: Scenes of Reading and Writing in Nineteenth-Century America* (Chicago: University of Chicago Press, 1993).

10. *Literary World* 1 (20 February 1847): 53.

11. *Literary World* 1 (3 April 1847): 198.

12. *Literary World* 1 (17 April 1847): 245.

13. *Literary World* 1 (29 May 1847): 390.

14. *Literary World* 1 (17 July 1847): 557.

15. *North American Review* 60 (January 1845): 75.

16. *North American Review* 60 (January 1845): 74, 75. The *North American's* reviewer, probably E. P. Whipple, seems to miss self-representational ironies characteristic of Byron's speakers. Frank Luther Mott notes that in the 1820s and 1830s the *North American Review* had been "inconsistent" on Byron; see his book *A History of American Magazines, 1850–1865* (Cambridge: Harvard University Press, 1938), 230.

17. *North American Review* 64 (April 1847): 426.

18. Harvard University's Houghton Library inventory of the Dickinson family's books lists bound *Harper's* volumes both from the Edward Dickinson household and from Austin Dickinson's home next door. The Dickinsons subscribed to *Harper's* continuously from its inception in 1850; see Jack L. Capps, *Emily Dickinson's Reading* (Cambridge: Harvard University Press, 1966), 128–29.

19. *Harper's New Monthly Magazine* 1 (August 1850): 341, 342.

20. *Harper's New Monthly Magazine* 4 (December 1851): 138. Dickinson's "Many a phrase has the English language—" describes "bright orthography's" emotional concussion in terms of joyful tears. "Thundering its Prospective— / Till I stir, and weep—" (Poem 276).

21. *Harper's New Monthly Magazine* 4 (December 1851): 138.

22. *The Hare-Bell,* ed. C. W. Everest (Hartford: Gurdon Robins, Jr., 1844). Dickinson's "Did the Harebell loose her girdle / To the lover Bee" (213) carries forward this analogical field for friendship speech, giving its figuration of intimacy a sexual intensity and social elevation: "Would the Eden *be* an Eden, / Or the *Earl—an Earl?*" On the popularity of annuals, see Lee Erickson, "The Poets' Corner: The Impact of Technological Changes in Printing on English Poetry, 1800–1850," *ELH* 52 (1985): 899–900.

23. *Harper's New Monthly Magazine* 2 (April 1851): 581, 583.

24. Richard Rabinowitz, *The Spiritual Self in Everyday Life: The Transformation of Personal Religious Experience in Nineteenth-Century New England* (Boston: Northeastern University Press, 1989), 180.

25. Rabinowitz, *Spiritual Self,* 164, 173.

26. Rabinowitz, *Spiritual Self,* 216.

27. Nina Baym, *Novels, Readers, and Reviewers* (Ithaca: Cornell University Press, 1984), 42.

28. Of course, persons in stories were not expected to carry the numinous force and passion of poetic genius. Having more potential as a religious experience than fiction, poetry seemed safely locked away, to anxious critics, from the more mundane pleasures (such as suspense) of the novel. Yet it is often hard to distinguish, in practice, in the literary reviews of Dickinson's early adulthood, between the desires of readers of the two genres for nearness to a valued other. In both genres authorially constructed best selves summon the best selves of readers. On Dickinson's attitudes toward intimacy and privacy, see Benfey, *Emily Dickinson.* The phrase "best self," used in several places in this essay, is Matthew Arnold's. Peter Dale elaborates on its meaning. Arnold, he feels, held "that religion is like poetry inasmuch as its value resides in an *emotional attitude,*" causing "attention to be redirected from what poetry is saying about truth, to how it is affecting the reader" (*The Victorian Critic and the Idea of History: Carlyle, Arnold, Pater* [Cambridge: Harvard University Press, 1977], 168).

29. *Harper's* 65 (June 1882): 126.

30. Capps, *Emily Dickinson's Reading,* 202, 204. The presence of both desires, for lonely vision and for affiliation, is especially apparent in Whitman's fashioning of a speaker who is a nurturing and inspiriting god-comrade.

31. Jane P. Tompkins, "The Reader in History: The Changing Shape of Literary Response," *Reader-Response Criticism: From Formalism to Post-Structuralism,* ed. Jane P. Tompkins (Baltimore: Johns Hopkins University Press, 1981), 217, 218.

32. Tompkins, "Reader in History," 218.

33. Literary friendship culture accounts, too, for the heartfelt reception Dickinson received from her 1890s audience, readers of her own generation for whom her volumes were commonly issued in delicate bindings suitable for gift giving. The friendship ethos is reflected in her editors' strategic placement of "This is my letter to the World" as the "prelude" poem to Dickinson's first (1890) volume. Her first reviewers wrote delightedly of that poem and of the poet's overall "comprehending sympathy" expressed in lines that "quiver with the intensity of her feeling." For these reviewers' phrases, see *Emily Dickinson's Reception in the 1890s: A Documentary History,* ed. Willis J. Buckingham (Pittsburgh: University of Pittsburgh Press, 1989), 128, 59. For an overall study of her early recognition, see Buckingham, "Poetry Readers and Reading in the 1890s: Emily Dickinson's First Reception," in *Readers in History,* ed. James L. Machor (Baltimore: Johns Hopkins University Press, 1993), 164–79.

34. Lawrence Buell describes a division in antebellum New England culture (especially at the highbrow level) between the artist as seer and "skepticism about art's authority" (*New England Literary Culture: From Revolution through Renaissance* [Cambridge: Cambridge University Press, 1986], 72). On the

nineteenth-century debate in the United States between elite and egalitarian cultural values, see also Lawrence W. Levine, *Highbrow/Lowbrow: The Emergence of Cultural Hierarchy in America* (Cambridge: Harvard University Press, 1988). This essay notices a parallel dualism—namely, that establishment American reviewing of the period continued to honor an elitist portrait of the poet as visionary while also sanctioning (on behalf of its growing middle-class readership) an egalitarian literary personalism framed within the ethos of domestic "friendship."

35. Allen Tate, "New England Culture and Emily Dickinson" (1932), rptd. in *The Recognition of Emily Dickinson*, ed. Caesar R. Blake and Carlton F. Wells (Ann Arbor: University of Michigan Press, 1964), 158. Although the friendship ethos was not gender specific, it arose early in the century, when women in large numbers entered the literary marketplace. Literary friendship appears to have taken its impetus from women and received its fullest expression among them. Louise Moulton's "I grow more and more in love" cannot be duplicated in directness and ardor among male (to the extent that they can be identified) reviewers of Dickinson during the 1890s.

36. Dickinson often sent letter-poems to accompany small presents. On "nourishment" and "rapture," see Capps, *Emily Dickinson's Reading*, 187; and Margaret Dickie, *Lyric Contingencies: Emily Dickinson and Wallace Stevens* (Philadelphia: University of Pennsylvania Press, 1991), 55–74.

37. On syntactically abbreviated forms of nonvocalized speech for oneself, see Lev Semenovich Vygotsky, "Thought and Word" in *Thought and Language*, ed. and trans. Eugenia Hanfmann and Gertrude Vakar, 119–53 (Cambridge: Massachusetts Institute of Technology Press, 1962).

38. See especially William Shurr's bibliographical essay appended to his edition of "new poems" drawn from Dickinson's letters: *New Poems of Emily Dickinson* (Chapel Hill: University of North Carolina Press, 1993), 103–6.

39. I am grateful to Robert Weisbuch for his suggestion that, during a time of controversy over slavery, Dickinson's choice of the word *auction* may carry heightened connotations of depersonalization of human beings as objects of commercial exchange.

40. Rebecca Patterson, *Emily Dickinson's Imagery*, ed. Margaret H. Freeman (Amherst: University of Massachusetts Press, 1979), 187. "Region of lovelessness" is Patterson's gloss for "further North" in this poem. "In general," she says, "the North and its associated symbols represent chastity, asceticism, deprivation, suffering, isolation, and death" (185).

41. Christopher Benfey suggests that Dickinson's expressions of small size and small voice may reflect an anorexic fantasy; see *Emily Dickinson*, 102–3. Heather Thomas believes she had the disease; see her essay "Emily Dickinson's 'Renunciation' and Anorexia Norvosa," *American Literature* 60 (1988): 205–25.

42. This essay does not intend to offer exhaustive new explications or to argue that poems once thought to be about death or love or nature are secretly about reading. "My Life had stood," for example, does not explicitly make

an equivalence between the speaker and a writer or between the "Master" and a reader. I am suggesting, rather, that dramas of meeting and service in many Dickinson poems bear a relation to her literary culture's constructions of readership.

43. On the sentimental literary friendship ethos manifested in popular enthusiasm (among female readers) for Elizabeth Barrett Browning's *Aurora Leigh,* see Susan K. Harris, "Responding to the Text(s): Women Readers and the Quest for Higher Education," in Machor, *Readers in History,* 265. On the extremely favorable general reception *Aurora Leigh* received, see John Evangelist Walsh, *The Hidden Life of Emily Dickinson* (New York: Simon and Shuster, 1971), 92–93. Note especially that Ada Parker's response, quoted by Harris, resembles Dickinson's and expresses a combination of heroic and intimate roles implicit in the reader-poet relationship: "I long to possess her poems—to have them by my pillow with the most precious of my books, as a personal inspiration to faith and courage. She drinks at a fountain whose waters cannot fail, and her words are full of hope and healing." In her accounts of reading Dickinson seems to reflect the idea that "possession" has an edge for writers it does not for readers, who, after all, do the possessing. On ambivalence about possession, see Joanne Dobson's discussion of "Good to hide and hear 'em hunt" (Poem 842): one can select being found, can enjoy being found, yet in being found one is captured, "fitted" (*Dickinson and the Strategies of Reticence,* 104–5). Notice also the sacramental imagery in Parker's "healing waters." Dickinson's similar, highly personal, accounts of interest in Barrett Browning's life and work have been widely noted.

44. "Within the political order of Dickinson's verse," Erkilla argues, "the multitude and the democratic masses are consistently demonized" (*The Wicked Sisters: Women Poets, Literary History, and Discord* [New York: Oxford University Press, 1992], 50).

45. For another view of the relation between the two poems, see Robert Weisbuch, *Emily Dickinson's Poetry* (Chicago: University of Chicago Press, 1975), 35–36.

46. See Christopher Benfey on Dickinson's "trusting uncertainty" about human relationships (*Emily Dickinson,* 113); and Joanne Dobson on "the self-in-relation" as fundamental to literary desire in antebellum America ("The American Renaissance Reenvisioned," in *The [Other] American Tradition: Nineteenth-Century Women Writers,* ed. Joyce Warren [New Brunswick: Rutgers University Press, 1993], 170).

Dickinson and the Public

Karen Dandurand

It may seem anomalous even to suggest that there was a public audience for Dickinson's poems during her lifetime. The idea that she was known as a poet only to a few close friends has been widely held. True, it was Dickinson's intention that her poems be kept private, that they not become "public property," as they would if she published. As I have argued previously, one reason she chose not to publish was to protect herself from the attention and curiosity that publication involved. Yet, as she herself and others indicated, despite her efforts to maintain her "barefoot rank," she became known as a writer, and, consequently, there were demands for her poems and curiosity about her life. A larger audience than we have thought was aware of her as a poet during at least the last two decades of her life, though members of this audience usually maintained some reticence about commenting publicly on her in keeping with the private channels through which they had come to know of her work. Present evidence does not make it possible fully to reconstruct this audience, of course, but we can see its general outlines as well as find evidence concerning specific people who knew Dickinson's poetry (if, in some cases, not the identity of its author) long before the first book of her poems appeared in 1890.

The Audience for the Published Poems

Only ten of Dickinson's poems were published in her lifetime, all anonymously, yet, although most readers would not have known the identity of the author, each poem had a potential readership of thousands. (See the appendix to this essay for a list of first printings and reprints of Dickinson poems published in her lifetime.) The poems were published and reprinted in papers that were nationally prominent and had large circulations. Most important, perhaps, is the *Springfield Daily Republican* because all but three of the ten poems either were originally published or were reprinted there. By the 1860s, when five Dickinson poems appeared in its pages, the *Republican* was nationally recognized as a leader in new approaches to journalism and was sold on newsstands throughout the Northeast. According to the masthead, it often had a circulation of fifteen thousand copies by the first years of the Civil War. As I have noted elsewhere, the *Round Table* during its fairly short existence was a much noticed, rather avant-garde, and controversial publication; it claimed an international circulation.[1] The *Brooklyn Drum Beat,* in which three of Dickinson's poems appeared, printed six thousand copies a day during the two weeks it was published, in conjunction with the fund-raising fair to aid the U.S. Sanitary Commission. In addition to sales at the fair and by Brooklyn dealers, it was sold by subscription, with copies going to people throughout the country.

With the poems that appeared in the *Drum Beat* (and probably also the one in the *Round Table*), we can go beyond mere circulation figures and identify a particular audience—an especially literary and sophisticated one—made up of the other writers whose works were published there. In addition to the paid subscribers, *Drum Beat* editor Richard Salter Storrs evidently sent all the issues of the paper to writers who contributed to it. Louisa May Alcott, whose two-part sketch "A Hospital Lamp" appeared the week before the first of Dickinson's poems, noted in her journal for February 1864: "Mr. Storrs D.D. wrote for a sketch for his little paper 'The Drum Beat,' to be printed during the Brooklyn Sanitary Fair. . . . He sent me another friendly letter & all the daily papers as they came out."[2] Her comments suggest that the potential audience for the three Dickinson poems in the *Drum Beat* included, in addition to Alcott, Oliver Wendell Holmes, William Cullen Bryant, Edward Everett, R. H. Stoddard, Edna Dean Procter, George W. Bungay, Alfred B. Street, Caroline Chesebro, John G. Palfrey, Charles Eliot Norton, and Theodore Tilton. There were also other contributors who cannot be identified; many works besides Dickinson's poems appeared anonymously or were signed only by initials. Helen Hunt (Jackson) also may have been among the *Drum Beat* authors, although a poem bearing her later characteristic signature "H. H." cannot be definitely identified as hers.[3]

A similar audience of authors who contributed to the volume would have existed in 1878 for Dickinson's poem in *A Masque of Poets.* In addition, of course, to Helen Hunt Jackson, the contributors included Bronson Alcott, Louisa May Alcott, Thomas Bailey Aldrich, William

Ellery Channing, Annie Fields, James T. Fields, Sidney Lanier, George Parsons Lathrop (editor of the book), Rose Hawthorne Lathrop, James Russell Lowell, Louise Chandler Moulton, Christina Rossetti, F. B. Sanborn, Edmund Stedman, Celia Thaxter, and Sarah Woolsey ("Susan Coolidge").[4] Although he did not contribute to the book, as several of his Concord neighbors did, Ralph Waldo Emerson may have taken a particular interest in "Success is counted sweetest," attributed to him by several reviewers. Though we cannot be sure that Emerson read *A Masque of Poets,* we can assume that each of the anonymous contributors to the volume would have been sent a complimentary copy, as Dickinson was. Publisher Thomas Niles's letter to Dickinson makes clear that she received a copy of *A Masque,* for which she politely wrote to thank him, without referring to the fact that her poem was in the book.[5]

In 1864 the absence of any explicit comment from Dickinson on the unparalleled publication of five of her poems within two months may suggest a similar pattern. It seems that Dickinson, like Alcott, would have received copies of the *Drum Beat* and so would have seen her poems in print there. And, since her family subscribed to the *Springfield Daily Republican,* she probably would have seen that two of her poems were reprinted and would have understood what this implied—that the poems might reappear again, in other newspapers: they had become "public property."

Since newspaper poetry no longer holds the place in popular culture it had in Dickinson's time, we must understand how it functioned then if we are to appreciate the significance of the newspaper publications as a factor in reconstructing her contemporary audience and her attitude toward that audience. Poetry was a regular feature of most mid-nineteenth-century newspapers. It was common for readers to clip or copy poems they liked from the newspapers, putting them in scrapbooks, sometimes even memorizing them, and often sharing them with friends. Dickinson herself participated in this practice when in 1856 she began a letter to Mary Warner by quoting the entire text of a poem by John Pierpont (L 183).[6]

When a poem had been published in one newspaper, others might freely reprint it, frequently but not always citing the paper in which it had first appeared. The source of a reprinted poem was sometimes identified only as an "exchange," and, occasionally, a poem was reprinted with a note saying that the editor did not know where it had first appeared. There was no telling how many miles a poem might travel or for how many weeks, even years, its circulation might continue once it began to "go the rounds of the papers."

The phenomenon whereby a poem printed in one newspaper was reprinted in another and then in a third, and so on, was well known to Dickinson, as it was to all nineteenth-century readers of popular literature. Her familiarity with the practice is indicated in one of her earliest letters, written to Abiah Root in 1846, in which she asks, "Have you seen a beautiful piece of poetry which has been going through the papers lately?" (L 12).[7] Dickinson would have understood that her poems were "going through the papers" in 1864. Two years later she may have expected that would happen (or perhaps she knew it was happening, though reprints of the poem have not yet come to light) when "A narrow fellow in the grass" was first published, placed prominently on the front page of the *Springfield Daily Republican*. If, in fact, "The Snake" "went the rounds of the newspapers," that would explain why when Dickinson wrote to Higginson a month after the initial publication she prefaced her defense, "Lest you meet my Snake" (L 316). She would seem to have little reason to fear he would see a poem published a month before unless she knew or suspected it was being reprinted.

It was even possible for authors of newspaper poetry to become well-known on the basis of a single poem that appeared again and again in the newspapers or for such a poem to be widely known though many of its readers might not know the author's name. Publication of poems in newspapers was often the means of creating reader interest and demand for a collection; though Dickinson's poems were not published for that purpose and no volume was forthcoming while she lived, interest and demand may have been created nonetheless.

Indeed, references in the 1890s to publication of her poems in newspapers about twenty-five years earlier are suggestive of the public audience those poems had in the 1860s. In his first review of *Poems* (1890), a month after its publication, John White Chadwick commented, "Of three or four poems that were printed in her lifetime, we recognize only the first, which came out in 'A Masque of Poets,' . . . and 'A Service of Song,' which appeared in the short-lived *Round Table*, with certain differences from the form given here, unless our memory fails."[8] A month later, in another review, Chadwick remarked more fully:

Of the three or four poems published [in Dickinson's lifetime], one I have treasured in my memory for more than twenty years, not knowing whose it was, having read it in the *Round Table.* . . . I doubt not that many others, when I quote it, will say as Robert Collyer said to me, "Oh, is that her's? I've loved it all these years."—and then resolve that they must know the fountain from which came those few clear drops. ("Emily Dickinson," *Unity* 26, 22 January 1891, 171; rpt. in Buckingham, *Emily Dickinson's Reception,* 103)

While Chadwick knew the poem without knowing who had written it, Charles Goodrich Whiting recalled and quoted another poem he identified as Dickinson's before its book publication later in the 1890s. In one of the earliest reviews of *Poems,* Whiting wrote in the *Springfield Republican,* in which "A narrow fellow in the grass" had first appeared on 14 February 1866:

A touch of humor will have been noticed rarely in these verses [in *Poems*], and certainly Emily Dickinson had not a little of this quality in her nature. A verse of hers published in *The Republican* many years ago concerning "the snake" was an illustration thereof. We can but imperfectly recall it to memory, but it concluded with these lines. . . .

He went on to quote the last four lines of the poem, getting it right except for *I* rather than *But* at the beginning ("The Literary Wayside," *Springfield Republican,* 16 November 1890; rpt. in Buckingham, *Emily Dickinson's Reception,* 20). Whiting's comment indicates that, though the poem was published anonymously, some people connected with the newspaper knew its authorship. Whiting was evidently a member of the *Republican* staff in 1866 but not yet in a position of any authority, and there is no reason to believe he was the one directly responsible for publishing the poem.[9]

These are just a few documented instances from the 1890s of public familiarity with Dickinson's poems published in newspapers of the 1860s. I would argue, however, that there were, as Chadwick suggested, many other readers who would recognize poems they had known for years.

"Private" Sharing of Unpublished Poems

Dickinson is often thought of as having a very small, very private audience—the "few friends" with whom she shared poems enclosed in letters to them. While this view of her carefully selecting and limiting her audience is, I think, essentially correct, we may underestimate the significance, and to some extent the size, of this private audience. First, of course, it is commonly accepted that we have only a fraction of the letters Dickinson wrote, with whole series of letters known to have been lost or destroyed.[10] No doubt, poems were included in many letters now destroyed, lost, or perhaps still extant but not discovered. We can only conjecture about these readers of her poems. But we can look more closely at the way known recipients shared her writings, thus enlarging her audience. In the case of the correspondents known to have received the greatest number of poems—Susan Dickinson, Thomas Wentworth Higginson, and Samuel Bowles—there is, for each, evidence that they shared Dickinson's letters and poems with others. Moreover, there is no reason to suppose that the particular instances that have come to light are unparalleled.

The idea of friends sharing Dickinson's letters and poems may seem shocking, even unethical, to our late twentieth-century sensibilities. But it seems not an uncommon practice in the nineteenth century, and one Dickinson followed herself. Early letters from her to Abiah Root and Austin Dickinson include references to sharing letters she had received (there was an "inner circle" to whom letters usually could be shown) as well as warnings not to let anyone else read a letter she regarded as particularly confidential.[11] Her comment to Louise and Fanny Norcross in 1861 indicates that they had sent her their letters from some unidentified correspondents: "It was pretty to lend us the letters from the new friends. It gets us acquainted. We will preserve them carefully" (L 230). It seems likely that she, in turn, showed or read to them letters she received, as is suggested by Dickinson's report of her unsuccessful attempt to locate a passage Louise asked for: "The beautiful words for which Loo asked were that genius is the ignition of affection. . . . Precisely as they were uttered I cannot give them, they were in a letter that I do not find" (L 691). Evidently, she had previously read to them (or let them read) the missing or misplaced letter, or at least that passage.

There are several well-documented instances in which Dickinson's correspondents shared her poems and letters with others. This broadening of her audience is significant, not merely in terms of increasing numbers but also because her correspondents, many of whom were themselves involved in the literary world, also had friends who were influential in that realm. The evidence is most extensive in the case of Higginson, but we can also be sure that Samuel Bowles, Susan Dickinson, and Helen Hunt Jackson talked about Dickinson's poetry and shared poems and letters sent to them.

Even Fanny and Louise Norcross, who in the 1890s annoyed Mabel Todd by their unwillingness to allow her to see the poems and letters sent to them by Dickinson, may have read to friends their cousin's poems and passages from her letters while Dickinson was living, as Fanny, in a letter to Higginson, reported having done in the 1890s (Bingham, *Ancestors' Brocades,* 142). If they shared Dickinson's poems earlier, this would suggest an important addition to her audience, since, as Martha Ackmann has shown, their circle of friends included prominent literary people. Information Ackmann provides about the Norcrosses' activities in Concord gives a basis for suggesting (though Ackmann does not explicitly do so) that Fanny Norcross might have presented Dickinson's poems at an 1878 meeting of the Concord "Saturday Club." The invited membership of this organization included, in addition to Fanny and Louise Norcross, Bronson Alcott, Louisa May Alcott, William Ellery Channing II, Ednah Dow Cheney, Ellen Emerson, Lydian Emerson, Ralph Waldo Emerson, Daniel Chester French, and Frank Sanborn.[12]

Susan Dickinson was said to have read Emily Dickinson's poems to her guests after the poet's death, a practice evidently begun years before. Her sharing of poems in her possession is especially significant because, by the early 1880s, she had over two hundred poems—the greatest number sent to any of Dickinson's known correspondents. The one documented instance of Susan reading Dickinson's poems to an appreciative visitor while the poet was alive is suggestive of others; there is no reason to think this was an isolated and rare incident.

In early February 1882 Mabel Loomis Todd, who had arrived in Amherst less than six months before, wrote in her diary of an afternoon visit at the home of her new friend Susan Dickinson: "She read me some strange poems by Emily Dickinson. They are full of power."[13] Todd's letter to her parents in late March suggests that by then she was familiar with enough Dickinson poems to have a sense of the poet's "characteristic" style. It is clear that Todd had not gotten the poems to which she referred directly from Dickinson, since she seemed to be commenting on her first letter from the poet, which she called "a very odd & characteristic note." She continued, telling her mother and father, "I am going to bring it [the note] when I come, and also some of her poems to show you" (qtd. in Leyda, *Years and Hours,* 2:361). Presumably, she had gotten

the poems from Susan Dickinson. Todd's promise to share these poems
with her parents illustrates how poems might be disseminated: Dickin-
son's correspondent (in this case, Susan) would share a poem received
from her with a friend; that person in turn might pass it on to another.
The chain of transmission was potentially endless.

Springfield Republican editor Samuel Bowles, in addition to having
been directly responsible for the publication of at least some of the Dickin-
son poems that appeared in his newspaper, also shared her letters and
poems with friends. Bowles apparently made a common practice of al-
lowing others to read letters sent to him and having his letters passed on
by the recipients. For example, in an 1862 letter to Susan Dickinson he
said, "Your sister sent me a sweet, bright letter this morning," adding: "I
will send you the letter next time. I want to show it to Mary" (qtd. in
Leyda, *Years and Hours,* 2:46).[14] Later that year, writing from Paris to
Austin and Susan, he said, "My life, outward & inward, has been spread
before you ad nauseam, if you have taken the trouble to read my letters in
the paper & to Mary" (2:58). Apparently, even letters to his wife were not
so private that they could not be read by others.

Earlier I had speculated that in 1861 Bowles shared Dickinson's
letters and poems with Mary Elwell Storrs.[15] Evidence I have discovered
since then indicates that this was in fact the case. In the fall of 1861
Bowles became acquainted with Mary Storrs and her husband, Richard
Salter Storrs, at a Northampton water cure, where she and Bowles were
being treated. Bowles wrote enthusiastically about the Storrses to Austin
and Susan Dickinson. Based on these and other circumstances, I had
suggested that Mary Storrs might have become familiar with some of
Dickinson's work at that time. Her letter to Mabel Todd thirty years later
confirms this conjecture: "I think I have not told you that I used to see
notes from E.D. written to Mr. Sam Bowles, and was at that time greatly
struck with her power and genius—Mr. B was at Dr. Denniston's at N.
while I was there at one time."[16] Storrs's "used to see" may refer not only
to the months during which she and Bowles were at the water cure but
also to later years. By March 1862 Bowles was referring to the Storrses as
among the "old friends" he visited while in New York, and references to
them in other letters indicate that his visits to their Brooklyn home were
regularly repeated.[17]

Helen Hunt Jackson discussed and promoted Dickinson's poetry with
the two men who played probably the most influential roles in her own
literary career, Higginson and Thomas Niles. There are also indications

that she talked about Dickinson and her poems with others. In a few instances we know that she had discussions about Dickinson with mutual friends or acquaintances because Jackson mentions them in letters to Dickinson. For instance, in 1876 she wrote about a visit from John Dudley: "A very clever man— . . . a Mr. Dudley of Milwaukee, spent a day with us last week, and we talked about you" (L 444a). It seems likely that Jackson would have talked about Dickinson with others she knew to be mutual friends or acquaintances, including Samuel Bowles and Josiah Gilbert Holland, with both of whom Jackson had at some point a friendly author-editor relationship. We know from his letters to Dickinson that Jackson talked with Thomas Niles, her publisher and friend, about Dickinson's poems, enlisting him in her efforts to persuade Dickinson to publish.

Jackson and Higginson discussed Dickinson's poetry and corresponded about it, if intermittently, over a period of many years, beginning in 1866. Higginson wrote in 1890 that he showed Helen Hunt (Jackson) Dickinson's poetry in about 1866 (Leyda, *Years and Hours,* 2:111). In February of that year the recently widowed Helen Hunt moved into the Newport boardinghouse where the Higginsons lived, and, according to his diary, in the months that followed he and she became frequent companions.[18] Though he did not record having shown her Dickinson's letters and poems, it seems that his memory was correct in placing that event in this year. In sharing the poems, he evidently gave her copies or allowed her to copy them. At least some of the Dickinson poems in the "little manuscript volume" to which Jackson refers in a letter to Dickinson seem likely to derive, as Johnson suggests in a note to Jackson's next letter, from the manuscripts Higginson had (L 444a; L 476a n).

Jackson was eager to reciprocate by sending on to Higginson poems Dickinson sent to her. In an 1879 letter Jackson asked Dickinson for "permission to send it [a poem she refers to as Dickinson's "Blue bird"] to Col. Higginson to read"; she added that, along with knowing the poem "by heart," she considered sending it to Higginson her "testimonial to its merit." Although Jackson emphasized her request in a postscript—"Write & tell me if I may pass the Blue Bird along to the Col?"—Dickinson did not acknowledge it in her response (L 601a; L 602). It is not clear whether Jackson sent "Before you thought of Spring" to Higginson, but she did send a letter-poem received earlier in the year to him, adding on the manuscript a note of her own commenting on it (L 601). At least one other Dickinson letter to Jackson was also sent to him, as we know because it remained among his papers (L 937).

The sharing of Dickinson's writings between Helen Hunt Jackson and Higginson was noted by William Jackson in response to Mabel Todd's query about Dickinson's letters to his late wife: "I have not yet given up finding them for I am quite sure they were all preserved by Mrs. Jackson. Possibly she may have sent them to Mr. Wentworth Higginson who was in correspondence with her about Emily Dickinson's writings" (qtd. in Bingham, *Ancestors' Brocades,* 153). Helen Jackson's comment in a letter to Higginson in 1881 indicates that the two of them had a familiarity with Dickinson's work that allowed her ideas to be referred to as one might refer to the works of a published writer: "Isn't that an odd thing? or rather, would it not be if anything were? while nothing is in this world—see E.D.—" (qtd. in Leyda, *Years and Hours,* 2:349).

Higginson was the most active of Dickinson's correspondents in sharing her poems with others—or, at least, there is the most evidence that he did so. And he was eager to discuss Dickinson and was always trying to learn more about her, as shown by the many references he made to such inquiries and his casual mentions of his correspondence with her, which imply that he had discussed her work before with those to whom he addressed these comments.[19]

One almost imagines Higginson asking everyone he met whether they knew Dickinson and could tell him anything about her. Soon after she began writing to him, it seems, he sought out her uncle William Dickinson and talked with him about her.[20] Higginson wrote in 1869 that, although she and her uncle struck him as totally unlike each other, "It brought you nearer e[ven] to know that you had an actual [?] uncle," and added, "But I have not seen him [for] several years, though I have seen [a lady] who once knew you, but could [not] tell me much" (L 330a). Johnson asserted that the woman referred to is Helen Hunt Jackson; while this is possible, there are other possibilities, among them any mutual acquaintance who spent a summer in Newport. After Higginson finally visited Dickinson in Amherst in 1870 he was still seeking additional information about her. He wrote to his wife: "I talked with Prest Stearns of Amherst about her—& found him a very pleasant companion in the cars. . . . Dr. S. says her sister is proud of her" (L 342b). In this letter he sent his wife a "picture of Mrs. Browning's tomb," which Dickinson had given him, saying she had gotten it from Josiah Gilbert Holland. Given Higginson's determination to learn more about Dickinson, it seems likely, knowing that Holland was her friend, that he would have queried Holland about her when an opportunity presented itself.

In addition to seeking information about Dickinson, Higginson shared the poems and letters she sent him with his friends and family. References to Dickinson in letters to his sisters make clear that he had told them about Dickinson and that they were familiar with her poems.[21] Besides the conversations and correspondence with Helen Hunt Jackson, discussed earlier, he seems to have read Dickinson's poems and letters to other friends in Newport, where he lived from the mid-1860s until the late 1870s. Among his close friends there were journalist and lecturer Kate Field, Julia Ward Howe, and Theodora Woolsey and her sister Sarah Woolsey, who published under the name Susan Coolidge. Although there are no comments on Dickinson in the letters to Field that I have seen, the fact that he was acting as Field's literary mentor (she was trying her hand at fiction and poetry) at the same time that he was advising and sharing Dickinson's poems with Jackson suggests he might have followed the same pattern with Field. That the Woolseys were familiar with Dickinson's letters to him is clear from a comment to his sister in 1876 saying that at a recent party the Woolseys "wrote some funny things for different guests" and that his was a parody of a letter from Dickinson (L 481n). Dora Woolsey indicated that she (and presumably her sister) also knew Dickinson's poems from that time. After *Poems* was published in 1890 she wrote to Higginson thanking him for a copy of the book, in which many poems were, as she called them, "my old familiars."[22] Sarah Woolsey's familiarity with Dickinson's writings may have been shared also with Helen Hunt Jackson; Jackson's biographer refers to Woolsey as Jackson's closest friend during a period of more than twenty years.[23]

Higginson's sharing of Dickinson's writings and seeking information about her does not, I believe, contradict the view I have argued elsewhere that he understood and supported her decision not to publish or, at least, "to delay" doing so. Yet he apparently saw his position as Dickinson's "safest friend," to whom she turned for protection against pressure to give her poems up to public demands, as not inconsistent with the private sharing of her "portfolio" poems. He used the term *poems of the portfolio* in the essay he wrote to introduce the poems shortly before the first book was to appear in 1890, and it was applied to them in a description of his 1875 reading before the New England Women's Club, probably suggested by his use of that term in his presentation. He evidently regarded his reading of the poems as "private" even when his audience numbered more than a hundred, so long as the event was closed to the general public and the press.

On 29 November 1875 at the "Woman's Club" Higginson talked about and read poems by "Two Unknown Poetesses," Dickinson and his sister Louisa (who had died the summer before). The fact that he did so and that the audience was very much interested by Dickinson's poems has long been known, but the full name of that organization, and therefore the significance of his presentation, was not recognized before my identification of it in 1984.[24]

Jay Leyda first brought to our attention the following entry in Higginson's diary for 29 November 1875: "At Woman's Club in aftn.—read verses by L.S.H. & E.D." (*Years and Hours,* 2:239). Leyda quotes as well Higginson's letter of 30 November to his sister Anna: "Yesterday afternoon, at the Woman's Club I talked about 'Two Unknown Poetesses'—namely Louisa & Emily Dickinson of Amherst; & read poems by both. . . . Afterwards I read some of E. Dickinson's (not giving the name) & their weird & strange power excited much interest" (2:239). Leyda adds no further identification of the Woman's Club.[25] That the New England Women's Club was the group to which Higginson presented Dickinson's poems is indicated by the following announcement on the front page of the *Woman's Journal* for 27 November 1875: "New England Women's Club—Monday, November 29, at 3:30 P.M., Col. T. W. Higginson will address the club."

Because newspaper reporters were excluded from club meetings, there is no published account of Higginson's lecture and the audience's reaction except for a brief reference in the club's annual report appearing in the *Woman's Journal* the following summer. The report noted that on 29 November 1875 Higginson accepted the club's invitation to choose any topic he wished and he talked about and read the poems of his sister "and also some of another friend, of remarkable strength and originality" (*Woman's Journal,* 15 July 1876). There is no detailed account of Higginson's reading in the extant papers of the New England Women's Club, but there is this brief record:

Mon. Nov. 29th 3:30 p.m.
According to previous agreement the Art & Lit Com[tee] took charge of this afternoon & Mr T. W. Higginson read to crowded rooms from "port-folio poems"—such as could only be privately enjoyed in this way—& wh. seemed to be highly appreciated by those who were thus enabled to hear them.[26]

Although there is no record of the number of people present, Higginson addressed "crowded rooms," and, while there is no indication of exactly who made up his audience, it potentially included many of the leaders of literary Boston and, indeed, some of the major writers of the time.

The membership of the New England Women's Club in the mid-1870s included many writers, reform activists, and women distinguished in other fields. Indeed, a partial listing of the club's members reads like a compendium of notable women in nineteenth-century New England: Julia Ward Howe (longtime president of the club), Louisa May Alcott, Ednah Dow Cheney, Kate Field, Annie Fields, Mary Peabody Mann, Abby W. May, Maria Mitchell, Lucretia Mott, Louise Chandler Moulton, Elizabeth Palmer Peabody, Harriet Hanson Robinson, Lucy Stone, Adeline D. T. Whitney, and Anne Whitney. Some other members are best known by association with their more famous husbands: the wives of Oliver Wendell Holmes, N. P. Willis, and Henry James as well as Lidian Emerson and her daughter Ellen. The club also had "honorary members"—men who could attend meetings but not vote or hold office—including Bronson Alcott, Ralph Waldo Emerson, Henry James, George Ripley, and John Greenleaf Whittier.[27] These well-known names are important because they evoke images, radically different from those given by earlier references, not only of the audience to which Higginson thought it appropriate to present Dickinson's poems but also the audience among which her poems "excited much interest."

Some of the less-well-known names on the New England Women's Club membership rolls may be significant, too, for a different reason. In the record book of members during the club's first forty years two consecutive entries appear for the period 1870–78, both of them reading simply "Norcross, Miss." While the lack of first names or initials makes it impossible to identify them with certainty, these entries may refer to Dickinson's cousins, Louise and Fanny Norcross. If they are the Norcrosses listed, and if they were present at Higginson's reading, they would have recognized the poems as their cousin's—and Dickinson may have learned not only that Higginson read and talked about her poems to the New England Women's Club but also that his large audience, including some of the literary leaders of the day, found the poems extremely interesting. Of course, we can only speculate about whether Dickinson learned of Higginson's reading. But I would suggest that later requests for her poems may have resulted from his reading of them in this important "private" forum.

Though he stresses that he did not reveal her name, at least a few in his audience might have known it because he had earlier shared the poems with them. Others may have recognized poems that had been published; although there is no record of which poems he read, the more than fifty poems Higginson had by 1875 included five of the ten that had appeared in print.[28]

That Higginson recalls his reading of Dickinson's poems nine years later shows not only that it was significant to him but also that he assumed that members of his audience would remember it. His reference indicates, I think, that he considered the presentation a success. Writing on 15 December 1884 to Eva Channing in response to an invitation to address the New England Women's Club in January, Higginson suggested:

> I could fill 45 minutes interestingly, I think, with readings from the poems of Miss [Ellen Harper?], which are practically unpublished—she who wrote "I slept & dreamed that life was Beauty" & is known to most people only by that. . . . I should only read, with comments: as I once did with two other women poets before the Club.[29]

A postscript to a follow-up letter two weeks later may suggest that his 1875 reading aroused an almost uncomfortable level of curiosity—or perhaps that on that occasion, too, he had asked that the nature of his presentation not be announced in advance. He cautioned, "Don't say anything in the notice about my reading *ms. poems.*"[30]

Dickinson's Awareness of a Public Audience

Dickinson was aware of public interest in her work, both through requests she received for poems to publish and through expressions of curiosity about herself that reached her. As she told Higginson, she was "Often . . . troubled by entreaty" for her poems (L 488). Susan Dickinson is the first to comment in print on requests Dickinson received to publish. In her obituary of the poet Susan wrote, "Many saw and admired her verses, and in consequence frequently notable persons paid her visits, hoping to overcome the protest of her own nature and gain a promise of occasional contributions at least, to various magazines" (qtd. in Leyda, *Years and Hours,* 2:473). Among "notable persons" whose efforts became known to Susan were, very likely, the "two Editors of

Journals" who, Dickinson reports to Higginson, visited in the winter of
1861–62 and, as she puts it, "asked me for my Mind" (L 261).[31] Higgin-
son, too, commented in his first biographical account of Dickinson on
requests she had received: "Sometimes . . . her verses found too much
favor for her comfort, and she was urged to publish. In such cases I was
sometimes put forward as a defense."[32] He then quoted from her letters
to him about two entreaties for publication during the last decade of her
life: Helen Hunt Jackson's request for a poem to be included in *A Masque
of Poets* and the request in response to which, she told Higginson, "I have
promised three Hymns to a charity" (L 674).

In rare instances she allowed her poems to be published on behalf of
charities—three poems in about 1880 (published texts not yet located),
because she could not refuse to "aid unfortunate Children," and three
poems in the *Drum Beat* in 1864, because she could not refuse to "help the
sick and wounded soldiers." More often, a comment to Louise Norcross
suggests, she resisted even such entreaties. In 1872 Dickinson was asked
by a "Miss P——" to, as she put it, "aid the world by my chirrup more."
"I replied declining. She did not write to me again—she might have been
offended, or perhaps is extricating humanity from some hopeless ditch."
Her comment on why she cannot quote the request verbatim suggests it
was one of many: "I . . . always burn such letters, so I cannot obtain it
now" (L 380). These persistent solicitations of her poetic contributions
suggest that she was more widely known as a poet than has usually been
realized.

And, as the protests of other authors suggest, a public that knew
the writings would not be satisfied until it also knew about the writer.
Gail Hamilton satirized such intrusions in the preface to her first book
in 1862:

> If any person writes a book or an article, and prefixes his name, he,
> in a manner, makes an unconditional surrender of himself. The pub-
> lic has perhaps the shadow of a right to ascertain and announce his
> birthplace, his residence, his wife, the color of his eyes, the length of
> his beard, the precocity of his childhood, the college at which he was
> graduated, the hotel in which he is spending the summer months,
> and similar items—startling, if true—which are so dear to the pub-
> lic. . . . The moment you get hold, by fair means or foul, of the
> outermost fibre of the shred of the husk of the semblance of a fact,
> you go straightway and put it in the newspapers.[33]

As Hamilton indicated, the newspapers claimed and exercised the right to learn and report all they could about authors, asserting the public's desire and right to know. "Personal intelligence is always interesting, and that relating to authors, peculiarly so," the *Springfield Daily Republican* stated in a preface to a 19 May 1852 reprint of a *New York Times* article "giving the pecuniary success of prominent authors in this country."

From an early point in her life Dickinson expressed acute awareness of the curiosity of "the public" about herself. In 1850 she observed that her failure to participate in the benevolent work of the "Sewing Society" "must puzzle the public exceedingly" (L 30). While this early remark may express simply what she perceived as her public role resulting from her family's prominence in the community, as time went on it seems more likely that she saw the curiosity as prompted by her lifestyle and her work. Ten years later she wrote to her cousin Louise Norcross, "Won't you tell 'the public' that at present I wear a brown dress with a cape if possible browner, and carry a parasol of the same!" (L 228). Her comment to Higginson in 1869, "My life has been too simple and stern to embarrass any. / 'Seen of Angels' scarcely my responsibility" (L 330), may be a gentle reproof of his attempts to gain more information about her.

Of course, curiosity and demands on her would have been more widespread and more frequent had Dickinson given herself up to the public as a published writer. The public would have wanted a portrait of the poet who responded to Higginson's request for one: "I had no portrait, now. . . . I noticed the Quick wore off those things, in a few days, and forestall the dishonor" (L 268). Indeed, when Dickinson's poems were published in the 1890s the editors received requests for her portrait and were bombarded with queries about her life. In publishing his essay "Emily Dickinson's Letters" in 1891, Higginson said he was responding to public demand following from the success of her *Poems:* "One result of this glare of publicity has been a constant and earnest demand by her readers for further information in regard to her. . . . [I]t has been urged upon me very strongly that her readers have the right to know something more of this gifted and most interesting woman" ("Emily Dickinson's Letters," 444).

Had Dickinson acquiesced to the publication of a volume of her poems, or even to their regular publication in a newspaper or magazine, she would have risked subjecting herself to such demands while she lived. An interview with a reporter sent to write a piece on "Miss Emily Dickinson in Her Amherst Home"—indeed, the very possibility of such an encounter—would have been particularly distressing to the poet, who by the early 1860s was already finding it difficult to meet friends face to face.

Her contemporary Louisa May Alcott described, with a sensibility in some ways strikingly similar to Dickinson's, the infringements on privacy that accompanied literary fame—dangers of which Dickinson would have been well aware. Alcott wrote in her journal in 1869, the year after *Little Women* was published: "People begin to come and stare at the Alcotts. Reporters haunt the place to look at the authoress, who dodges into the woods *à la* Hawthorne."[34] The following month Alcott expressed her reactions to the indignities attending celebrity in a letter published in the *Springfield Republican* of 5 May 1869, which Dickinson may well have read. Headed "latest news from Concord / Nurse Periwinkle Frees Her Mind" and signed "Tribulation Periwinkle," it describes the sufferings of the "Concordians" as "each spring brings, with the robins, a flock of reporters":

> No spot is safe, no hour is sacred, and fame is beginning to be considered an expensive luxury by the Concordians. Their plaints are pathetic, though many of the performances behind the scenes are decidedly comic, for . . . some of these haunted ones step out of the back window when the hunter enters the front door, others take refuge in the garret, while the more timid flee into the wilderness and do not emerge until a bell is rung to inform them that the peril is past. It is whispered that one irascible spinster, driven to frenzy by twenty-eight visitors in a week, proposed to get a garden engine and "play away" whenever a suspicious stranger was seen entering her gates.[35]

Alcott recorded three years later that public curiosity continued to be strong; note that her sister May played a role similar to Lavinia Dickinson's: "May makes a lovely hostess, and I fly round behind the scenes, or skip out of the back window when ordered out for inspection by the inquisitive public."[36] A month later, when May has gone away "for rest," Alcott wrote:

> I say "No," and shut the door. People *must* learn that authors have some rights; I can't entertain a dozen a day, and write the tales they demand also. . . .

Reporters sit on the wall and take notes, artists sketch me as I pick pears in the garden, and strange women interview Johnny [her nephew] as he plays in the orchard.

It looks like impertinent curiosity to me, but it is called "fame," and considered a blessing to be grateful for, I find. Let 'em try it. (*Journals*, 183)

As Dickinson wrote:

How dreary—to be—Somebody!
How public—like a Frog—
To tell your name—the livelong June—
To an admiring Bog!

(Poem 288)

Although Dickinson did not publish and thus submit herself to the "blessings" of fame Alcott sardonically described, it is clear that the public was aware of Dickinson as an author. In the summer of 1878 comments about Dickinson appeared in a series of articles in several newspapers speculating whether she was the author of stories published earlier in the decade by Helen Hunt Jackson under the pseudonym Saxe Holm. The article that initiated the flurry of speculation described Dickinson's way of life, though without naming her. It suggested

that the author may be a person long shut out from the world and living in a world of her own; that perhaps she is a recluse. . . . [W]e may imagine her to be a member of one of those "sleepy and dignified" New England families . . . ; of a timid nature; separated from the outside world, devoted to literature and flowers. We cannot refrain, also, from picturing her robed in white. (*Springfield Daily Republican*, 25 June 1878; qtd. in Leyda, *Years and Hours*, 2:296)

A few days later the *Springfield Union* speculated "that she answers in private life to the honored name of Dickinson." On 31 July, in the Amherst *Record*, Dickinson was fully identified by name:

The person referred to by the *Union*, we suppose, is the daughter of the late Hon. Edward Dickinson, a lady of superior culture and education, and who has for many years secluded herself from society for the purpose of indulging in literary tastes and pursuits. Helen Hunt . . . has been an intimate friend of Miss Emily Dickinson from childhood.

Finally, an editorial note in the *Republican* of 3 August responded: "We happen to *know* that no person by the name of Dickinson is in any way responsible for the Saxe Holm stories" (qtd. in Leyda, *Years and Hours,* 2:297). The speculation, however, was not put to rest by this pronouncement; references to Dickinson's supposed connection with the Saxe Holm stories appeared at the time of her death and again in reviews of her poems in the 1890s.[37]

Clearly, the myths about Dickinson were already well established in her lifetime, both in print and in local talk. Soon after her arrival in Amherst in 1881 Mabel Todd reported to her parents about Dickinson:

I must tell you about the *character* of Amherst. It is a lady whom the people call the *Myth*. She is a sister of Mr. Dickinson, & seems to be the climax of all the family oddity. She has not been outside of her own house in fifteen years. . . . She dresses wholly in white, & her mind is said to be perfectly wonderful. She writes finely, but no one *ever* sees her. . . .

No one knows the cause of her isolation, but of course there are dozens of reasons assigned. (Qtd. in Leyda, *Years and Hours,* 2:357)

In light of the diligence used to find out about the reclusive poet, evidenced here both on the part of the local gossips and of those official gossips, the newspapers, perhaps we need to reconsider Dickinson's hiding from publicity. Her comments on public curiosity are, perhaps, not just the hyperbolic utterances of an overly sensitive recluse. Written requests for poems such as the one from "Miss P———" could, of course, be burned. But strangers lurking about to observe one in the garden are another matter. Indeed, maybe one of those reporters did come to the door hoping to write a piece on Miss Emily Dickinson, the Amherst poet.

APPENDIX: POEMS PUBLISHED IN DICKINSON'S LIFETIME, INCLUDING REPRINTS

"'Sic transit gloria mundi'" (Poem 3), titled "A Valentine," *Springfield Daily Republican,* 20 February 1852.

"Nobody knows this little rose" (Poem 35), titled "To Mrs_____, with a Rose," *Springfield Daily Republican*, 2 August 1858.

"I taste a liquor never brewed" (Poem 214), titled "The May-Wine," *Springfield Daily Republican*, morning and evening editions, 4 May 1861. Reprinted, *Springfield Weekly Republican*, 11 May 1861.

"Safe in their Alabaster Chambers" (Poem 216), titled "The Sleeping," *Springfield Daily Republican*, 1 March 1862. Reprinted, *Springfield Weekly Republican*, 8 March 1862.

"Blazing in gold, and quenching in purple" (Poem 228), titled "Sunset," *Drum Beat*, 29 February 1864. Reprinted, *Springfield Daily Republican*, 30 March 1864. Reprinted, *Springfield Weekly Republican*, 2 April 1864.

"Flowers—well if anybody" (Poem 137), titled "Flowers," *Drum Beat*, 2 March 1864. Reprinted, *Springfield Daily Republican*, 9 March 1864. Reprinted, *Springfield Weekly Republican*, 12 March 1864. Reprinted, *Boston Post*, 16 March 1864.

"These are the days when birds come back" (Poem 130), titled "October," *Drum Beat*, 11 March 1864.

"Some keep the Sabbath going to Church" (Poem 324), titled "My Sabbath," *Round Table*, 12 March 1864.

"Success is counted sweetest" (Poem 67), untitled, *Brooklyn Daily Union*, 27 April 1864.

"A narrow fellow in the grass" (Poem 986), titled "The Snake," *Springfield Daily Republican*, 14 February 1866. Reprinted, *Springfield Weekly Republican*, 17 February 1866.

"Success is counted sweetest" (Poem 67), titled "Success," in *A Masque of Poets*, ed. George Parsons Lathrop (Boston: Roberts Brothers, 1878), 174. Quoted in full in review, *Literary World*, 10 December 1878.

NOTES

1. Karen Dandurand, "New Dickinson Civil War Publications," *American Literature* 56 (1984): 26–27.
2. Louisa May Alcott, *The Journals of Louisa May Alcott*, ed. Joel Myerson, Daniel Shealy, and Madeleine B. Stern (Boston: Little, Brown, 1989), 128. Alcott's comments also add support to the argument I made in "New Dickinson Civil War Publications" that Dickinson would have been asked for her contributions to the *Drum Beat* and that her poems would not have been published without at least her tacit agreement (22–23).
3. The poem, titled "A Charade," does not appear in collections of Helen Hunt Jackson's poems, nor is it in the extensive list of her publications in Ruth Odell, *Helen Hunt Jackson* (New York: D. Appleton-Century, 1939). If it is hers, it would be her earliest publication. The poem's ephemeral nature may

explain why she would not have included it in her collections. She knew Storrs through their Amherst College connections, and William Francis Williams, his assistant on the *Drum Beat,* was an editor of the *New York Evening Post,* in which her first-known publications appeared the following year.

4. The list of contributors to *A Masque of Poets* is based on Aubrey H. Starke, "An Omnibus of Poets," *Colophon* 4, no. 16 (March 1934): 12 unnumbered pages. Starke's identification derives from notes in a copy of the book owned by Louise Chandler Moulton.

5. Emily Dickinson, *The Letters of Emily Dickinson,* 3 vols., ed. Thomas H. Johnson and Theodora Ward (Cambridge: Belknap Press of Harvard University Press, 1958), 626 (L 573d). Subsequent references to *Letters* will appear parenthetically in the text.

6. This poem, as Johnson notes, "was popular in the early forties when it appeared . . . in a number of newspapers and gift books" (L 183n). Though we cannot be sure of Dickinson's source, it should be added that the poem was still being reprinted in newspapers in the 1850s.

7. Dickinson may well have quoted "Are We Almost There." An ellipsis appears after she gives the title of the poem; the original text cannot be restored, as the manuscript is no longer extant, and the published text is based on the 1931 edition.

8. *Christian Register* 69 (18 December 1890): 828; reprinted in *Emily Dickinson's Reception in the 1890s: A Documentary History,* ed. Willis J. Buckingham (Pittsburgh: University of Pittsburgh Press, 1989), 63. The *Round Table* publication of "Some keep the Sabbath going to Church" had not been mentioned by the editors of *Poems* or in previous reviews; in fact, it appears that Higginson and Todd were not aware of the 1864 publication, since it is only after Chadwick's review that Todd searched for the poem in the *Round Table* at the Amherst College Library. Millicent Todd Bingham, *Ancestors' Brocades: The Literary Debut of Emily Dickinson* (New York: Harper and Brothers, 1945), 106.

9. George S. Merriam, *The Life and Times of Samuel Bowles,* 2 vols. (New York: Century, 1885), 2:68; Richard Hooker, *The Story of an Independent Newspaper: One Hundred Years of the Springfield Republican, 1824–1924* (New York: Macmillan, 1924), 125.

10. See Thomas H. Johnson, "Notes on the Present Text," in *Letters,* xxiii–iv; and Richard B. Sewall, "A Note on the Missing Correspondences," *The Life of Emily Dickinson,* 2 vols. (New York: Farrar, Straus and Giroux, 1974), 750–51.

11. In 1846 Dickinson adds, in a postscript to Abiah, "Please not let S. or any one see this letter. It is only for you. I carried your letter to Abby, & we read it together. I shall show it to no one else, of course" (L 11). Similarly, writing to Austin in 1848, she closes, "Please not to show this letter for it is strictly confidential" (L 22). In contrast, a letter to Abiah from Mt. Holyoke includes a report that she shared part of Abiah's last letter with her cousin Emily Norcross, a promise to share a letter from Eliza Coleman with Abiah, and a

reference to Abby Wood's writing that she had seen a letter (to some unidenti-
fied person) from Abiah (L 18).

12. Martha Ackmann, "The Matrilineage of Emily Dickinson" (Ph.D. diss.,
    University of Massachusetts, 1987), 250–55.

13. Jay Leyda, *The Years and Hours of Emily Dickinson,* 2 vols. (New Haven: Yale
    University Press, 1960), 2:361. Subsequent references appear parenthetically
    in the text.

14. Leyda suggests that the reference is to Susan's sister Martha Gilbert Smith;
    however, the term *sister* might refer, instead, to Susan's sister-in-law Emily
    Dickinson.

15. See Karen Dandurand, "Why Dickinson Did Not Publish" (Ph.D. diss.,
    University of Massachusetts, 1984), 19.

16. Mary E. Storrs to Mabel Todd, postscript dated 17 May 1892, to letter dated
    16 May 1892, Yale University Library.

17. The quoted phrase is in a letter from Bowles to Austin and Susan Dickinson,
    Houghton Library, Harvard University; Bowles refers to visiting the Storrses
    in other unpublished manuscript letters to Austin and Susan and in a letter to
    Maria Whitney, 12 April 1866, quoted in Merriam, *Life and Times of Samuel
    Bowles,* 2:48–49.

18. Higginson diary for 1866, Houghton Library. Entries for 30 March, 9 April,
    10 May, 20 May, 22 May, 26 May, 28 May, 29 May, and 6 June record
    rowing, sailing, walking, and other local excursions with Helen Hunt (some-
    times also with Kate Field) as well as a trip to Boston.

19. For example, Higginson writes to Edward Tuckerman, 26 August 1868: "I
    have always dreamed of coming to Amherst, to see you & my unseen corre-
    spondent Emily Dickinson—besides the aerolites & bird tracks" (Leyda,
    Years and Hours, 2:132).

20. Higginson, "Emily Dickinson's Letters," *Atlantic Monthly* 68 (1891): 444.

21. See, for example, Higginson's comments on his 1870 and 1873 visits with
    Dickinson in letters to his sisters (L 342b; L 405n). A reference in a letter to
    his mother (18 April 1862) indicates that his sister Louisa was staying with
    him when he received Dickinson's first letter (Leyda, *Years and Hours,* 2:55).

22. Dora [Theodora] Woolsey to Higginson, 12 December [1890], Amherst Col-
    lege Library.

23. Odell, *Helen Hunt Jackson,* 59, 71.

24. Dandurand, "Why Dickinson Did Not Publish," 161.

25. Subsequently, Higginson's reading of the poems is cited by Klaus Lubbers
    and Anna Mary Wells, who refer to the group as the "Boston Woman's
    Club." While both credit Higginson's reading as evidence of his regard for
    Dickinson's poems, they are condescending toward his audience, referring to
    them as "the Boston ladies." Klaus Lubbers, *Emily Dickinson: The Critical
    Revolution* (Ann Arbor: University of Michigan Press, 1968), 8, 232; Anna
    Mary Wells, *Dear Preceptor: The Life and Times of Thomas Wentworth Higginson*
    (Boston: Houghton Mifflin, 1963), 239–40.

26. New England Women's Club papers, Schlessinger Library, Radcliffe College.

27. New England Women's Club papers, Schlessinger Library, Radcliffe College.

28. Thomas H. Johnson, ed., app. 2, "Tabulation of Recipients," *Poems of Emily Dickinson*, 1198. The five poems he had that were published by 1875 were "Success is counted sweetest" (Poem 67), "Safe in their Alabaster Chambers" (Poem 216), "Blazing in gold, and quenching in purple" (Poem 228), "Some keep the Sabbath going to Church" (Poem 324), and "A narrow fellow in the grass" (Poem 986).

29. Higginson to Channing, 15 December 1884, Sophia Smith Collection, Smith College.

30. Higginson to Channing, 2 January [1885], Sophia Smith Collection, Smith College. Higginson dated the letter 2 January 1884, but clearly it follows the one cited in note 29.

31. I have suggested that this may be a reference to Samuel Bowles and Richard Salter Storrs ("Why Dickinson Did Not Publish," 54–55).

32. Higginson, "Emily Dickinson's Letters," 451.

33. Gail Hamilton (Mary Abigail Dodge), *Country Living and Country Thinking* (Boston: Ticknor and Fields, 1862), iv–v.

34. Alcott, *Journals*, 171.

35. Alcott, *Letters*, 126–28.

36. Alcott, *Journals*, 183.

37. An obituary notice published on 17 May 1886 in the *Northampton Daily Herald* says, "She was supposed by many of her friends to have been the author of the Saxe Holme [*sic*] stories" and goes on to suggest that she and Helen Hunt Jackson might have coauthored them (Leyda, *Years and Hours*, 2:472). For reviews in the 1890s, see Buckingham, *Emily Dickinson's Reception*, 12, 48, 88.

Contributors

Willis J. Buckingham is Professor of English at Arizona State University. He is the editor of *Emily Dickinson: An Annotated Bibliography* and *Emily Dickinson's Reception in the 1890s: A Documentary History*. Currently, he is at work on a study of Dickinson's relationship to the reading culture of her generation.

Karen Dandurand is Associate Professor of English at Indiana University of Pennsylvania, where she teaches nineteenth-century American literature and women's literature. She is an editor of *Legacy: A Journal of American Women Writers* and has edited *Dickinson Scholarship: An Annotated Bibliography*. She is also the author of various articles on Dickinson.

Betsy Erkkila, Professor of English at Northwestern University, is most recently the author of *The Wicked Sisters: Women Poets, Literary History and Discord*. She is also the author of *Whitman the Political Poet* and *Walt Whitman among the French: Poet and Myth*.

Virginia Jackson is Assistant Professor of English at Boston University. She has published essays on Dickinson and Emerson and is completing a book entitled *Dickinson's Misery*.

Charlotte Nekola is Associate Professor of English at William Patterson College of New Jersey. She recently wrote *Dream House: A Memoir*, selected for the Graywolf Press Rediscovery series, and coedited *Writing Red: An Anthology of Women Writers, 1930–1940*.

Martin Orzeck was until recently an instructor at the University of Pennsylvania, where he taught nineteenth-century and modern literature. He organized panels on "Dickinson and Audience" and on "Edgar Allan Poe and Audience" for the Modern Language Association. He has also taught English and American literature at Temple, Auburn, and Arizona State universities.

David Porter, Professor of English, Emeritus, of the University of Massachusetts, Amherst, has written extensively on literary innovation in American and British literature and is the author of *Emerson and Literary Change* and *Dickinson: The Modern Idiom*. He has directed several international conferences on the nature of Dickinson's achievement and serves as consultant to research institutes and foundations.

Robert Regan is Professor of English at University of Pennsylvania, where he teaches nineteenth-century American literature. He has edited *Poe: A Collection of Critical Essays* and authored *Unpromising Heroes: Mark Twain and His Characters* as well as various articles on nineteenth-century American literature.

Richard B. Sewall, Professor of English, Emeritus, of Yale University is remembered by generations of students for his lectures, for his distinguished teaching in the classroom, and for his inspiring role as Master of Ezra Stiles College. Professors of literature everywhere are indebted to him for the instructional value of the text he edited, *Short Stories for Study,* and for the enduring insights in his book *The Vision of Tragedy*. His book *The Life of Emily Dickinson* was awarded the National Book Award for biography.

R. McClure Smith teaches in the English Department at George Washington University. He has authored several articles on Dickinson and Hawthorne and is currently at work on a book, *The Seductions of Emily Dickinson*.

Stephanie A. Tingley is Associate Professor of English at Youngstown State University, where she teaches American literature, film, women's literature, and composition. She completed her doctorate at University of Illinois at Urbana-Champaign and is currently working on a book-length critical study of Dickinson's letters, entitled *A Fairer House than Prose*.

Robert Weisbuch is Thurnau Professor of English, Associate Vice President for Research, and Associate Dean of the Graduate School at the University of Michigan. He is the author of two books: *Emily Dickinson's Poetry* and *Atlantic Double-Cross*. He is also the author of numerous essays on American Romanticism.